PHILIP'S FOUNDATION ATLAS

i	Symbols
ii–iii	Scale and Direction
iv–v	Latitude and Longitude
vi	Map Reading from Aerial Photographs: Edinburgh
vii	Map Reading from Aerial Photographs: St Ives
viii	Map Reading from Satellite Imagery: North-east England
ix	Map Reading from Satellite Imagery: North Wales

BRITISH ISLES SECTION

2–3	British Isles from Space
4–5	England and Wales
6	Scotland
7	Ireland
8	British Isles: Relief
9	British Isles: Counties and Regions
10	British Isles: Climate and Weather
11	British Isles: Geology and Water
12	British Isles: Food
13	British Isles: Energy
14	British Isles: Trade and Industry
15	British Isles: People
16	British Isles: Travel and Leisure

REGIONAL STUDIES SECTION

18–19	Europe from Space
20–21	European Themes
22–23	Italy: Thematic
24–25	Japan: Thematic
26–27	Kenya: Thematic
28–29	South Africa: Thematic
30–31	Brazil: Thematic
32	The Arctic and Antarctica

WORLD MAP SECTION

34	Europe
35	Scandinavia
36–37	Western Europe
38–39	Southern Europe
40–41	Russia and Northern Asia
42	Asia
43	Japan
44–45	South Asia
46–47	Africa
48	Australia and New Zealand
49	Pacific Ocean
50	North America
51	South America
52–53	United States of America
54–55	Mexico, Central America and the West Indies
56	Polar Regions
57	The Solar System and the Earth
58–59	World: Relief
60–61	World: Political
62–63	World: Climate
64	World: Environment
65	World: Tectonics
66–67	World: People
68–69	World: Quality of Life
70	World: Resources
71	World: Energy
72	Seasons and Time Zones
73–80	Index

SUBJECT LIST

Acid rain	20
Aerial photography	vi, vii
Age structure	26, 30
Agriculture	12, 20, 29, 31, 70
Barley	12
Cape Peninsula, South Africa	28
Climate graphs	10, 62
Climate regions	20
Coal	71
Deforestation	31, 64
Desertification	64
Earthquakes	25, 65
Electricity	13
Employment	14, 21, 69
Energy production and consumption	13, 71
Family size	67
Fishing	12, 70
Food intake	69
Fuels	13, 71
Great Rift Valley, Kenya	26
Illiteracy	68
Industrial accidents	64
Industry	23, 25, 29
Land use	12, 20, 27, 70
Life expectancy	67
Manufacturing	14
Minerals	70
Mining	15, 29, 66
Motorways	16
Mount Fuji, Japan	25
Mount Kenya, Kenya	27
Natural disasters	64
Natural gas	13, 71
Natural vegetation	20, 27, 64
Oil	13, 71
Ozone holes	32
Pollution	20, 64
Population	25
Population change	15, 66
Population density	15, 66
Population per doctor	69
Ports	14
Railways	16
Rainfall	10, 20, 63
Satellite imagery	viii, ix, 2, 3, 18, 23, 24, 25, 26, 27, 28, 30, 31, 32
Services	14, 21
Sunshine hours	10
Temperature	10, 20, 62
Tokyo, Japan	24
Tourism	16
Trade	14, 21
Transport	21
Type of goods traded	26
Unemployment	14, 23
Urban population	66
Volcanoes	25, 65
Water supply	11, 68
Wealth	21, 68
Weather map	10
Wheat	12
Wildlife	27
Young and old	15

Published by Heinemann Educational,
a division of Reed Educational and Professional Publishing Ltd,
Halley Court, Jordan Hill, Oxford OX2 8EJ
OXFORD MADRID ATHENS FLORENCE PRAGUE CHICAGO
PORTSMOUTH NH (USA) MEXICO CITY SÃO PAULO SINGAPORE
KUALA LUMPUR TOKYO MELBOURNE AUCKLAND NAIROBI
KAMPALA IBADAN GABORONE JOHANNESBURG

in association with Philip's,
a division of Octopus Publishing Group Limited,
2–4 Heron Quays, London E14 4JP

Copyright © 2001 Philiip's
Cartography by Philip's
First published 1989; this edition published 2001
Reprinted 2002, 2003

A catalogue record for this book is available from
the British Library.
ISBNs 0 435 35017 X (paper); 0 435 35016 1 (cased)
Printed in Hong Kong
Details of other Philip's titles and services can be
found on our website at: www.philips-maps.co.uk

Philip's World Atlases are published in
association with The Royal Geographical
Society (with The Institute of British
Geographers).
   The Society was founded in 1830 and
given a Royal Charter in 1859 for 'the
advancement of geographical science'.
Today it is a leading world centre for
geographical learning – supporting
education, teaching, research and
expeditions, and promoting public
understanding of the subject.
   Further information about the Society
and how to join may be found on its
website at: www.rgs.org

Below is a slice through the map of England and Wales on page 4. It is used here to explain the meaning of the lines, colours and symbols.

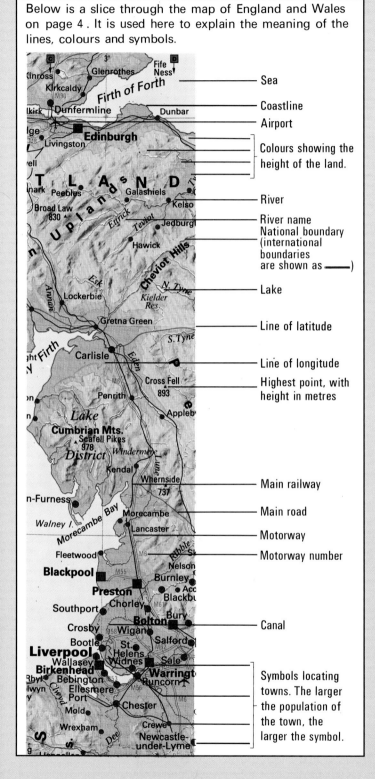

- Sea
- Coastline
- Airport
- Colours showing the height of the land.
- River
- River name National boundary (international boundaries are shown as ——)
- Lake
- Line of latitude
- Line of longitude
- Highest point, with height in metres
- Main railway
- Main road
- Motorway
- Motorway number
- Canal
- Symbols locating towns. The larger the population of the town, the larger the symbol.

HEIGHT OF LAND

There is an explanation like the one on the right on every page where different colours are used to show the height of the land above sea level. There is also a colour for land below sea level.

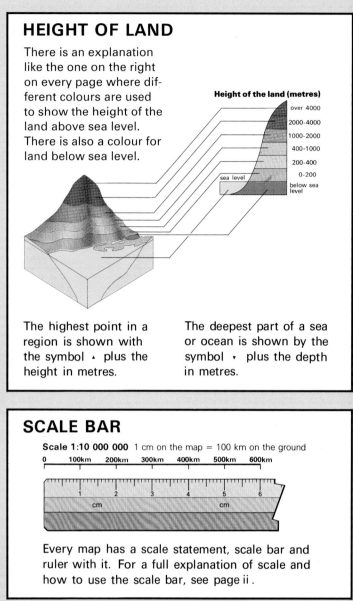

Height of the land (metres)

| over 4000 |
| 2000-4000 |
| 1000-2000 |
| 400-1000 |
| 200-400 |
| 0-200 |
| below sea level |

sea level

The highest point in a region is shown with the symbol ▴ plus the height in metres.

The deepest part of a sea or ocean is shown by the symbol ▾ plus the depth in metres.

SCALE BAR

Scale 1:10 000 000 1 cm on the map = 100 km on the ground

0 100km 200km 300km 400km 500km 600km

Every map has a scale statement, scale bar and ruler with it. For a full explanation of scale and how to use the scale bar, see page ii.

SCALE COMPARISON MAP

BRITISH ISLES
On same scale

This map, or one of England and Wales appears on the maps of the continents at the same scale as the main map. They give an idea of size.

LOCATOR MAP

There is a small map such as this on every map page. The red area shows how the main map fits into its larger region.

PICTURE ACKNOWLEDGEMENTS
© **Crown Copyright** p.vii/back cover (map extract and photograph)
© **Patricia and Angus Macdonald** p.vi
© **Courtesy of NPA Group, Edenbridge, UK** p.viii, p.ix, p.2 (top left), p.2 (centre), p.18 (bottom left/back cover), p.18 (bottom right), p.27, pp.58–59
© **Science Photo Library** /JBP/NRSC p.32 (top left), p.32 (centre), /CNES, 1989 Distribution Spot Image p.26, /Geospace p.23, /M-SAT Ltd p.2 (top right), p.2 (bottom), /NOAA p.32 (top right), p.32 (bottom), /NRSC Ltd p.28, p.31, /Photo Library International pp.18–19 (top), /RESTEC, Japan p.24, p.25, /Tom Van Sant/Geosphere Project, Santa Monica p.17, /WORLD-SAT Productions/NRSC p.3
© **Tony Stone Images** p.30
Photographs page 63 (top to bottom): **Britstock-IFA; Zefa Pictures; Robert Harding Picture Library; Finnish Tourist Board; Robert Harding Picture Library; Tony Stone Images**

Types of Scale

In this atlas the scale of the map is shown in three ways:-

1. **A written statement** - this tells you how many kilometres on the Earth are represented by one centimetre on the map.

1cm on the map = 20km on the ground

2. **Ratio** - this tells you that one on the map represents two million of the same unit on the ground.

1:2 000 000

3. **Scale** - this shows you the scale as a line or bar with a section of ruler beneath it.

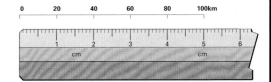

How to measure distance

The map on the right is a small part of the map of Southern Europe which is on page 38 in the World Map section of the atlas.

The scale of the map extract is shown below:

Scale 1:10 000 000   1cm on the map = 100km on the ground

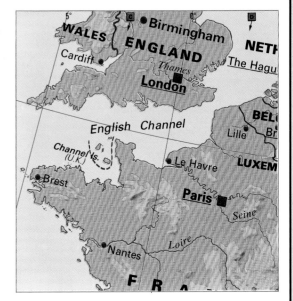

To measure the distance from London to Paris you can use any of the three methods described above.

For example:-

Using the written statement

Using the scale above you can see that 1cm on the map represents 100km on the ground.

Measure the distance on the map between London and Paris. You will see that this is about 3.5cm.

If 1cm = 100km

then 3.5cm = 350km   (3.5 x 100)

Using the Ratio

Using the scale above you can see that the ratio is 1:10 000 000

We know that the distance on the map between the cities is 3.5cm and we know from the ratio that 1cm on the map = 10 000 000cm on the ground. We multiply the map distance by the ratio.

= 3.5 x 10 000 000cm
= 35 000 000cm
= 350 000m
= **350km**

Using the Scale

We know that the distance on the map between the cities is 3.5cm.

Using the scale, measure 3.5cm along this (or use the yellow section of ruler as a guide) and read off the distance.

Using these 3 methods now work out the distance between London and Birmingham on the map above. Your teacher could tell you if your answer is correct.

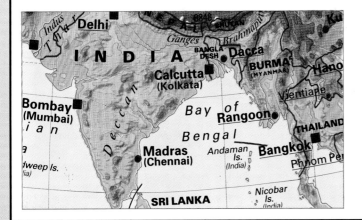

The map on the left is an extract from the map of Asia on page 42 in the World Map section of the atlas. Below, you can see the scale of this map. Calculate the distance between Calcutta and Bangkok.

Scale 1:45 000 000   1cm on the map = 450km on the ground

Different Sizes of Scale

The table on the right shows the distances between London - Paris and Bangkok - Calcutta. The map distances are both 3.5cm but the actual distances are very different. This is because the maps are at different scales.

	Map Distance	Scale	Actual Distance
London - Paris	3.5cm	1:10 000 000	350km
Bangkok - Calcutta	3.5cm	1:45 000 000	1 575km

On the continent maps, in the World Map section of this atlas, are Scale Comparison maps. These show you the size of the British Isles drawn at the same scale as the main map on that page. This is to give you an idea of the size of that continent.

Below are three maps which appear in this atlas.

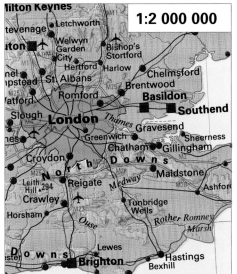

1:2 000 000

1:7 000 000

1:20 000 000

The maps all show London, but the map above shows much more detail than the maps on the right. The map above is a larger scale map than the maps on the right.

Large Scale means a **large** map of a **small** area

Small Scale means a **small** map of a **large** area

Notice how the ratios are getting larger as the scale of the map gets smaller.

Direction on the Maps

On most of the atlas maps, North is at the top of the page. Longitude lines run from South to North. These usually curve a little because the Earth is a globe and not a flat shape.

Points of the Compass

Below is a drawing of the points of the compass. North, East, South and West are called **cardinal points**. Direction is sometimes given in degrees. This is measured going clockwise from North. To help you remember the order of the compass points try to learn this sentence:
Naughty **E**lephants **S**quirt **W**ater

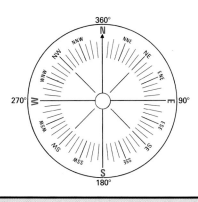

Using a Compass

Compasses have a needle with a magnetic tip. The tip is attracted towards the Magnetic North Pole which is close to the North Pole. The compass tells you where North is. You can see the Magnetic North Pole on the diagram below.

THE MAGNETIC NORTH POLE

Activities

Look at the map below.
If Keswick is South of Edinburgh then:
• Armagh is _____ – _____ of Oxford.
• Fort William is _____ of Edinburgh.
• Ilfracombe is _____ of Oxford.
Look at the map on pages 4 – 5 of the British Isles section.
• Which is the most Southerly town shown in England ?
• Which is the most Westerly town shown in Wales ?

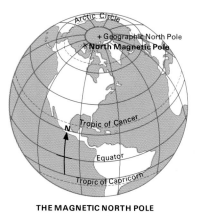

1:12 000 000

iv Latitude and Longitude

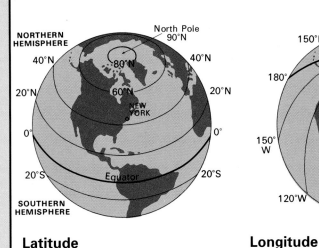

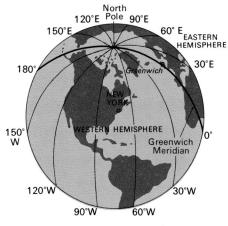

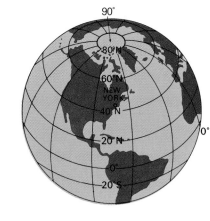

Latitude

Lines of latitude cross the atlas maps from East to West. The Equator is at 0. All other lines of latitude are either North of the Equator, or South of the Equator. Line 40°N is almost half way towards the North Pole. The North Pole is at 90°N.

At the Equator a degree measures about 110km.

Special latitude lines

Some special latitude lines are shown on maps. The diagrams in the World Map section on page 40 show that the sun is only overhead vertically in the tropical regions. These regions are between 23°30' North and South of the Equator. On maps these are shown as blue dotted lines. The **Tropic of Cancer** is at 23°30'N and the **Tropic of Capricorn** is at 23°30'S.

In the North and South Polar regions there are places where the Sun does not rise or set above the horizon at certain times of the year. These places are also shown by a blue dotted line. The **Arctic Circle** is at 66°30'N and the **Antarctic Circle** is at 66°30'S.

Longitude

Lines of longitude run from North to South. These lines meet at the North Pole and the South Pole. Longitude 0 passes through Greenwich. This line is also called the Greenwich Meridian. Lines of longitude are either East of 0 or West of 0. There are 180 degrees of longitude both East and West of 0.

Using latitude and longitude

Latitude and longitude lines make a grid. You can find a place if you know its latitude and longitude number. The latitude number is either North or South of the Equator. The longitude number is either East or West of the Greenwich Meridian.

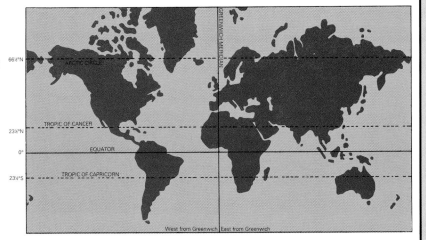

Latitude and longitude in this atlas

In this atlas lines of latitude and longitude are blue.

On large scale maps such as those in the British Isles section, pages 4 – 7, there is a line for every degree. On smaller scale maps only every other, every fifth or even tenth line is shown.

The map on the right shows the British Isles. The latitude and longitude lines are numbered at the edges of the map. The bottom of the map shows whether a place is East or West of Greenwich. The side of the map tells you how far North from the Equator the line is.

Around the edges of the map are small yellow pointers with letters and numbers in. Columns made by longitude lines have letters, rows made by latitude lines have numbers.

In the index at the end of the atlas places have number-letter references as well as latitude and longitude numbers.

On the map opposite, London is in rectangle **8M** (this is where row 8 crosses with column M). Edinburgh is in **4J** and Dublin is in **6F**.

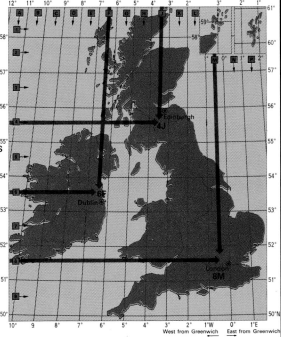

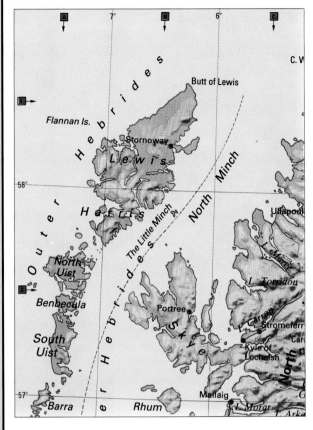

How to find a place

The map on the left is an extract from the map of Scotland on page 6 of the British Isles section. If you want to find Stornoway in the atlas you must look in the index. Places are listed alphabetically. You will find the following entry:

Stornoway............**6   1B** 58°N 6°W

The number in **bold** type is the page number where the map appears. The figure and letter which follow the page number give the grid rectangle on the map in which the feature appears. Here we can see that Stornoway is on page 6 in the rectangle where row 1 crosses column B.

The latitude and longitude number corresponds with the numbered lines on the map. The first set of figures represent the latitude and the second set represent the longitude. The unit of measurement for latitude and longitude is the degree (°) which is divided into minutes ('). Here, only full degrees are given.

Latitude and longitude can be used to locate places more accurately on smaller scale maps such as those in the World Map section.

All rivers are indexed to their mouth or confluence and in the index they are followed by the symbol

Making Maps

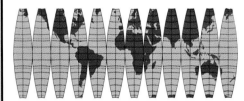

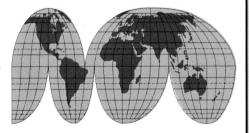

One of the greatest problems in making maps is how to draw the curved surface of the globe on a flat piece of paper. The map above shows one way of putting the globe onto paper, but because it splits up the land and sea it is not very useful.

The map above is better. It is a good map because it shows the correct size of places. It is an **equal area** map. For example, Australia is the correct size in relation to North America and Europe is the correct size in relation to Africa.

Comparing areas is a useful way of checking the accuracy of maps. Comparing Greenland (2.2 million km²) with Australia (7.7 million km²) is a good 'area test'.

A better shape at the edges of the map can be made by splitting the map (above).

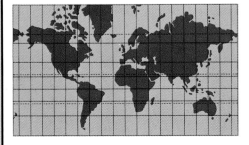

The map on the left is called **Mercator**. It has been used since the 16th century. The area scale is not equal area. All sea and air maps are drawn on this type of map.

The scale of distances is difficult to put on a map. On the above map the Equator and Greenwich Meridian are true to scale.

On the Mercator map, scale is correct along the Equator but is less correct towards the Poles.

In this atlas most maps are reasonable for area and scale. Latitude lines are curves and longitude lines are straight lines or curves.

Edinburgh Street Map
Key to Map Symbols

- Place of Interest
- ✝ Place of Worship
- Pedestrian Street
- — Shopping Street
- → One Way Street
- ⓌⓁ Public Toilets
- 🄳 Tourist Information Centre
- 🄿 Car Park
- 🚂 Station
- ✳ View Point

COPYRIGHT GEORGE PHILIP

Scale 1:10 000 1 cm on the map and aerial photograph = 100 metres on the ground

0   500 metres   1 km

O.S. Pathfinder Map of St. Ives

Key to Map Symbols

Roads and Paths

A 31 (T)	Trunk or main road
B 3074	Secondary road
	Road more than 4 metres wide
	Road less than 4 metres wide
	Other road, drive or track
....	Path
- - - - - - - - -	Public right of way

Railways

	Single track
	Cutting, embankment

Symbols

▪ ▴ +	Place of worship
▢ ▭	Building, important building
⚲ ⚲	Lighthouse, beacon
△	Triangulation pillar
○ W, Spr	Well, spring
⌢⌢⌢	Cliff
▢	Water, sand and shingle

Vegetation

	Coniferous forest
	Non-coniferous forest
	Coppice
	Orchard
	Scrub
	Bracken, rough grassland

Heights

˙116	Spot heights in metres
	Contours are in 5 metre intervals

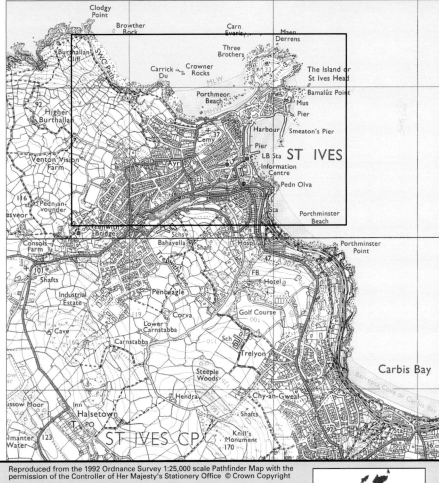

Scale of photograph 1:10 000

500 metres

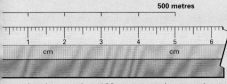

cm on the photograph = 100 metres on the ground

Scale of map 1:25 000

0   500 metres   1 km   1.5 km

1 cm on the map = 250 metres on the ground

St. Ives

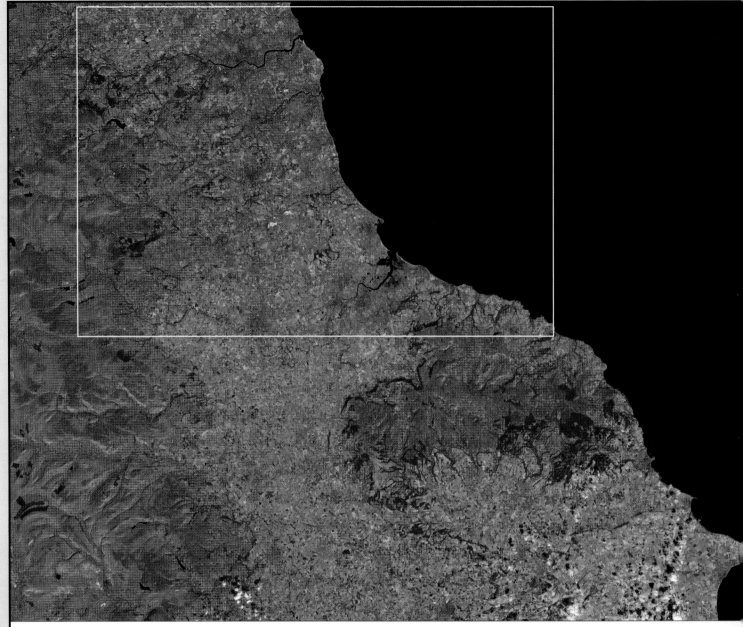

Landsat images

The satellite images on these pages are produced by the Landsat 5 spacecraft, launched by NASA in 1984. It travels around the Earth at a height of over 700km. It is able to scan every part of the Earth's surface once every 16 days. The data is transmitted back to Earth where it is printed in false colours to make certain features stand out.

On these pages grass and crops appear red, soils and exposed rock light blue, woodland dark red, moorland brown, water black and built up areas dark-grey. The image on page viii shows North-East England and the image on page ix shows North Wales. Both images are recorded in late September. Comparing the maps with the images helps to identify specific features on the images.

COPYRIGHT GEORGE PHILIP

Scale 1:760 000 1 cm on the map and satellite image = 7.6 km on the ground

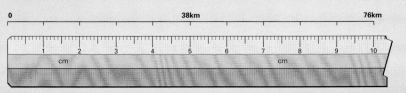

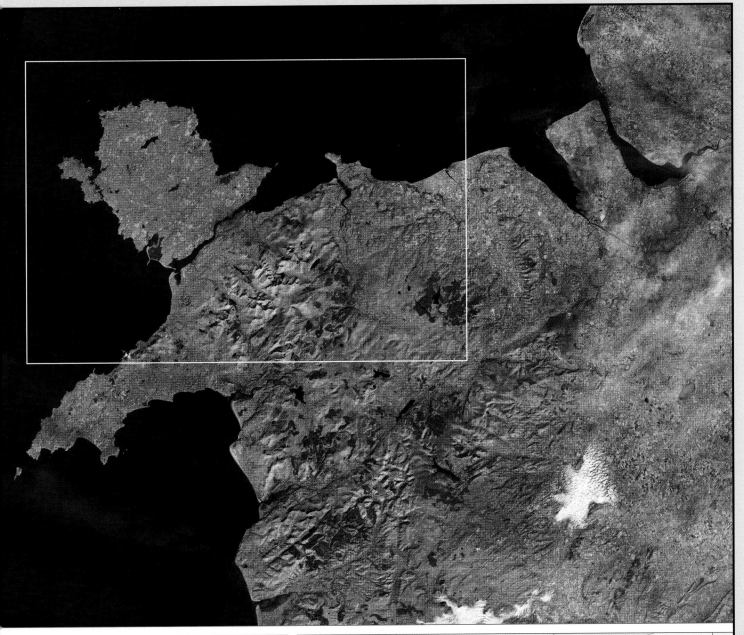

Key to Map Symbols

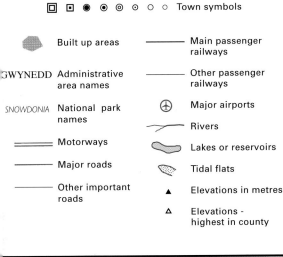

▣ ▣ ● ◉ ◎ ⊙ ○ ○ Town symbols

Built up areas	Main passenger railways
GWYNEDD Administrative area names	Other passenger railways
SNOWDONIA National park names	✈ Major airports
Motorways	Rivers
Major roads	Lakes or reservoirs
Other important roads	Tidal flats
	▲ Elevations in metres
	△ Elevations - highest in county

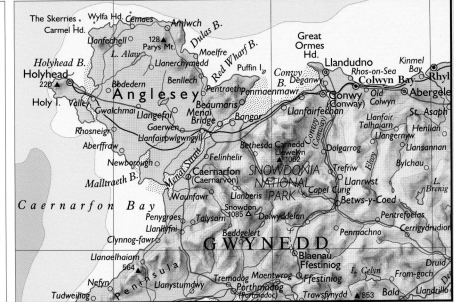

Scale 1:760 000   1 cm on the map and satellite image = 7.6 km on the ground

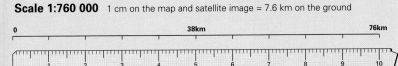

0   38km   76km

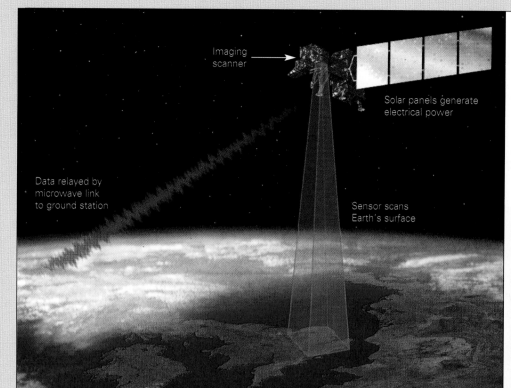

Imaging scanner

Solar panels generate electrical power

Data relayed by microwave link to ground station

Sensor scans Earth's surface

▼ Western Scotland
The brown region indicates the sparsely-populated Highland region lying north of Glasgow. Around the rugged coastline (which includes the Firth of Clyde, Firth of Lorn and Loch Fyne), the islands of Mull (centre left), Jura (lower left) and Islay (bottom left) form part of the Hebrides archipelago.

▲ Earth Observation Satellites
Powered by outstretched solar panels, Earth Observation Satellites such as the one shown (above) record images of the Earth's surface and relay the images digitally to ground-receiving stations.

▶ The Thames Basin and London
This Landsat satellite image clearly shows the extent of the Greater London conurbation. The runways of Heathrow Airport are clearly visible at centre left.

◀ Southern England
This true-colour satellite image shows the Isle of Wight (bottom left) separated from the mainland by the Solent. Parts of the counties of Hampshire and West Sussex appear on the image, with the major towns of Southampton (far left), Portsmouth (lower left) and Brighton (lower right) all clearly visible.

The British Isles seen from space

A mosaic of data gathered by Landsat satellites, the colours on this image have been processed to match the natural tone of the landscape. The large amount of agricultural land in the UK is reflected by the extensive brownish green on the image. In Scotland, snow-covered mountains are seen, with dark green coniferous forests below the snow line. Most of Ireland has a mid-green colour which indicates the presence of rich pasture.

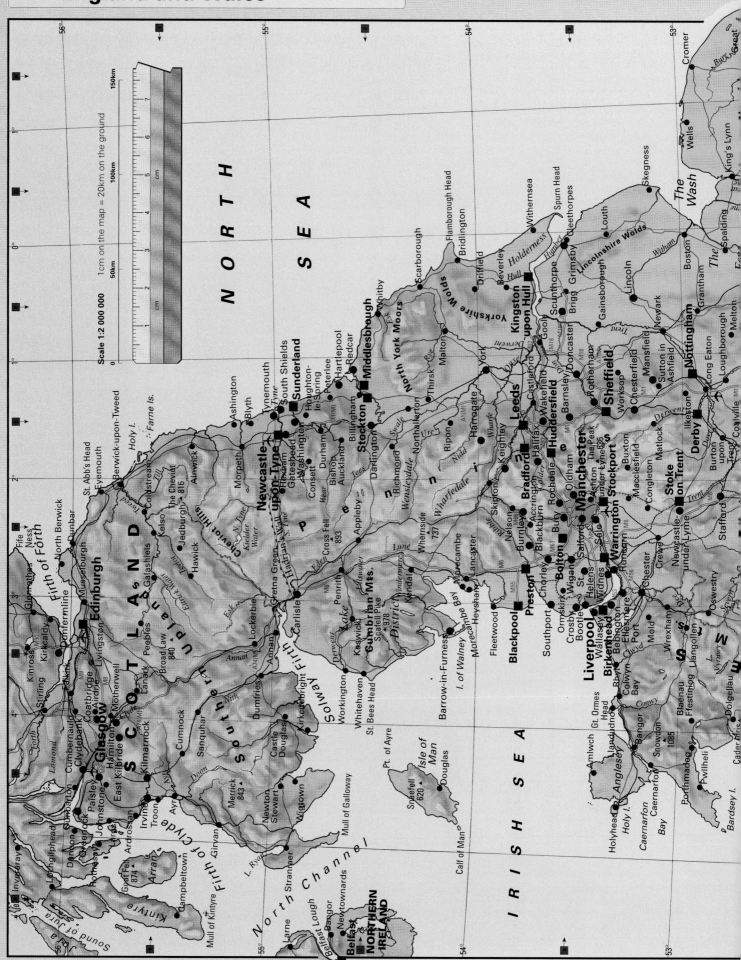

COPYRIGHT GEORGE PHILIP LTD

Height of the land (metres)

over 1000
400-1000
200-400
100-200
0-100
below sea level

sea level

○ Over 500 000 inhabitants
■ 100 000 - 500 000 inhabitants
● 50 000 - 100 000 inhabitants
· Under 50 000 inhabitants

London Capital cities underlined

M6 — Motorways
— Main Roads
— Railways
✈ International Airports
- - - Canals
∴ Historical sites
— Country boundaries

See page 9 for counties

Scilly Isles
On same scale

St. Ives
Penzance
Land's End
Scilly Isles
St. Mary's

ENGLAND

Lowestoft
Aldeburgh
Ipswich
Felixstowe
Harwich
Bury St. Edmunds
Thetford
Clacton
Colchester
Newmarket
Ely
Cambridge
Bishop's Stortford
Harlow
Huntingdon
St. Neots
Bedford
Letchworth
Stevenage
Hertford
Welwyn Garden City
St. Albans
Brentwood
Basildon
Southend
Sheerness
Gravesend
Gillingham
Chatham
Rochester
Maidstone
Margate
Herne Bay
Canterbury
Deal
Dover
Folkestone
Ashford
Hastings
Bexhill
Eastbourne
Beachy Head
Newhaven
Brighton
Hove
Lewes
Tonbridge
Royal Tunbridge Wells
Reigate
Crawley
Horsham
Worthing
Littlehampton
Bognor Regis
Selsey Bill
Chichester
London
Greenwich
Kingston
Croydon
Leith Hill 294▲
Guildford
Woking
Staines
Windsor
Slough
Maidenhead
High Wycombe
Watford
Hemel Hempstead
Aylesbury
Luton
Milton Keynes
Northampton
Wellingborough
Kettering
Corby
Rugby
Banbury
Oxford
Stratford-upon-Avon
Evesham
Cheltenham
Gloucester
Cirencester
Swindon
Newbury
Reading
Basingstoke
Andover
Winchester
Eastleigh
Southampton
Fareham
Portsmouth
Havant
Gosport
Newport
Isle of Wight
St. Catherine's Pt.
Bournemouth
Poole
Swanage
Portland Bill
Weymouth
Dorchester
Lyme Regis
Sidmouth
Exmouth
Exeter
Tiverton
Torquay
Torbay
Dartmouth
Start Pt.
Newton Abbot
Plymouth
Dartmoor
High Willhays 621▲
Bodmin
Bodmin Moor
Brown Willy 419▲
Bude
Barnstaple
Bideford
Ilfracombe
Minehead
Dunkery Beacon 520▲
Exmoor
Taunton
Bridgwater
Bristol
Bath
Mendip Hills
Weston-super-Mare
Bridgwater Bay
Yeovil
Salisbury
Salisbury Plain
Stonehenge
Trowbridge
Bridport
St. Austell
Truro
Falmouth
Newquay
St. Ives
Penzance
Land's End
Lizard

WALES

Aberystwyth
Cardigan Bay
Cardigan
Fishguard
St. David's Head
Milford Haven
Haverfordwest
Pembroke
Carmarthen
Carmarthen Bay
Llanelli
Swansea
Port Talbot
Neath
Aberdare
Rhondda
Pontypridd
Merthyr Tydfil
Brecon Beacons 886▲
Brecon
Abergavenny
Ebbw Vale
Pontypool
Cwmbran
Newport
Cardiff
Barry
Monmouth
Ross-on-Wye
Hereford
Great Malvern
Worcester
Kidderminster
Redditch
Stourbridge
Dudley
West Bromwich
Birmingham
Solihull
Coventry
Sutton Coldfield
Nuneaton
Hinckley
Warwick
Plynlimon 752▲
Llandovery
Llandrindod Wells
Builth Wells
Hay-on-Wye
Newtown
Rhayader

FRANCE

Dieppe
Rouen
Le Havre
Caen
Cherbourg
C. de la Hague
Alderney
Guernsey
St. Peter Port
Sark
Jersey
St. Helier
Channel Islands (U.K.)

ENGLISH CHANNEL

Strait of Dover

East from Greenwich
West from Greenwich

Thames Estuary

North Downs
South Downs
Chiltern Hills
Cotswolds

Rivers: Waveney, Little Ouse, Stour, Cam, Great Ouse, Nene, Cherwell, Thames, Avon, Windrush, Kennet, Test, Itchen, Arun, Ouse, Rother, Medway, Romney Marsh, Exe, Teign, Dart, Tamar, Taw, Torridge, Yeo, Tone, Teifi, Tywi, Usk, Wye

Orkney Is.
On same scale

Shetland Is.
On same scale

Scale 1:2 000 000   1cm on the map = 20km on the ground

COPYRIGHT GEORGE PHILIP LTD

| 0 | 50km | 100km | 150km | 200km |

ATLANTIC

OCEAN

SCOTLAND

North Channel

Malin Head
Tory I.
Inishowen Pen.
Giants Causeway
Rathlin I.
Campbeltown
Mull of Kintyre
L. Ryan
Bloody Foreland
Buncrana
Moville
Coleraine
Ballycastle
Errigal 752
Letterkenny
Londonderry
Ballymoney
Trostan 554
Mts. of Antrim
Aran I.
Strabane
Ballymena
Larne
Stranraer
Rossan Pt.
Foyle
Sperrin Mts.
Bann
Antrim
Carrickfergus
Donegal
Sawel 683
Main
Belfast L.
Bangor
Killybegs
Omagh
NORTHERN
Cookstown
L. Neagh
Belfast
Lagan
Newtownards
Donegal Bay
Bundoran
Ballyshannon
Ulster
IRELAND
Dungannon
Lisburn
Ards Pen.
Lower L. Erne
Portadown
Lurgan
Ballyquintin Pt.
Erris Hd.
Enniskillen
Armagh
Banbridge
Downpatrick
Mullet Pen.
Sligo B.
Upper L. Erne
Monaghan
Newry
Slieve Donard 852
Dundrum Bay
Killala B.
Sligo
L. Allen
Belturbet
Annalee
Cootehill
Mourne Mts.
Warrenpoint
Collooney
Finn
Ballina
L. Conn
Boyle
Cavan
Carrickmacross
Dundalk
Achill I.
Castlebar
Charlestown
Carrick-on-Shannon
Louth
Dundalk Bay
IRISH
Clare I.
Clew Bay
Knock
Castlerea
Longford
Blackwater
Drogheda
SEA
Inishturk
Westport
Claremorris
An Uaimh
Balbriggan
Inishbofin
Mweelrea 819
Ballinrobe
Roscommon
Mullingar
Boyne
Swords
Clifden
L. Mask
Tuam
Inny
Ireland's Eye
Slyne Hd.
L. Corrib
Connacht
Athlone
Leinster
Howth Head
Galway
Ballinasloe
Edenderry
Liffey
Dublin
Inishmore
Loughrea
Shannon
Bog of Allen
Naas
Dun Laoghaire
Aran Is.
Galway Bay
Gort
IRELAND
Birr
Tullamore
Kildare
Bray
Hags Hd.
L. Derg
Port Laoise
Athy
Poulaphouca Res.
Lugnaquilla 926
Wicklow
Milltown Malbay
Ennis
Roscrea
Carlow
Wicklow Mts.
Kilkee
Killaloe
Nenagh
Tullow
Mizen Head
Kilrush
Keeper Hill 694
Thurles
Kilkenny
Mt. Leinster 796
Arklow
Loop Hd.
Limerick
Cashel
Enniscorthy
Gorey
Mouth of the Shannon
Listowel
Newcastle West
Tipperary
Cahir
Carrick-on-Suir
New Ross
Kerry Hd.
Galtymore 920
Clonmel
Wexford
Tralee Bay
Munster
Mitchelstown
Knockmealdown Mts.
Waterford
Rosslare
Brandon Mt. 953
Tralee
Kanturk
Fermoy
Tramore
Carnsore Pt.
Dingle
Maine
Mallow
Blackwater
Dungarvan
Hook Hd.
Saltee Is.
Dunmore Hd.
Killarney
Boggeragh Mts.
St. David's Hd.
Dingle Bay
Macgillycuddy's Reeks 1041
Carrauntoohill
Blarney
Cork
Youghal
WALES
Valencia I.
Cahirciveen
Kenmare
Lee
West Passage
Cobh
St. George's Channel
Castletown Bearhaven
Caha Mts.
Bantry
Bandon
Crow Hd.
Beara
Clonakilty
Bantry Bay
Skibbereen
Old Head of Kinsale
Clear I.
C. Clear
Fastnet Rock

CELTIC SEA

West from Greenwich

COPYRIGHT GEORGE PHILIP LTD

Height of the land (metres)

over 1000
400-1000
200-400
100-200
0-100
sea level
below sea level

Over 500 000 inhabitants
100 000 - 500 000 inhabitants
50 000 - 100 000 inhabitants
Under 50 000 inhabitants

Dublin Capital cities underlined

M6 Motorways
Main Roads
Railways
International Airports
Canals
Country boundaries

Scale 1:4 600 000   1 cm on the map = 46 km on the ground

100km   200km   300km   400km

**HIGHEST MOUNTAINS,
LARGEST LAKES &
LONGEST RIVERS**

England
Scafell Pike   978m
Windermere   14.8km²
Thames   346km
Severn   354km

Wales
Snowdon   1085m
Trawsfynydd L.   4.9km²
Tywi   109km
Severn   354km

Scotland
Ben Nevis   134 m
Loch Lomond   69.9km²
Tay   188km

Northern Ireland
Slieve Donard   852m
Lough Neagh   396.0km²
Bann   128.7km

Ireland
Carrauntoohil   1042m
Lough Corrib   176.0km²
Shannon   354km

Shetland Is.

Fair I.

ATLANTIC

OCEAN

Orkney Is.

C. Wrath

Pentland Firth
Duncansby Hd.

Lewis

Outer Hebrides

St. Kilda

Harris

North Uist

South Uist

Skye

Rhum

Coll

Tiree

Mull

Jura

Islay

Inner Hebrides

Arran

1182

Moray Firth

Spey

L. Ness

Cairn Gorm
1245

Dee

Kinnairds Head

North West Highlands

Ben Nevis
1342

1214

1124

Grampian Mts

Tay

L. Lomond

Firth of Forth

Clyde

Firth of Clyde

North Channel

Southern Uplands

830

Tweed

The Cheviot
816

Malin Hd.

752

554

683

Bann

L. Neagh

544

Donegal Bay

L. Erne

Mourne Mts

Slieve Donard
852

843

Mull of Galloway

Solway Firth

893

Tyne

NORTH SEA

Great Britain

Ireland

Achill I.

819

L. Corrib

L. Ree

Boyne

Liffey

Shannon

Shannon

L. Derg

Barrow

Suir

Blackwater

953

920

Carrauntoohil
1041

Dingle Bay

Bantry Bay

C. Clear

Galway Bay

Aran Is.

Wicklow Mts
926

Isle of Man

IRISH SEA

Scafell Pike 978
Lake District

Windermere

454

Flamborough Hd.

Pennines

Tees

Aire

Humber

Liverpool Bay

Mersey

The Peak
636

Anglesey

Snowdon
1085

Dee

Trawsfynydd L.

Cardigan Bay

Cambrian Mts

Tywi

Brecon Beacons
886

Severn

Wye

Trent

The Wash

The Fens

Nene

Ouse

315

Avon

330

Severn

Cotswolds

297

Chiltern Hills

Thames

North Foreland

St. George's Channel

St. David's Hd.

Bristol Channel

Exmoor

Salisbury Plain

North Downs

South Downs

Beachy Hd.

Strait of Dover

618
Dartmoor

Lyme Bay

Portland Bill

Isle of Wight

CELTIC

SEA

Land's End

Scilly Is.

Lizard

ENGLISH CHANNEL

Channel Is.
Guernsey

Jersey

France

Somme

Seine

West from Greenwich 0° East from Greenwich

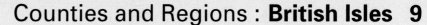

COUNTRY FACTS

Country Name	Area (square kilometres)	Inhabitants (thousands 1999)	Capital City or Town
UNITED KINGDOM	**240 883**	**59 509**	**LONDON**
of which England	129 652	49 753	London
Wales	20 628	2 937	Cardiff
Scotland	77 097	5 119	Edinburgh
N. Ireland	13 532	1 692	Belfast
*Isle of Man	572	72	Douglas
* Jersey	116	85	St. Helier
* Guernsey	63	59	St. Peter Port
IRELAND	**68 896**	**3626**	**DUBLIN**

Crown Dependencies which are not part of the U.K.

The map shows the 6 counties in Northern Ireland, the 32 unitary authorities in Scotland, the 22 unitary authorities in Wales and the 87 unitary authorities in England as of 1st April 1998. Authorities which are too small to name on the map are numbered and listed separately.

SCOTLAND
1. ABERDEEN CITY
2. DUNDEE CITY
3. WEST DUNBARTONSHIRE
4. EAST DUNBARTONSHIRE
5. CITY OF GLASGOW
6. INVERCLYDE
7. RENFREWSHIRE
8. EAST RENFREWSHIRE
9. NORTH LANARKSHIRE
10. FALKIRK
11. CLACKMANNANSHIRE
12. WEST LOTHIAN
13. CITY OF EDINBURGH
14. MIDLOTHIAN

● Capital cities

The Channel Islands and the Isle of Man are dependencies of the Crown and have their own parliaments. They are not part of the United Kingdom.

WALES
15. SWANSEA
16. NEATH PORT TALBOT
17. BRIDGEND
18. RHONDDA CYNON TAFF
19. MERTHYR TYDFIL
20. CAERPHILLY
21. BLAENAU GWENT
22. TORFAEN
23. CARDIFF
24. NEWPORT

ENGLAND
25. HARTLEPOOL
26. DARLINGTON
27. STOCKTON-ON-TEES
28. MIDDLESBROUGH
29. REDCAR AND CLEVELAND
30. BLACKPOOL
31. BLACKBURN WITH DARWEN
32. HALTON
33. WARRINGTON
34. KINGSTON UPON HULL
35. NORTH EAST LINCOLNSHIRE
36. STOKE-ON-TRENT
37. TELFORD AND WREKIN
38. DERBY CITY
39. CITY OF NOTTINGHAM
40. LEICESTER CITY
41. RUTLAND
42. PETERBOROUGH
43. MILTON KEYNES
44. LUTON
45. NORTH SOMERSET
46. CITY OF BRISTOL
47. BATH AND N. E. SOMERSET
48. SWINDON
49. READING
50. WOKINGHAM
51. WINDSOR AND MAIDENHEAD
52. SLOUGH
53. BRACKNELL FOREST
54. THURROCK
55. SOUTHEND-ON-SEA
56. MEDWAY
57. PLYMOUTH
58. TORBAY
59. POOLE
60. BOURNEMOUTH
61. SOUTHAMPTON
62. PORTSMOUTH
63. BRIGHTON AND HOVE

COPYRIGHT GEORGE PHILIP LTD

Weather is measured in terms of rainfall, temperature, cloudiness, sunshine and wind over a short period of time, usually less than a day. Climate is the average of the weather over a longer period, usually 30 years.

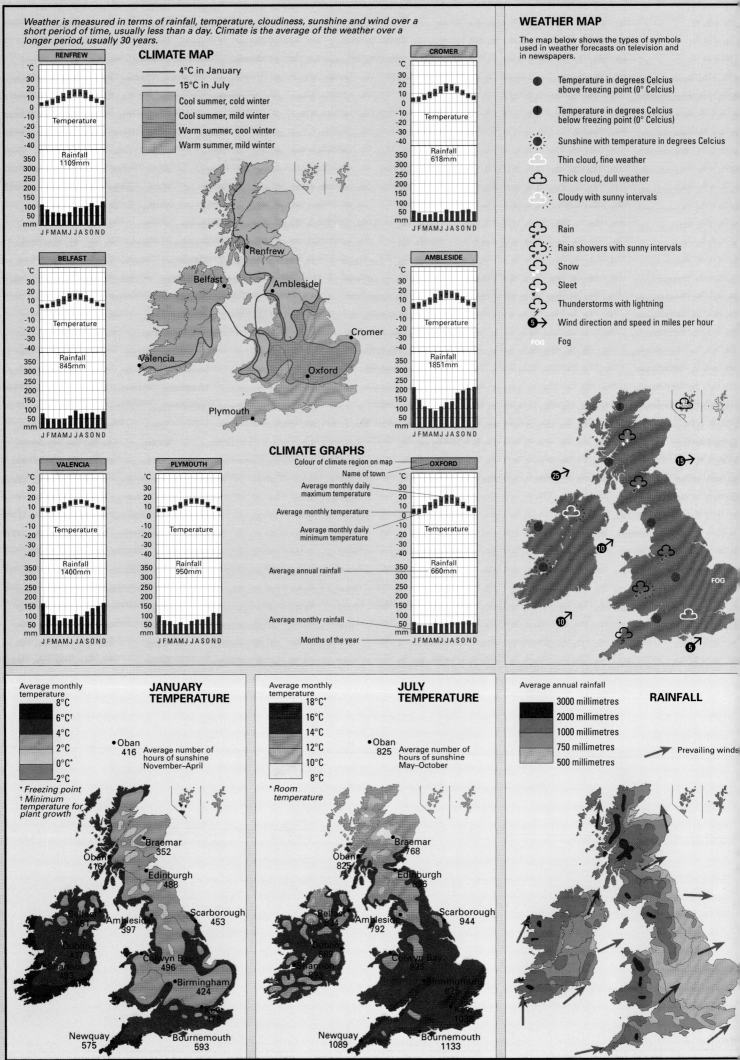

CLIMATE MAP

— 4°C in January
— 15°C in July
Cool summer, cold winter
Cool summer, mild winter
Warm summer, cool winter
Warm summer, mild winter

RENFREW — Temperature / Rainfall 1109mm
CROMER — Temperature / Rainfall 618mm
BELFAST — Temperature / Rainfall 845mm
AMBLESIDE — Temperature / Rainfall 1851mm
VALENCIA — Temperature / Rainfall 1400mm
PLYMOUTH — Temperature / Rainfall 950mm
OXFORD — Temperature / Rainfall 660mm

CLIMATE GRAPHS

Colour of climate region on map
Name of town
Average monthly daily maximum temperature
Average monthly temperature
Average monthly daily minimum temperature
Average annual rainfall
Average monthly rainfall
Months of the year

WEATHER MAP

The map below shows the types of symbols used in weather forecasts on television and in newspapers.

- Temperature in degrees Celcius above freezing point (0° Celcius)
- Temperature in degrees Celcius below freezing point (0° Celcius)
- Sunshine with temperature in degrees Celcius
- Thin cloud, fine weather
- Thick cloud, dull weather
- Cloudy with sunny intervals
- Rain
- Rain showers with sunny intervals
- Snow
- Sleet
- Thunderstorms with lightning
- Wind direction and speed in miles per hour
- FOG — Fog

JANUARY TEMPERATURE

Average monthly temperature
8°C
6°C†
4°C
2°C
0°C*
-2°C

* Freezing point
† Minimum temperature for plant growth

Average number of hours of sunshine November–April

Oban 416
Braemar 352
Edinburgh 488
Scarborough 453
Belfast
Ambleside 397
Dublin
Colwyn Bay 496
Shannon
Birmingham 424
Kew 470
Newquay 575
Bournemouth 593

JULY TEMPERATURE

Average monthly temperature
18°C*
16°C
14°C
12°C
10°C
8°C

* Room temperature

Average number of hours of sunshine May–October

Oban 825
Braemar 768
Edinburgh 896
Scarborough 944
Belfast
Ambleside 792
Dublin
Colwyn Bay 995
Shannon
Birmingham 875
Kew 1038
Newquay 1089
Bournemouth 1133

RAINFALL

Average annual rainfall
3000 millimetres
2000 millimetres
1000 millimetres
750 millimetres
500 millimetres
Prevailing winds

GEOLOGY

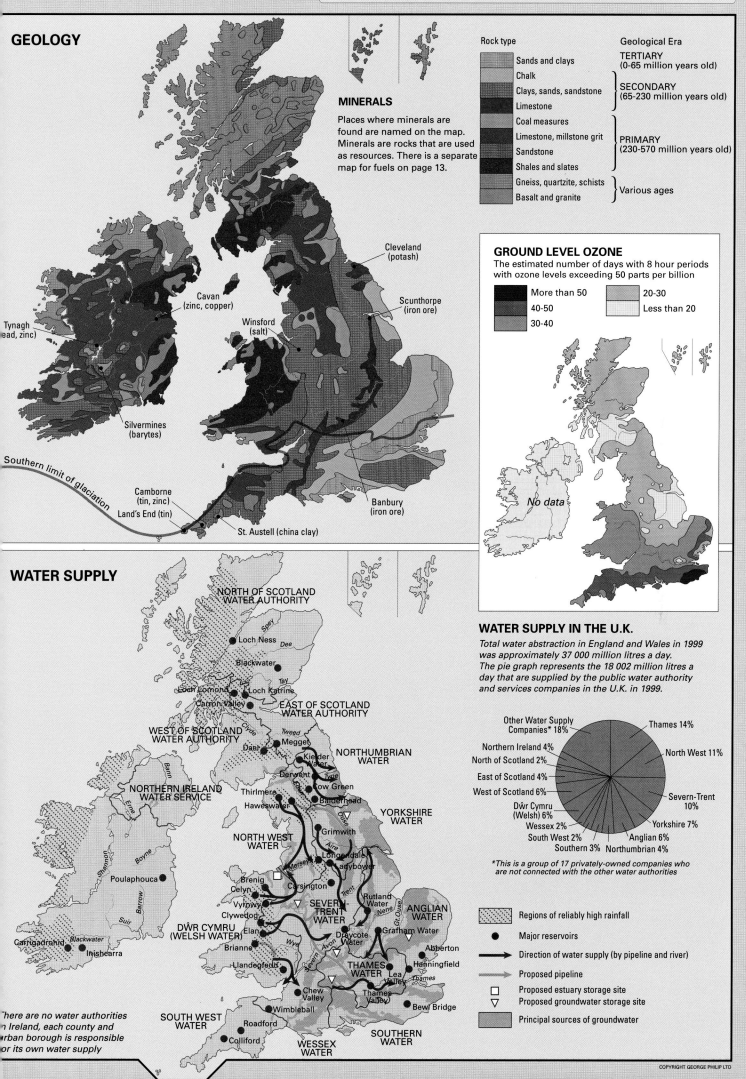

MINERALS

Places where minerals are found are named on the map. Minerals are rocks that are used as resources. There is a separate map for fuels on page 13.

Cleveland (potash)

Cavan (zinc, copper)

Scunthorpe (iron ore)

Winsford (salt)

Tynagh (lead, zinc)

Silvermines (barytes)

Southern limit of glaciation

Camborne (tin, zinc)

Land's End (tin)

Banbury (iron ore)

St. Austell (china clay)

Rock type	Geological Era
Sands and clays	TERTIARY (0–65 million years old)
Chalk	
Clays, sands, sandstone	SECONDARY (65–230 million years old)
Limestone	
Coal measures	
Limestone, millstone grit	PRIMARY (230–570 million years old)
Sandstone	
Shales and slates	
Gneiss, quartzite, schists	Various ages
Basalt and granite	

GROUND LEVEL OZONE

The estimated number of days with 8 hour periods with ozone levels exceeding 50 parts per billion

- More than 50
- 40-50
- 30-40
- 20-30
- Less than 20

No data

WATER SUPPLY

NORTH OF SCOTLAND WATER AUTHORITY

Spey

Loch Ness Dee

Blackwater

Tay

Loch Lomond Loch Katrine

Carron Valley

EAST OF SCOTLAND WATER AUTHORITY

Clyde

WEST OF SCOTLAND WATER AUTHORITY

Tweed

Megget

Daer

Kielder Water

NORTHUMBRIAN WATER

Derwent Tyne

Cow Green

Thirlmere

Baldershead

Haweswater

Bann

NORTHERN IRELAND WATER SERVICE

YORKSHIRE WATER

Grimwith

NORTH WEST WATER

Ouse

Aire

Erne

Longdendale

Ladybower

Mersey

Boyne

Shannon

Poulaphouca

Brenig

Celyn

Carsington

Trent

Rutland Water Nene

ANGLIAN WATER

Barrow

Vyrnwy

Ouse Gt

Clywedog

SEVERN-TRENT WATER

Grafham Water

Suir

DŴR CYMRU (WELSH WATER)

Elan

Draycote Water

Abberton

Carrigadrohid Blackwater

Inishcarra

Brianne

Wye

Avon

Severn

Hanningfield

Llandegfedd

THAMES WATER

Lea Valley Thames

Chew Valley

Thames Valley

Bewl Bridge

Wimbleball

SOUTH WEST WATER

Roadford

SOUTHERN WATER

Colliford

WESSEX WATER

There are no water authorities in Ireland, each county and urban borough is responsible for its own water supply

WATER SUPPLY IN THE U.K.

Total water abstraction in England and Wales in 1999 was approximately 37 000 million litres a day. The pie graph represents the 18 002 million litres a day that are supplied by the public water authority and services companies in the U.K. in 1999.

Other Water Supply Companies* 18%

Northern Ireland 4%

North of Scotland 2%

East of Scotland 4%

West of Scotland 6%

Dŵr Cymru (Welsh) 6%

Wessex 2%

South West 2%

Southern 3%

Thames 14%

North West 11%

Severn-Trent 10%

Yorkshire 7%

Anglian 6%

Northumbrian 4%

*This is a group of 17 privately-owned companies who are not connected with the other water authorities

- Regions of reliably high rainfall
- ● Major reservoirs
- → Direction of water supply (by pipeline and river)
- → Proposed pipeline
- □ Proposed estuary storage site
- ▽ Proposed groundwater storage site
- Principal sources of groundwater

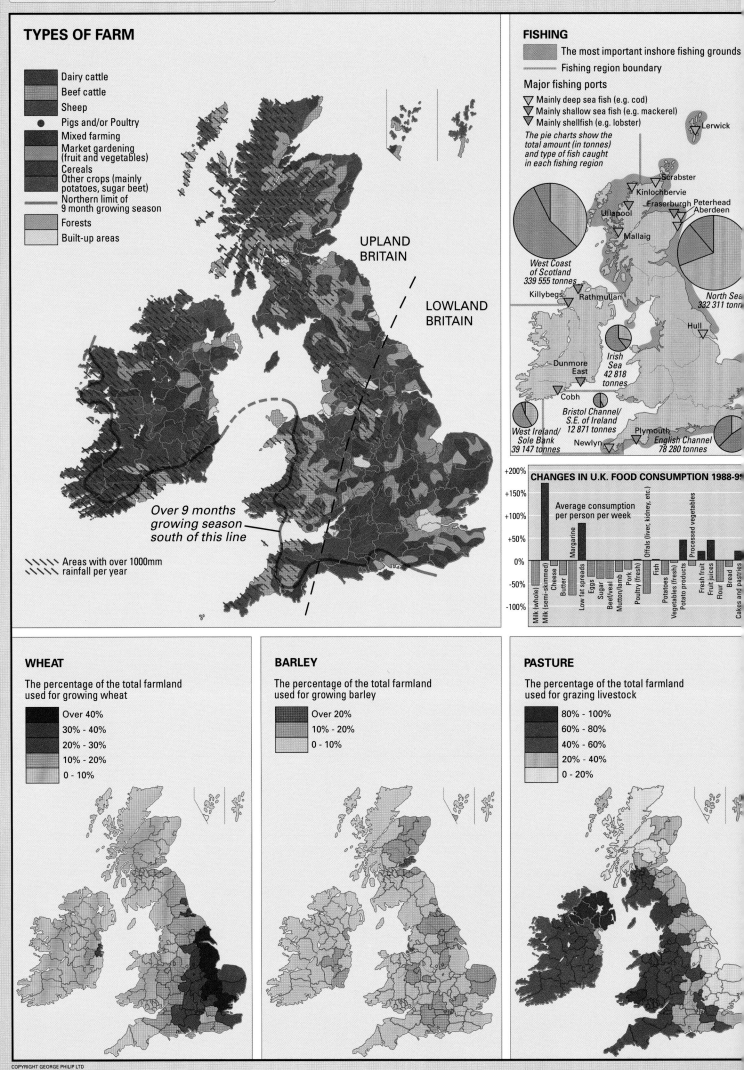

TYPES OF FARM

- Dairy cattle
- Beef cattle
- Sheep
- Pigs and/or Poultry
- Mixed farming
- Market gardening (fruit and vegetables)
- Cereals
- Other crops (mainly potatoes, sugar beet)
- Northern limit of 9 month growing season
- Forests
- Built-up areas

UPLAND BRITAIN

LOWLAND BRITAIN

Over 9 months growing season south of this line

Areas with over 1000mm rainfall per year

FISHING

- The most important inshore fishing grounds
- Fishing region boundary

Major fishing ports

- ▽ Mainly deep sea fish (e.g. cod)
- ▽ Mainly shallow sea fish (e.g. mackerel)
- ▽ Mainly shellfish (e.g. lobster)

The pie charts show the total amount (in tonnes) and type of fish caught in each fishing region

Lerwick
Scrabster
Kinlochbervie
Fraserburgh Peterhead
Ullapool Aberdeen
Mallaig
West Coast of Scotland 339 555 tonnes
Killybegs Rathmullan
North Sea 332 311 tonnes
Hull
Dunmore East
Irish Sea 42 818 tonnes
Cobh
Bristol Channel/ S.E. of Ireland 12 871 tonnes
West Ireland/ Sole Bank 39 147 tonnes
Newlyn
Plymouth
English Channel 78 280 tonnes

CHANGES IN U.K. FOOD CONSUMPTION 1988-9

Average consumption per person per week

+200% +150% +100% +50% 0% -50% -100%

Milk (whole), Milk (semi-skimmed), Cheese, Butter, Margarine, Low fat spreads, Eggs, Sugar, Beef/veal, Mutton/lamb, Pork, Poultry (fresh), Offals (liver, kidney, etc.), Fish, Potatoes, Vegetables (fresh), Potato products, Processed vegetables, Fresh fruit, Fruit juices, Flour, Bread, Cakes and pastries

WHEAT

The percentage of the total farmland used for growing wheat

- Over 40%
- 30% - 40%
- 20% - 30%
- 10% - 20%
- 0 - 10%

BARLEY

The percentage of the total farmland used for growing barley

- Over 20%
- 10% - 20%
- 0 - 10%

PASTURE

The percentage of the total farmland used for grazing livestock

- 80% - 100%
- 60% - 80%
- 40% - 60%
- 20% - 40%
- 0 - 20%

ENERGY SOURCES

- ▬ Coalfield
- ● Coal-fired* power station (over 1000MW in U.K., over 500MW in Ireland)
- ▬ Peat-cutting area in Ireland
- ● Peat-fired* power station (over 100MW)
- ▲ Oilfield
- ▬ Oil pipeline (with terminal)
- ● Oil-fired power station (over 1000MW in U.K., over 500MW in Ireland)
- ▲ Gasfield
- ▬ Gas pipeline (with terminal)
- ▬ International dividing line
- ☐ UK Sector

- ● Gas-fired* power station (over 1000MW in U.K., over 500MW in Ireland)
- ○ Combined cycle gas turbine** (over 1000MW)
- ○ Dual-fired power station* (over 1000MW in U.K., over 500MW in Ireland)
- ● Hydro-electric power station (over 40MW)
- ● Pumped storage scheme
- ● Nuclear power station (over 1000MW)

* Refers to the fuel that is being burnt to generate electricity (in dual-fired stations at least two types of fuel can be burnt, such as coal and oil or oil and gas)

**An efficient use of gas fuel where burnt gas from the main turbine is used to generate steam that is fed to a steam turbine

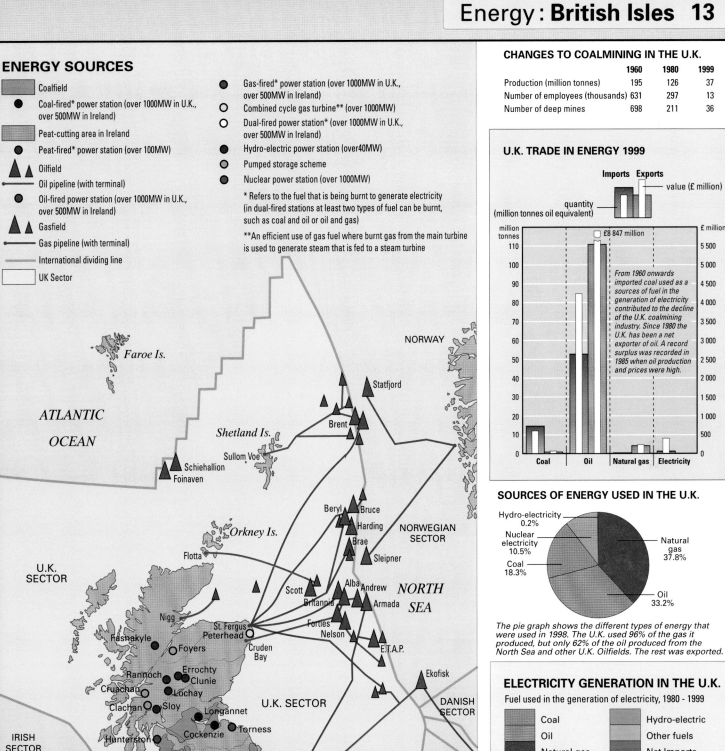

CHANGES TO COALMINING IN THE U.K.

	1960	1980	1999
Production (million tonnes)	195	126	37
Number of employees (thousands)	631	297	13
Number of deep mines	698	211	36

U.K. TRADE IN ENERGY 1999

From 1960 onwards imported coal used as a sources of fuel in the generation of electricity contributed to the decline of the U.K. coalmining industry. Since 1980 the U.K. has been a net exporter of oil. A record surplus was recorded in 1985 when oil production and prices were high.

SOURCES OF ENERGY USED IN THE U.K.

- Hydro-electricity 0.2%
- Nuclear electricity 10.5%
- Coal 18.3%
- Natural gas 37.8%
- Oil 33.2%

The pie graph shows the different types of energy that were used in 1998. The U.K. used 96% of the gas it produced, but only 62% of the oil produced from the North Sea and other U.K. Oilfields. The rest was exported.

ELECTRICITY GENERATION IN THE U.K.

Fuel used in the generation of electricity, 1980 - 1999

- Coal
- Oil
- Natural gas
- Nuclear
- Hydro-electric
- Other fuels
- Net Imports

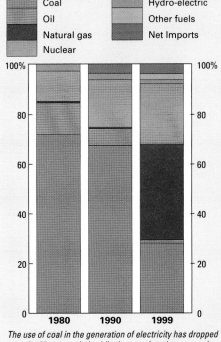

The use of coal in the generation of electricity has dropped over the 20 year period, while the use of nuclear power has increased by 58%.

PORTS

The weight of goods handled in millions of tonnes, 1999

5 10 20 50 millions of tonnes

● Mainly fuel oils ● Mainly general cargo

*The main container ports

Orkney

Sullom Voe

Forth

Clyde

Belfast

*Tees & Hartlepool

*Grimsby & Immingham

*Dublin Liverpool Hull

Shannon Manchester

Cork *Felixstowe

Milford Haven *London

Port Talbot *Dover

See map on page 16 for ferry routes

*Medway

Southampton

U.K. TRADE

Trade is balanced by money coming in for services such as banking and insurance

Total Imports 1999
£192 434 million

Food and Drink 8.6% Other Goods 3.8%
Fuel and Chemicals 12.6%
Machinery and Transport Equipment 46.0%
Manufactured Goods 29.0%

Total Exports 1999
£165 667 million

Food and Drink 6.0% Other Goods 2.3%
Fuel and Chemicals 19.8%
Machinery and Transport Equipment 47.5%
Manufactured Goods 24.4%

SERVICES

The percentage of the workforce employed in the service industry in 2000

Over 85% in services
80% – 85% in services
75% – 80% in services
70% – 75% in services
Under 70% in services

U.K. as a whole 73.5%
Ireland as a whole 74.3%

MINING, ENERGY AND WATER SUPPLY

✿ Over 10% of the workforce employed in mining, energy and water supply

U.K. as a whole 2.0%
Ireland as a whole 1.1%

All types of work are divided into three groups. Each group is called a type of industry.
1. Industry which produces raw materials. This includes farming, forestry, fishing, mining, energy and water supply.
2. Industry which manufactures goods out of raw materials. This includes metals, chemicals, engineering and textiles.
3. Industry which provides services not goods. This includes work in offices, tourism, transport, construction and government.

EMPLOYMENT

FARMING, FORESTRY AND FISHING

🚜 Over 10% of the workforce employed in farming, forestry and fishing in 2000

U.K. as a whole 1.4%
Ireland as a whole 7.8%

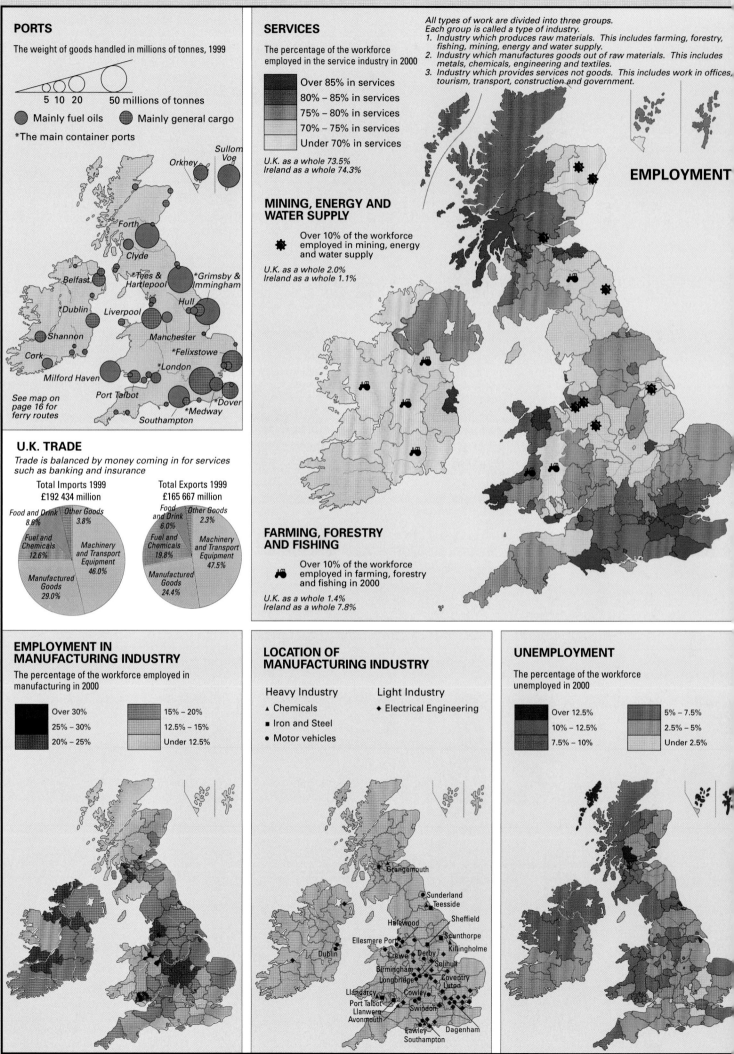

EMPLOYMENT IN MANUFACTURING INDUSTRY

The percentage of the workforce employed in manufacturing in 2000

Over 30%
25% – 30%
20% – 25%
15% – 20%
12.5% – 15%
Under 12.5%

LOCATION OF MANUFACTURING INDUSTRY

Heavy Industry
▲ Chemicals
■ Iron and Steel
● Motor vehicles

Light Industry
◆ Electrical Engineering

Grangemouth

Sunderland
Teesside

Halewood Sheffield

Ellesmere Port Scunthorpe
Killingholme

Dublin Crewe Derby
Birmingham Solihull
Longbridge Coventry
Luton
Llandarcy Cowley
Port Talbot Swindon
Llanwern
Avonmouth
Fawley Dagenham
Southampton

UNEMPLOYMENT

The percentage of the workforce unemployed in 2000

Over 12.5%
10% – 12.5%
7.5% – 10%
5% – 7.5%
2.5% – 5%
Under 2.5%

POPULATION FACTS

U.K. Population 1999	59 500 900
of which England	49 752 900
Scotland	5 119 200
Wales	2 937 000
N. Ireland	1 691 800
Ireland Population 1996	3 626 087

AGE STRUCTURE OF THE U.K. IN 1901 AND 1999

The age structure shows how old people are and the percentage in each age group that is male and female. The diagram is called a population pyramid. For example, in 1901, 20% of the female population was aged between 10-19. In 1999, about 12% were in this group.

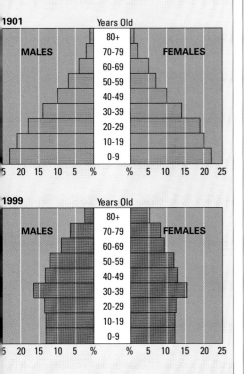

1901

MALES — FEMALES — Years Old: 80+, 70-79, 60-69, 50-59, 40-49, 30-39, 20-29, 10-19, 0-9

1999

MALES — FEMALES — Years Old: 80+, 70-79, 60-69, 50-59, 40-49, 30-39, 20-29, 10-19, 0-9

POPULATION DENSITY

Number of people per square kilometre in 1998 (Ireland and Isle of Man 1996)

- Over 1000
- 500 - 1000
- 200 - 500
- 100 - 200
- 50 - 100
- 25 - 50
- Under 25

The average density for the U.K. is 244 people per km². The average density for the Republic of Ireland is 52 people per km².

MAJOR CITIES
Population of major cities

- ⬤ Over 1 000 000
- ⬛ 400 000 – 1 000 000
- ● 200 000 – 400 000
- · 100 000 – 200 000

YOUNG PEOPLE

The percentage of the population under 16 years old in 1998 (under 15 in Ireland and Isle of Man 1996)

- Over 25%
- 20% - 25%
- 19% - 20%
- 18% - 19%
- Under 18%

% young by country U.K. 20.4% Ireland 23.7%

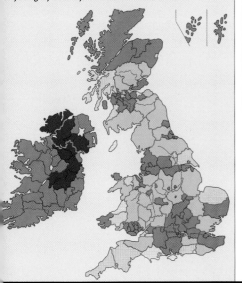

OLD PEOPLE

The percentage of the population over pensionable age* in 1998 (65 or over in Ireland 1996)

- Over 20%
- 17.5% - 20%
- 15% - 17.5%
- 12.5% - 15%
- 10% - 12.5%
- Under 10%

% old by country U.K. 18.1% Ireland 11.4%

Pensionable age in the U.K. and Isle of Man is 65 for males, 60 for females

POPULATION CHANGE

The percentage change in the number of people between 1981 and 1998 (Ireland and Isle of Man 1991 and 1996)

Gain
- Over 15%
- 10% - 15%
- 5% - 10%
- 0% - 5%

Loss
- 0% - 5%
- 5% - 10%
- 10% - 15%
- Over 15%

*% change by country
U.K. 5.1% gain
Ireland 2.9% gain*

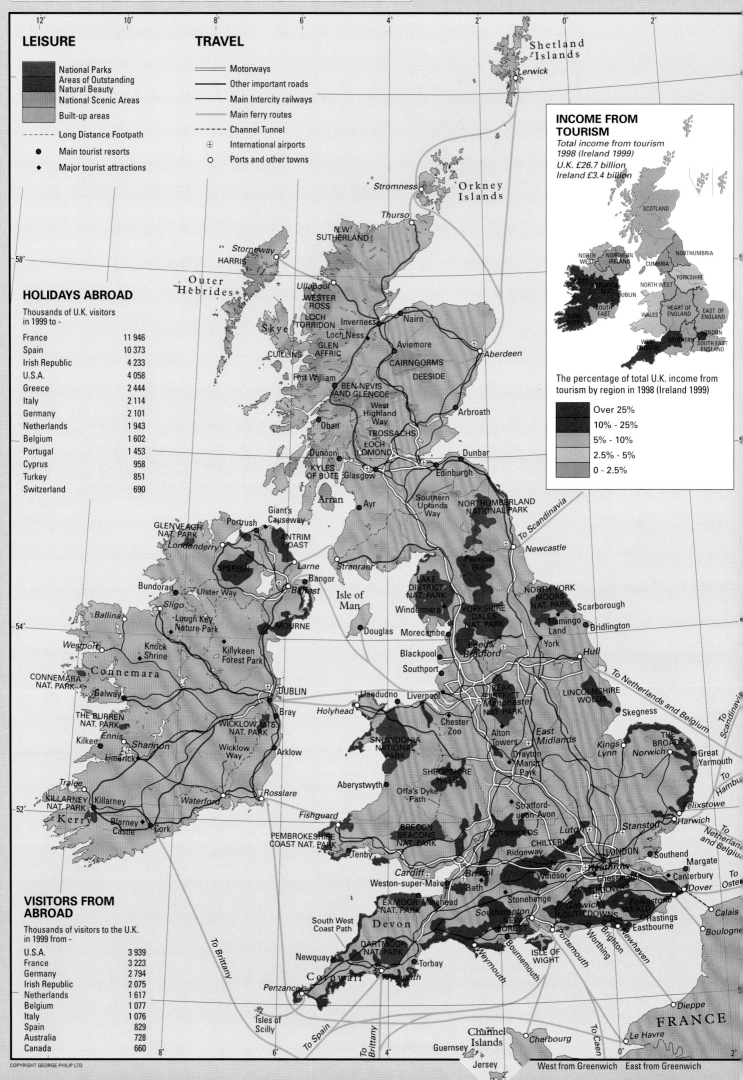

LEISURE

- ■ National Parks
- ■ Areas of Outstanding Natural Beauty
- ■ National Scenic Areas
- ■ Built-up areas
- ------ Long Distance Footpath
- ● Main tourist resorts
- ◆ Major tourist attractions

TRAVEL

- ═══ Motorways
- ━━━ Other important roads
- ─── Main Intercity railways
- ─── Main ferry routes
- ----- Channel Tunnel
- ⊕ International airports
- ○ Ports and other towns

HOLIDAYS ABROAD

Thousands of U.K. visitors in 1999 to -

France	11 946
Spain	10 373
Irish Republic	4 233
U.S.A.	4 058
Greece	2 444
Italy	2 114
Germany	2 101
Netherlands	1 943
Belgium	1 602
Portugal	1 453
Cyprus	958
Turkey	851
Switzerland	690

VISITORS FROM ABROAD

Thousands of visitors to the U.K. in 1999 from -

U.S.A.	3 939
France	3 223
Germany	2 794
Irish Republic	2 075
Netherlands	1 617
Belgium	1 077
Italy	1 076
Spain	829
Australia	728
Canada	660

INCOME FROM TOURISM

Total income from tourism 1998 (Ireland 1999)
U.K. £26.7 billion
Ireland £3.4 billion

The percentage of total U.K. income from tourism by region in 1998 (Ireland 1999)

- ■ Over 25%
- ■ 10% - 25%
- ■ 5% - 10%
- ■ 2.5% - 5%
- ■ 0 - 2.5%

COPYRIGHT GEORGE PHILIP LTD

West from Greenwich   East from Greenwich

REGIONAL STUDIES SECTION

Europe from Space 18–19
Satellite images of Europe and North Africa,
the Netherlands and Paris

European Themes 20–21
Climate Regions
Natural Vegetation
Land Use
Pollution
Wealth
Employment
Trade and Transport

Italy 22–23
Italy 1:5.5m
Age Structure of Italy
Industry
Italy from Space
Out of Work

Japan 24–25
Japan 1:5m
Tokyo
Volcanoes and Earthquakes
Mount Fuji
Population and Industry

Kenya 26–27
Kenya 1:8m
Great Rift Valley from Space
Age Structure of Kenya
Type of Goods Traded
Mount Kenya
Wildlife
Land Use and Natural Vegetation

South Africa 28–29
South Africa 1:8m
The Cape Peninsula from Space
Agriculture
Mining and Industry
Cross-section of South Africa

Brazil 30–31
Brazil 1:21m
Brazil from Space
Age Structure of Brazil
Mining and Industry
Agriculture and Deforestation

The Arctic and Antarctica 32
The Arctic and Antarctica from Space
Ozone Holes

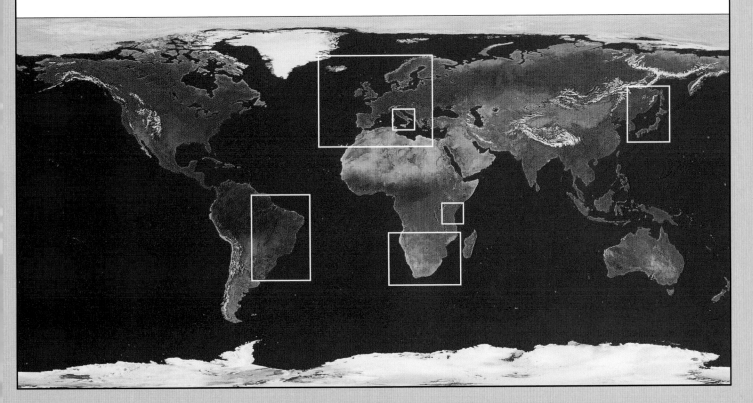

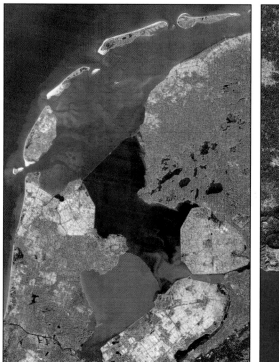

▶ Netherlands (right)
Following the construction of the Afluitsdijk Dam across the mouth of the IJsselmeer between 1927 and 1932, large areas of land were drained, forming new, fertile land for agriculture. This land, known as *polders*, is seen here in green.

▶ Naples (far right)
This image, processed to appear as natural colour, shows Naples on the north side of the bay. To the south-east (lower right) Mount Vesuvius can be seen.

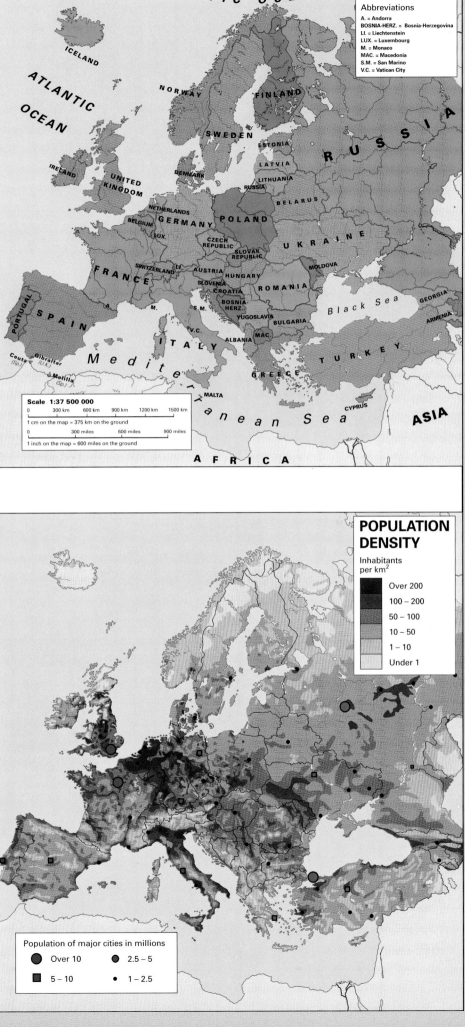

COUNTRIES

Abbreviations

A. = Andorra
BOSNIA-HERZ. = Bosnia-Herzegovina
LI. = Liechtenstein
LUX. = Luxembourg
M. = Monaco
MAC. = Macedonia
S.M. = San Marino
V.C. = Vatican City

Scale 1:37 500 000

| 0 | 300 km | 600 km | 900 km | 1200 km | 1500 km |

1 cm on the map = 375 km on the ground

| 0 | 300 miles | 600 miles | 900 miles |

1 inch on the map = 600 miles on the ground

POPULATION DENSITY

Inhabitants per km²

Over 200
100 – 200
50 – 100
10 – 50
1 – 10
Under 1

Population of major cities in millions

● Over 10
■ 5 – 10
● 2.5 – 5
• 1 – 2.5

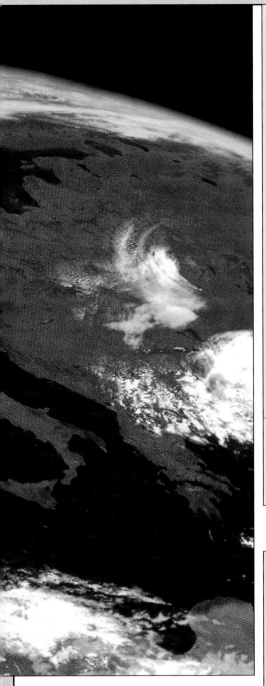

▲ Oblique satellite image of Europe and North Africa

The colours in this European Meteosat satellite image result from the different vegetation and surface temperatures. Europe is largely green indicating extensive agriculture, and orange from the forests and urban development, while North Africa is mainly brown, indicating the presence of arid desert. A number of weather systems, revealed as white clouds, cover the Atlantic Ocean (left on the image).

Comparing the maps (top, right and overleaf) with the oblique satellite image above will help identify specific countries and land use types.

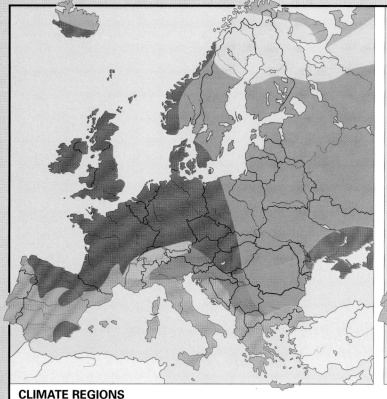

CLIMATE REGIONS

Polar climate (very cold and dry)

- Tundra: short cold summer

Continental climate (cold and wet)

- Subarctic: very short, cool summer
- Cool summer
- Warm summer

Mild climate (warm and wet)

- Wet all year, cool summer
- Wet all year, warm summer
- Warm, dry summer

Dry climate

- Steppe - dry all year, warm summer
- Mountain areas with cold, wet and exposed conditions

NATURAL VEGETATION

The map shows what vegetation would grow in the area if people did not live there

- Tundra: moss, lichen and herbs
- Needleleaf evergreen forest
- Mixed forest of broadleaf deciduous and needleleaf evergreen trees
- Broadleaf deciduous woodland
- Grassland
- Evergreen broadleaf and needleleaf trees, shrubs and herbs
- High mountains

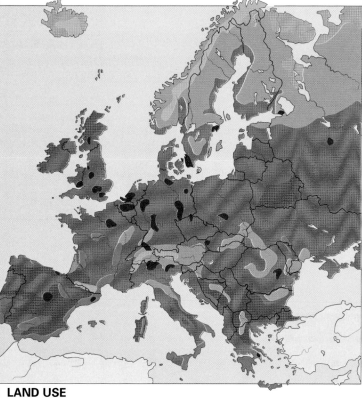

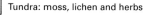

The seas and lakes are being polluted by:- chemical fertilizers, pesticides, sewage, industrial waste, radioactive waste and oil spillage

Acid rain is a form of air pollution. It is common in industrial areas where burning coal and petrol releases poisonous gases such as sulphur dioxide into the atmosphere. These gases can be carried long distances. They fall as acid rain, polluting lakes and killing plant life

LAND USE

This map shows how people use the land to support the population

- Urban areas: commercial, industrial and residential land use
- Nomadic herding
- Forestry
- Rough grazing: keeping sheep and goats on large unenclosed areas of natural vegetation
- Pasture: grazing animals such as beef and dairy cattle on sewn fields of grass
- Arable: growing crops in fields
- Fruit trees, vineyards, olives or flowers
- Unproductive land

POLLUTION

- Heavily polluted seas and lakes
- Moderately polluted seas and lakes
- Lightly polluted seas and lakes

Recent oil tanker accidents

- ▲ Over 100 000 tonnes oil spilt
- ▴ 10 000 - 100 000 tonnes oil spilt

 Areas heavily polluted by acid rain

Use of chemical fertilizers on agricultural land

- Over 300 kg per hectare
- 200 - 300 kg per hectare
- 100 - 200 kg per hectare
- 50 - 100 kg per hectare
- Under 50 kg per hectare

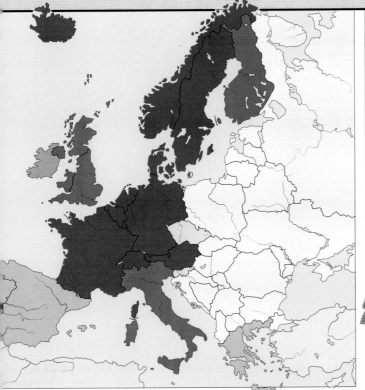

WEALTH

The value of total production divided by population 1997 (US$ per person)

- Over $25 000 per person
- $20 - 25 000 per person
- $15 - 20 000 per person
- $10 - 15 000 per person
- $5 - 10 000 per person
- Under $5 000 per person

Wealthiest countries

Luxembourg $45 380 per person
Switzerland $44 220 per person
Liechtenstein $33 000 per person

Poorest countries

Albania $750 per person
Moldova $540 per person
Bosnia-Herz. $300 per person

EMPLOYMENT

Employment can be divided into three groups: agriculture, industry and services. This map shows the countries with the highest percentage of people in each group

- Over 20% in agriculture (farming, forestry and fishing)
- Over 40% in industry (includes mining and manufacturing)
- Over 60% in services (includes gas, electricity and water supplies, tourism, banking, education)
- Employment is balanced between the groups (under 20% in agriculture, under 40% in industry, under 60% in services)

TRADE PARTNERS

- E U (European Union)

H Q Brussels

Founder members in 1957: Belgium, France, Luxembourg, W. Germany, Italy, Netherlands. U K, Ireland and Denmark joined in 1973, Greece in 1981, Spain and Portugal in 1986, Austria, Finland and Sweden joined in January 1995.

- E F T A (European Free Trade Association)

H Q Geneva. Founded in 1959.
Members in 1995:
Iceland, Liechtenstein, Norway and Switzerland.

- Not a member of any trade organisation

TOURISM

Tourism receipts as a percentage of G.N.P.

- Over 10% of G.N.P from tourism
- 5-10% of G.N.P from tourism
- 2.5-5% of G.N.P from tourism
- 1-2.5% of G.N.P from tourism
- 0.5-1% of G.N.P from tourism
- Under 0.5% of G.N.P from tourism

Tourist destinations

- Cultural & historical centres
- Coastal resorts
- Ski resorts
- Centres of entertainment
- Places of pilgrimage
- Places of great natural beauty

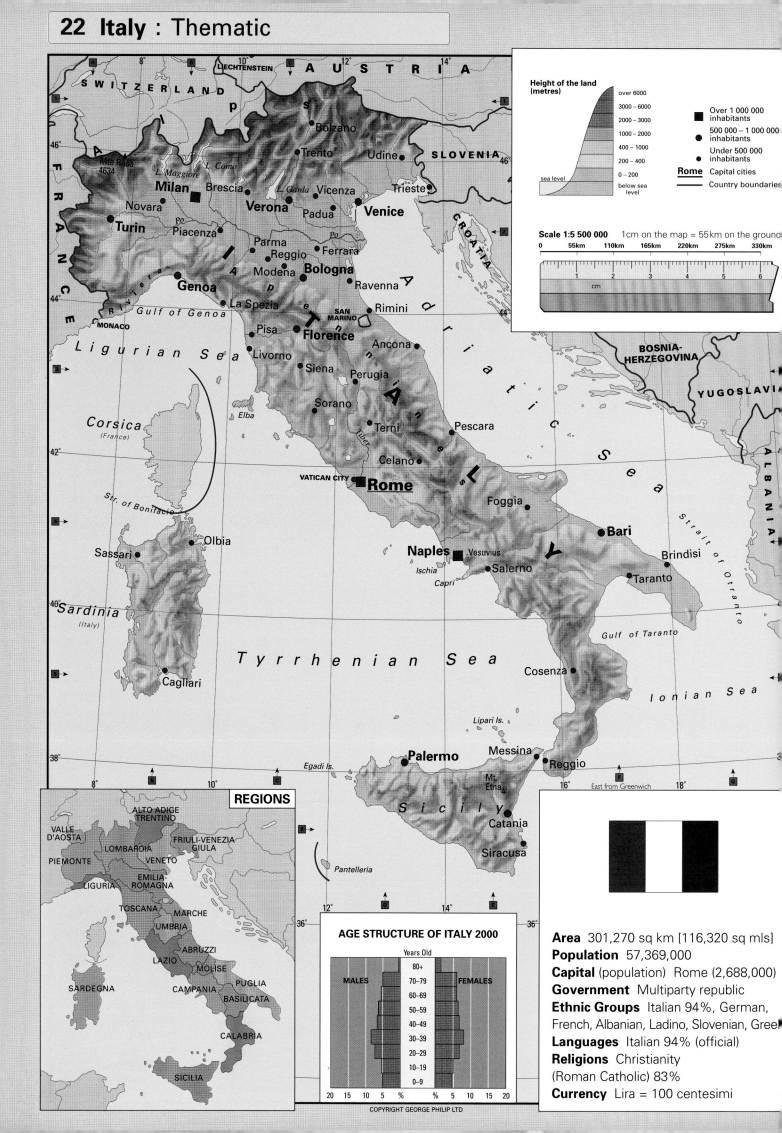

Height of the land (metres)

over 6000
3000 – 6000
2000 – 3000
1000 – 2000
400 – 1000
200 – 400
0 – 200
below sea level
sea level

■ Over 1 000 000 inhabitants
● 500 000 – 1 000 000 inhabitants
● Under 500 000 inhabitants
Rome Capital cities
— Country boundaries

Scale 1:5 500 000   1cm on the map = 55km on the ground

0   55km   110km   165km   220km   275km   330km

REGIONS

VALLE D'AOSTA
ALTO ADIGE TRENTINO
FRIULI-VENEZIA GIULIA
LOMBARDIA
PIEMONTE
VENETO
LIGURIA
EMILIA-ROMAGNA
TOSCANA
MARCHE
UMBRIA
ABRUZZI
LAZIO
MOLISE
CAMPANIA
PUGLIA
BASILICATA
SARDEGNA
CALABRIA
SICILIA

AGE STRUCTURE OF ITALY 2000

Years Old

MALES   FEMALES

80+
70–79
60–69
50–59
40–49
30–39
20–29
10–19
0–9

20 15 10 5 %   % 5 10 15 20

COPYRIGHT GEORGE PHILIP LTD

Area 301,270 sq km [116,320 sq mls]
Population 57,369,000
Capital (population) Rome (2,688,000)
Government Multiparty republic
Ethnic Groups Italian 94%, German, French, Albanian, Ladino, Slovenian, Greek
Languages Italian 94% (official)
Religions Christianity (Roman Catholic) 83%
Currency Lira = 100 centesimi

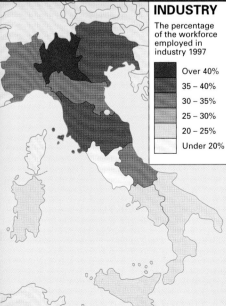

INDUSTRY

The percentage
of the workforce
employed in
industry 1997

- Over 40%
- 35 – 40%
- 30 – 35%
- 25 – 30%
- 20 – 25%
- Under 20%

▲ Italy

At the centre of the image lies Italy,
with the island of Sicily at its base. The
Alps are identified in white and green
to the north of Italy, and to the west of
the Tyrrhenian Sea are the islands of
Corsica and Sardinia. Albania and the
former Yugoslav republics of Slovenia,
Croatia and Bosnia-Herzegovina are to
be seen to the east across the Adriatic
Sea.

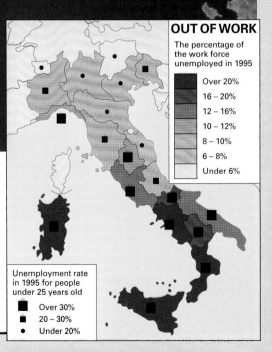

OUT OF WORK

The percentage of
the work force
unemployed in 1995

- Over 20%
- 16 – 20%
- 12 – 16%
- 10 – 12%
- 8 – 10%
- 6 – 8%
- Under 6%

Unemployment rate
in 1995 for people
under 25 years old

- ■ Over 30%
- ■ 20 – 30%
- ● Under 20%

SOUTHERN JAPAN
(See page 43 for rest of Japan)

Height of the land (metres)

over 4000	
2000–4000	
1000–2000	
400–1000	
200–400	
0–200	
sea level	
	below sea level

S E A   O F   J A P A N

Oki Is.

Nanao
Takaoka
Nagano
Utsunomiya
Hitachi
Matsuto
Toyama
Maebashi
Mito
Kanazawa
Takasaki
Ashikaga
Matsumoto
Takayama
Okaya
Kawagoe
Omiya
Fukui
Takefu
Ina
Kofu
Hachioji
Kawaguchi
Tsuruga
Maizuru
Gifu
Ichinomiya
Tokyo
Funabashi
Matsue
Tottori
Ogaki
Nagoya
Mt. Fuji 3776
Chiba Ch
Yonago
Kurayoshi
Kyoto
Otsu
Yokkaichi
Toyota
Numazu
Kawasaki
Tsuyama
Okazaki
Yokohama
Yokosuka
H O N S H U
Gotsu
Himeji
Amagasaki
Tsu
Shizuoka
Odawara
Hamada
Okayama
Kobe
Higashiosaka
Hamamatsu
Masuda
Kurashiki
Osaka
Sakai
Toyohashi
Ise Bay
Hiroshima
Fukuyama
Takamatsu
C. Daio
Yamaguchi
Kure
Imabari
Tokushima
Wakayama
Nii Is.
Ube
Tokuyama
Niihama
Miyake Is.
Shimonoseki
Hofu
Matsuyama
Tanabe
Nogata
SHIKOKU
Shingu
Kitakyushu
Buzen
Yawatahama
Kochi
Fukuoka
Beppu
C. Shiono
Karatsu
Kurume
Oita
Tosa Bay
Sasebo
KYUSHU
Saiki
Uwajima
C. Ashizuri
Omuta
Nagasaki
Kumamoto
Nobeoka
Yatsushiro

Inland Sea
Kii Channel
Bungo Channel

P A C I F I C
O C E A N

East from Greenwich

Sendai
Miyazaki
Miyakonojo
Kagoshima

Osumi Channel
Tanega I.

Population legend:

■ Over 5 000 000 inhabitants
● 1 000 000 – 5 000 000 inhabitants
• Under 1 000 000 inhabitants
<u>Tokyo</u> Capital cities underlined

Scale 1:5 000 000 — 1cm on the map = 50km on the ground

| 0 | 50km | 100km | 150km | 200km | 250km | 300km | 350km | 400km |

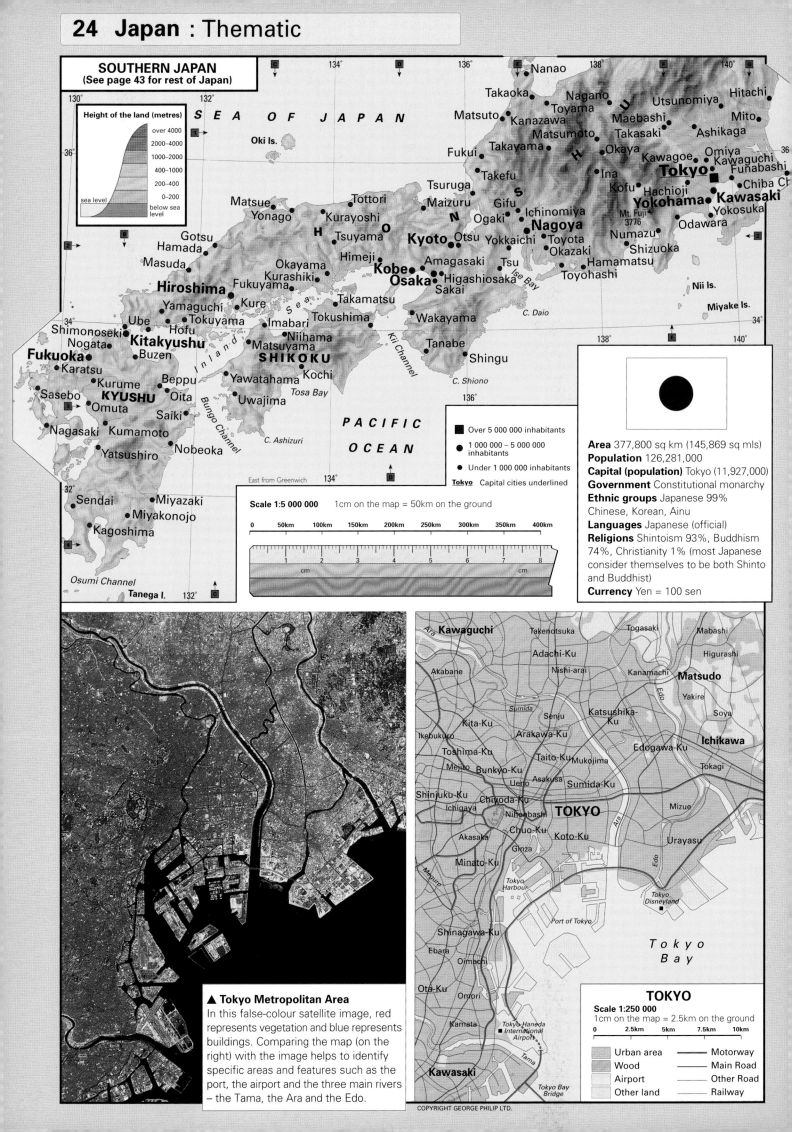

Area 377,800 sq km (145,869 sq mls)
Population 126,281,000
Capital (population) Tokyo (11,927,000)
Government Constitutional monarchy
Ethnic groups Japanese 99%
Chinese, Korean, Ainu
Languages Japanese (official)
Religions Shintoism 93%, Buddhism 74%, Christianity 1% (most Japanese consider themselves to be both Shinto and Buddhist)
Currency Yen = 100 sen

▲ Tokyo Metropolitan Area
In this false-colour satellite image, red represents vegetation and blue represents buildings. Comparing the map (on the right) with the image helps to identify specific areas and features such as the port, the airport and the three main rivers – the Tama, the Ara and the Edo.

TOKYO map labels:

Kawaguchi
Takenotsuka
Togasaki
Mabashi
Adachi-Ku
Higurashi
Akabane
Nishi-arai
Kanamachi
Matsudo
Ara
Yakire
Sumida
Senju
Katsushika-Ku
Soya
Kita-Ku
Arakawa-Ku
Edo
Ikebukuro
Ichikawa
Toshima-Ku
Taito-Ku
Edogawa-Ku
Mejiro
Mukojima
Tokagi
Bunkyo-Ku
Ueno
Asakusa
Shinjuku-Ku
Sumida-Ku
Mizue
Ichigaya
Chiyoda-Ku
TOKYO
Nihonbashi
Akasaka
Chuo-Ku
Koto-Ku
Urayasu
Ginza
Minato-Ku
Meguro
Tokyo Harbour
Tokyo Disneyland
Shinagawa-Ku
Port of Tokyo
Ebara
T o k y o   B a y
Ota-Ku
Oimachi
Omori
Kamata
Tokyo Haneda International Airport
Kawasaki
Tama
Tokyo Bay Bridge

TOKYO
Scale 1:250 000
1cm on the map = 2.5km on the ground

| 0 | 2.5km | 5km | 7.5km | 10km |

Urban area	Motorway
Wood	Main Road
Airport	Other Road
Other land	Railway

VOLCANOES AND EARTHQUAKES

- ● Epicentres of earthquakes greater than 7 on the Richter Scale (from 1600AD)
- ── Plate boundaries
- → Direction of movement
- ▨ Volcanic regions
- ▲ Active volcanoes
- ━ Coasts vulnerable to tidal waves

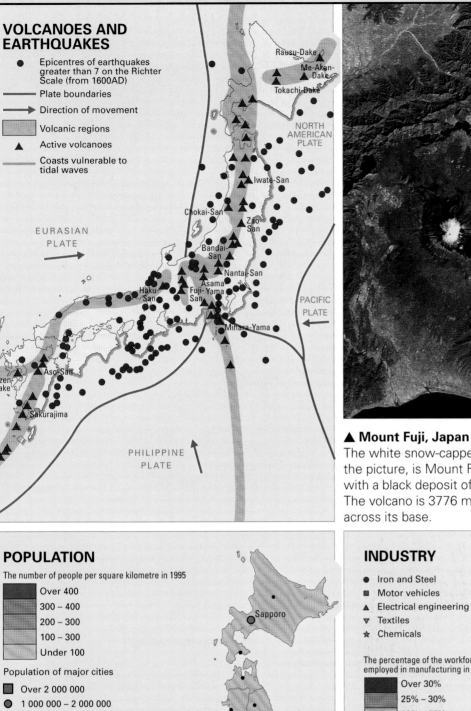

EURASIAN PLATE

NORTH AMERICAN PLATE

PACIFIC PLATE

PHILIPPINE PLATE

Rausu-Dake
Me-Akan-Dake
Tokachi-Dake
Iwate-San
Chokai-San
Zao-San
Bandai-San
Nantai-San
Asama
Haku-San
Fuji-Yama San
Mihara-Yama
Aso-San
Unzen-Dake
Sakurajima

▲ Mount Fuji, Japan

The white snow-capped feature, just below the centre of the picture, is Mount Fuji. The cone is seen as dark green, with a black deposit of ash from its 1707 eruption.
The volcano is 3776 metres high and 30 kilometres wide across its base.

POPULATION

The number of people per square kilometre in 1995

- Over 400
- 300 – 400
- 200 – 300
- 100 – 300
- Under 100

Population of major cities

- ■ Over 2 000 000
- ◉ 1 000 000 – 2 000 000
- ◉ 500 000 – 1 000 000
- • 250 000 – 500 000

Cities with populations over one million are named on the map

Sapporo

Kawasaki
Tokyo
Kyoto
Kobe
Nagoya
Yokohama
Hiroshima
Osaka
Kitakyushu
Fukuoka

AGE STRUCTURE OF JAPAN 2000

	Years Old	
MALES	80+	FEMALES
	70–79	
	60–69	
	50–59	
	40–49	
	30–39	
	20–29	
	10–19	
	0–9	

20 15 10 5 %   % 5 10 15 20

INDUSTRY

- ● Iron and Steel
- ■ Motor vehicles
- ▲ Electrical engineering
- ▼ Textiles
- ★ Chemicals

The percentage of the workforce employed in manufacturing in 1995

- Over 30%
- 25% – 30%
- 20% – 25%
- 15% – 20%
- Under 15%

JAPAN'S TRADE

Main exports Machinery, electrical, 36%, vehicles 20%, iron and steel 6%, chemicals 6%, textiles 3%, ships 2%.
Main export partners USA 31%, Hong Kong SAR 6%, South Korea 4%, China 4%, Germany 5%, UK 4%.
Main imports Petrol and petroleum products 18%, food and live animals 14%, machinery and transport equipment 11%, metals 10%, chemicals 8%, timber 4%.
Main import partners USA 24%, China 13%, Australia 5%, South Korea 4%, Indonesia 4%, Germany 4%.

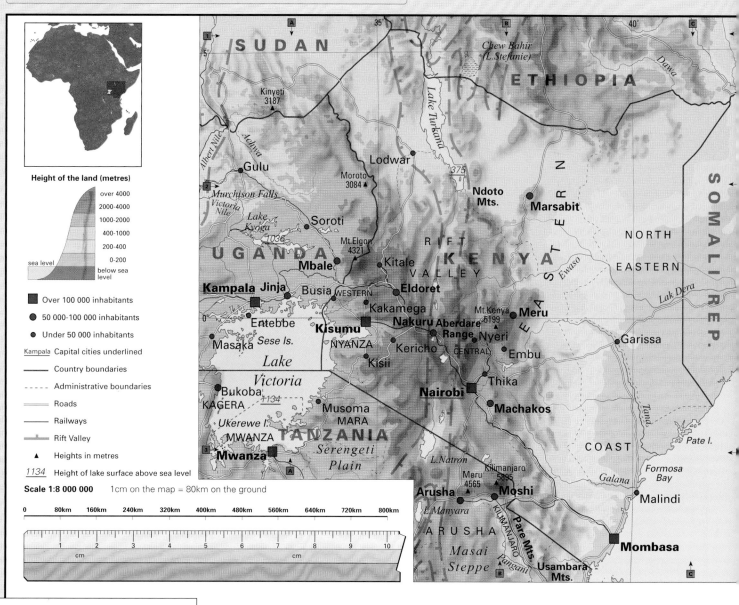

Height of the land (metres)

over 4000
2000-4000
1000-2000
400-1000
200-400
0-200
sea level
below sea level

■ Over 100 000 inhabitants
● 50 000-100 000 inhabitants
● Under 50 000 inhabitants

Kampala Capital cities underlined
—— Country boundaries
----- Administrative boundaries
═══ Roads
—— Railways
━━ Rift Valley
▲ Heights in metres
1134 Height of lake surface above sea level

Scale 1:8 000 000   1cm on the map = 80km on the ground

0 80km 160km 240km 320km 400km 480km 560km 640km 720km 800km

Area 580,370 sq km
[224,081 sq mls]
Population 28,240,000
Capital (population)
Nairobi (2,000,000)
Government Multiparty
republic
Ethnic groups Kikuyu
21%, Luhya 14%,
Luo 13%, Kamba 11%,
Kalenjin 11%
Languages Swahili and
English (both official)
Religions Christianity
(Roman Catholic 27%,
Protestant 19%, others
27%), traditional beliefs
19%, Islam 6%
Currency Kenya shilling
= 100 cents

TYPE OF GOODS TRADED
(important goods are named)

EXPORTS
Kenya Total Exports 1993, K£ 3,625 million

Coffee 15%
Tea 26%
Oil & gas 9%
Pyrethrum 1%
Pineapples 3%
Soda ash 2%
Cement 2%
Others 42%

IMPORTS
Kenya Total Imports 1993, K£ 5,056 million

Crude materials 4%
Others 6%
Mineral fuels (including crude oil) 33%
Chemicals 26%
Manufactured items (incl. machinery) 31%

▼ Great Rift Valley
The infrared satellite image shows
vegetation in red, water in blue/black and
bare ground and buildings in light blue.

AGE STRUCTURE OF KENYA 2000

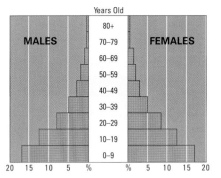

Years Old

MALES		FEMALES
	80+	
	70–79	
	60–69	
	50–59	
	40–49	
	30–39	
	20–29	
	10–19	
	0–9	

20 15 10 5 % % 5 10 15 20

◀ **Mount Kenya**

The satellite used to acquire this image
orbited at around 700 kilometres above
the Earth's surface. The dark green in this
image around the base of Mount Kenya
represents mountain forest while the
lighter greens on the higher slopes
represent bamboo forest and mountain
grasslands.
Mount Kenya is 5199m high, the second
highest mountain in Africa, after
Mount Kilimanjaro, Tanzania.

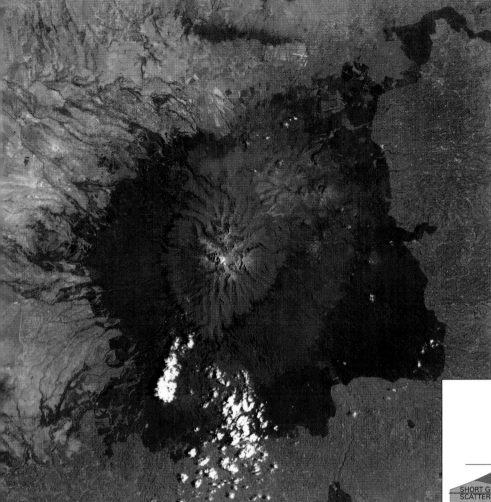

CHANGES IN VEGETATION WITH HEIGHT ON MOUNT KENYA

ROCK & SNOW — 4 500m
MOUNTAIN GRASSLAND AND BAMBOO FOREST — 3 000m
MOUNTAIN FOREST
SHORT GRASS SCATTERED TREES — TALL GRASS, SCATTERED TREES — 1 500m
DRY BUSH WITH TREES

WEST — EAST

WILDLIFE

Mt. Elgon
Samburu
Aberdare
Mt. Kenya
Masai Mara
Nairobi
Amboseli
Tsavo

■ National Park
■ Game Reserve

LAND USE & CROPS

CROPS

- ◉ Coffee
- 🌿 Maize
- ⚘ Tea

■ Woods and forests
■ Arable land
■ Rough grazing
■ Non-agricultural land

NATURAL VEGETATION

■ Mangrove forest
■ Coastal forest
■ Tall grass with scattered trees
■ Short grass with scattered trees
■ Poor grass, thorns, sand and bare rock
■ Dry bush with trees
■ Mountain forest and grassland
■ High mountain vegetation

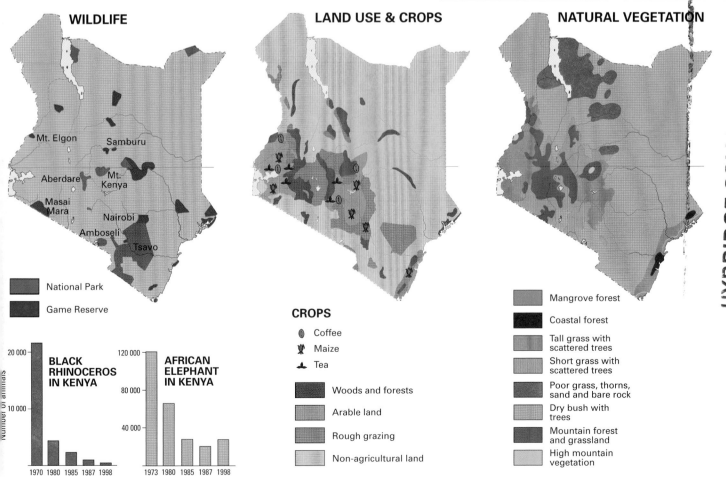

BLACK RHINOCEROS IN KENYA

20 000
10 000

Number of animals

1970 1980 1985 1987 1998

AFRICAN ELEPHANT IN KENYA

120 000
80 000
40 000

1973 1980 1985 1987 1998

▶ **Cape of Good Hope, South Africa**

This Landsat 4 image shows the area around the Cape Peninsula in South Africa. Arable land is shown in red and urban areas are shown in light blue, in a false-colour view.
Cape Town lies near the top of the peninsula, while the Cape of Good Hope is shown at the bottom. The dark area on the coast next to Cape Town represents the Table Mountain.

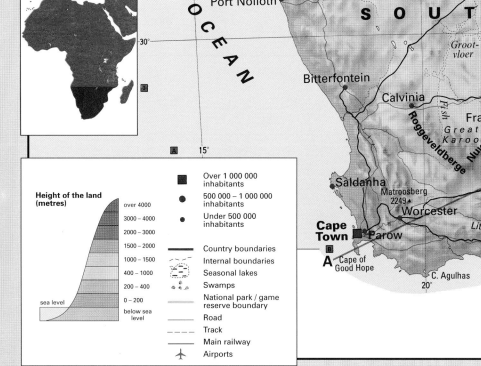

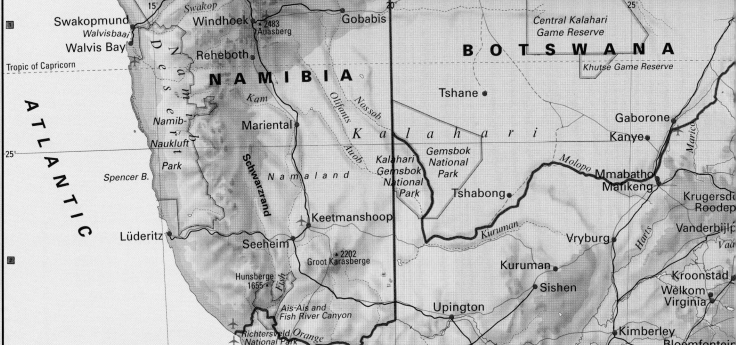

Height of the land (metres)

over 4000	
3000 – 4000	
2000 – 3000	
1500 – 2000	
1000 – 1500	
400 – 1000	
200 – 400	
0 – 200	
sea level	below sea level

- ■ Over 1 000 000 inhabitants
- ● 500 000 – 1 000 000 inhabitants
- • Under 500 000 inhabitants
- ▬▬ Country boundaries
- ····· Internal boundaries
- Seasonal lakes
- Swamps
- National park / game reserve boundary
- ▬▬ Road
- - - - Track
- ▬▬ Main railway
- ✈ Airports

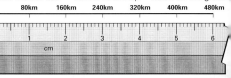

Scale 1:8 000 000   1cm on the map = 80km on the ground

0	80km	160km	240km	320km	400km	480km

cm

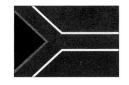

Area 1,219,916 sq km (470,566 sq mls)
Population 39,357,000
Capital (population) Cape Town (legislative, 2,350,000); Pretoria (administrative, 1,080,000); Bloemfontein (judiciary, 300,000)
Government Multiparty republic
Ethnic groups Black 76%, White 13%, Coloured 9%, Asian 2%
Languages Afrikaans, English, Ndebele, North Sotho, South Sotho, Swazi, Tsonga, Tswana, Venda, Xhosa, Zulu (all official)
Religions Christianity 68%, Hinduism 1%, Islam 1%
Currency Rand = 100 cents

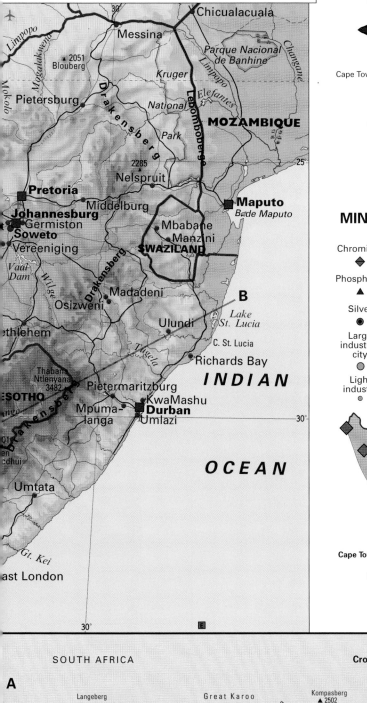

AGRICULTURE

- Arable land
- Plantation crops
- Non agricultural land
- Forest, woods and mangroves
- Rough grazing with some woods and trees
- Non agricultural land and some rough grazing

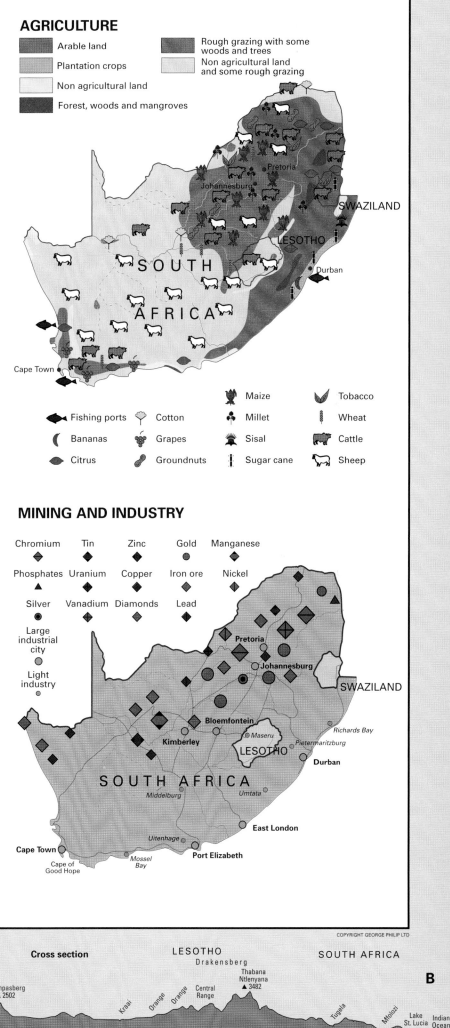

- Fishing ports
- Bananas
- Citrus
- Cotton
- Grapes
- Groundnuts
- Maize
- Millet
- Sisal
- Sugar cane
- Tobacco
- Wheat
- Cattle
- Sheep

MINING AND INDUSTRY

Chromium · Tin · Zinc · Gold · Manganese
Phosphates · Uranium · Copper · Iron ore · Nickel
Silver · Vanadium · Diamonds · Lead

- Large industrial city
- Light industry

SWAZILAND

Pretoria
Johannesburg
Bloemfontein
Kimberley
Maseru
LESOTHO
Richards Bay
Pietermaritzburg
Durban

SOUTH AFRICA

Middelburg
Umtata
East London
Uitenhage
Port Elizabeth
Mossel Bay
Cape Town
Cape of Good Hope

COPYRIGHT GEORGE PHILIP LTD

SOUTH AFRICA

Cross section

LESOTHO
Drakensberg

SOUTH AFRICA

A

Cape of Good Hope
Atlantic / False Bay
Langeberg
Bree
Touws
Great Karoo
Gamka
Sout
Kariega
Kompasberg ▲ 2502
Kraai
Orange
Orange
Central Range
Thabana Ntlenyana ▲ 3482
Tugela
Mfolozi
Lake St. Lucia
Indian Ocean

B

Scale 1:21 000 000   1cm on the map = 210km on the groun

| 0 | 210km | 420km | 630km | 840km | 1050km | 1260km |

VENEZUELA
SURINAM
GUYANA
FRENCH GUIANA
COLOMBIA
Orinoco
Boa Vista
AMAPÁ
RORAIMA
Macapá
Equator
Branco
Bragança
São Luís
Negro
Uaupés
Abaetetuba
Belém
Cametá
Japurá
Santarém
Amazon
Putumayo
Içá
Solimões
Manaus
L. Badajós
Altamira
Bacabal
Sobral
Fortaleza
A M A Z O N A S
Itaituba
Tapajós
Marabá
MARANHÃO
Teresina
Mossoró
RIO GRAND DO NORTE
Juruá
Purus
Madeira
Imperatriz
CEARÁ
Natal
Aripuanã
P A R Á
Juàzeiro do Norte
PARAÍBA
Joã Pes
Campina
Grande
ACRE
Pôrto Velho
Teles Pires
Xingu
PIAUÍ
PERNAMBUCO
Re
Rio Branco
B R
Juàzeiro
São Francisco
Garanhun
Maceló
RONDÔNIA
A Z
Tocantins
Araguaia
Sobradinho
Reservoir
ALAGOAS
SERGIPE
PERU
Mamoré
Guaporé
I L
TOCANTINS
B A H Í A
Aracaju
BOLIVIA
MATO GROSSO
Feira de
Santana
Salvador
Cuiabá
Vitória da
Conquista
Itabuna
Cáceres
Anápolis
Brasília
Ilhéus
Rondonópolis
Goiânia
GOIÁS
Montes
Claros
Teófilo
Otoni
MATO
GROSSO
DO SUL
Uberlândia
Governador Valadares
MINAS GERAIS
Belo Horizonte
ESPÍRITO
SANTO
São José do
Rio Prêto
Campo
Grande
Araçatuba
Ribeirão Prêto
Vitória
Dourados
Bauru
Piracicaba
Juiz de Fora
Campos
Paraná
Londrina
Campinas
Nova Iguaçu
Umuarama
São Paulo
Rio de Janeiro
Tropic of Capricor
PARANÁ
Santos
Ponta Grossa
PARAGUAY
Foz do
Iguaçu
Curitiba
São Francisco do Sul
Joinville
Florianópolis
SANTA
CATARINA
**ATLANTIC
OCEAN**
ARGENTINA
Passo
Fundo
RIO GRANDE
DO SUL
Caxias do Sul
Uruguaiana
Pôrto Alegre
Bagé
Pelotas
URUGUAY
Rio Grande
West from Greenwich

Height of the land (metres)

| over 4000 |
| 2000-4000 |
| 1000-2000 |
| 400-1000 |
| 200-400 |
| 0-200 |
| sea level |
| below sea level |

■ Over 5 000 000 inhabitants
● 1 000 000 – 5 000 000 inhabitants
• Under 1 000 000 inhabitants

Brasília Capital cities underlined
——— Roads
——— Railways

▲ **South America**
The Atacama Desert and Andes mountain chain (to the left) are depicted in yellow, while rainforest and grassland areas are shown in green.

AGE STRUCTURE OF BRAZIL 2000

Years Old

	80+	
MALES	70–79	FEMALES
	60–69	
	50–59	
	40–49	
	30–39	
	20–29	
	10–19	
	0–9	

20 15 10 5 % % 5 10 15 20

Area 8,511,970 sq km
[3,286,472 sq mls]
Population 159,500,000
Capital (population) Brasília (1,596,000)
Government Federal republic
Ethnic groups White 53%,
Mulatto 22%, Mestizo 12%, African
American 11%, Japanese 1%,
Amerindian 0.1%
Languages Portuguese (official)
Religions Christianity
(Roman Catholic 88%)
Currency Real = 100 centavos

MINING AND INDUSTRY

Chromium	Tin	Zinc	Gold
Bauxite	Copper	Iron ore	Manganese
	Coal	Oil	

EXPORTS
Brazil Total Exports 1998 $51,120.0 million

- Others 12.7%
- Food & live animals 20.3% (of which coffee 5.1%)
- Machinery 24.6% (of which motor vehicles 9.4%)
- Crude materials 15.5% (of which iron ore 7.2%)
- Fuel 0.7%
- Chemicals 6.2%
- Manufactured Goods 20.0% (of which iron and steel 7.2%)

IMPORTS
Brazil Total Imports 1998 $60,793.2 million

- Others 8.1%
- Food & live animals 8.4%
- Crude materials 3.1%
- Fuel 9.3%
- Machinery 43.8% (of which motor vehicles 9.5%)
- Chemicals 16.2%
- Manufactured Goods 11.1%

AGRICULTURE

	Industrial
	Arable land
	Plantation crops
	Pasture
	Forest, woods and mangroves
	Rough grazing

CROPS AND LIVESTOCK

Fishing ports	Cotton	Tea
Bananas	Groundnuts	Tobacco
Cacao	Maize	Cattle
Citrus fruit	Potatoes	Pigs
Coconuts	Rice	
Coffee	Sugar cane	

Map labels: Fortaleza, Recife, Salvador, Brasília, Belo Horizonte, São Paulo, Rio de Janeiro, Pôrto Alegre

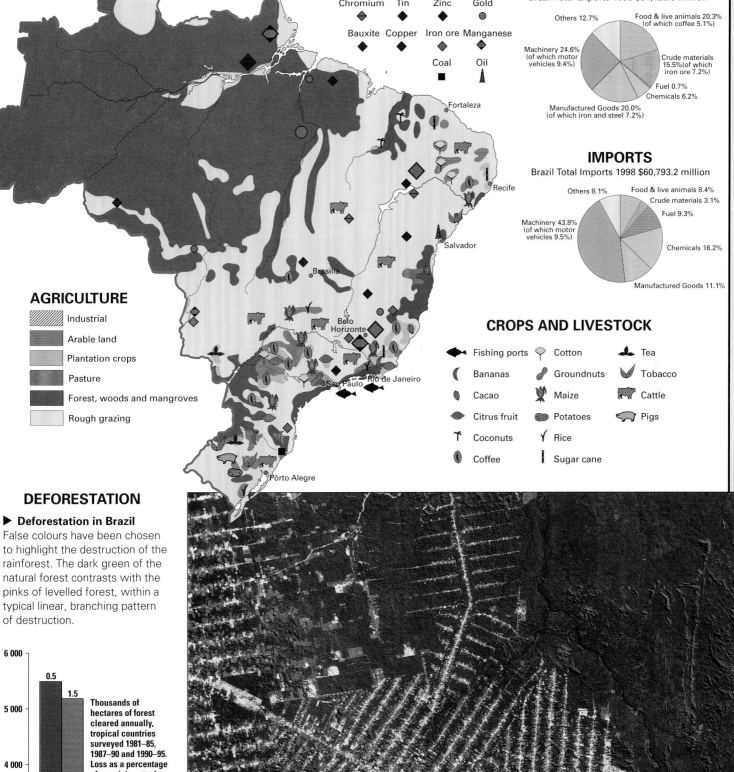

DEFORESTATION

▶ **Deforestation in Brazil**
False colours have been chosen to highlight the destruction of the rainforest. The dark green of the natural forest contrasts with the pinks of levelled forest, within a typical linear, branching pattern of destruction.

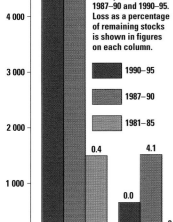

Thousands of hectares of forest cleared annually, tropical countries surveyed 1981–85, 1987–90 and 1990–95. Loss as a percentage of remaining stocks is shown in figures on each column.

- 1990–95
- 1987–90
- 1981–85

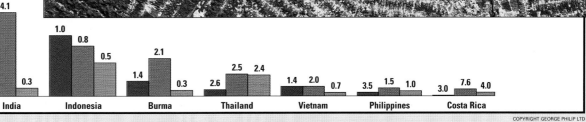

Deforestation chart values:

Country	1990–95	1987–90	1981–85
Brazil	0.5	1.5	0.4
India	0.0	4.1	0.3
Indonesia	1.0	0.8	0.5
Burma	1.4	2.1	0.3
Thailand	2.6	2.5	2.4
Vietnam	1.4	2.0	0.7
Philippines	3.5	1.5	1.0
Costa Rica	3.0	7.6	4.0

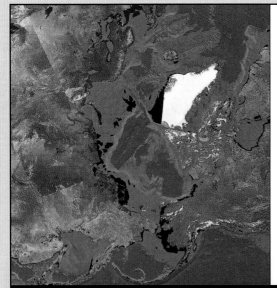

▶ Northern hemisphere 'ozone hole', 1995

Red, orange and yellow indicate high values of ozone concentration. The 'hole' is seen as the dark blue and purple patch at the centre. Here, ozone values are around 120DU (Dobson Units) or lower – normal levels are around 280DU.

◀ Arctic Ocean

The ocean bed is coloured according to depth: green for sea level to 3000 metres and blue for depths greater than 3000 metres.

▲ Antarctica

The colours on this satellite mosaic have been enhanced to reveal the large-scale structure of the ice cover over the continent. Most of the ice shown here covers land, with the exception of the Ross Ice Shelf (brown tint, lower left of centre) and the Ronne Ice Shelf (brown tint, left of centre). The permanent ice cover is over 3000 metres thick near the centre of the continent, and covers a total area of over 12.5 million square kilometres.

◀ Antarctic 'ozone hole', 1995

The image shows a large 'hole' at the centre, coloured in light blue, dark blue and purple. The lowest value of ozone recorded was 98DU.

WORLD MAP SECTION

Below is a slice through the map of Southern Europe on page 38 and 39. It is used here to explain the meaning of the lines, colours and symbols.

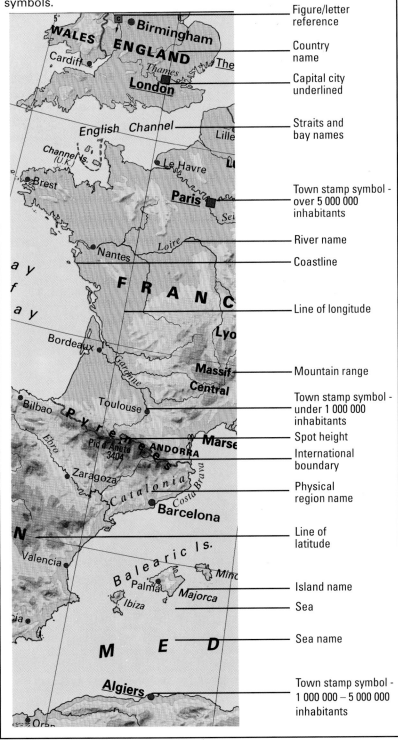

- Figure/letter reference
- Country name
- Capital city underlined
- Straits and bay names
- Town stamp symbol - over 5 000 000 inhabitants
- River name
- Coastline
- Line of longitude
- Mountain range
- Town stamp symbol - under 1 000 000 inhabitants
- Spot height
- International boundary
- Physical region name
- Line of latitude
- Island name
- Sea
- Sea name
- Town stamp symbol - 1 000 000 – 5 000 000 inhabitants

HEIGHT OF THE LAND & KEY

These explanation boxes appear on each map to show the height of the land above sea level and to explain some of the features on the map.

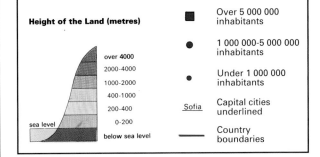

Height of the Land (metres)

over 4000
2000-4000
1000-2000
400-1000
200-400
0-200
sea level
below sea level

- ■ Over 5 000 000 inhabitants
- ● 1 000 000-5 000 000 inhabitants
- • Under 1 000 000 inhabitants
- Sofia — Capital cities underlined
- — Country boundaries

LOCATOR MAP

One of the two styles of map below will appear on each map page. The red area shows how the main map fits into the region around it.

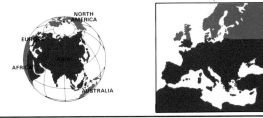

SCALE COMPARISON MAP

Where the map scale allows it, this map appears on map pages at the same scale as the main map, to give an idea of size.

BRITISH ISLES
On same scale

SCALE BAR

Scale 1:50 000 000   1cm on the map = 500km on the ground

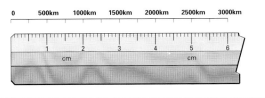

0   500km   1000km   1500km   2000km   2500km   3000km

CROSS SECTION

There is a cross section similar to the one below for each continent. These can be found on the relevant map pages.

FRANCE   ITALY   YUGOSLAVIA   ROMANIA

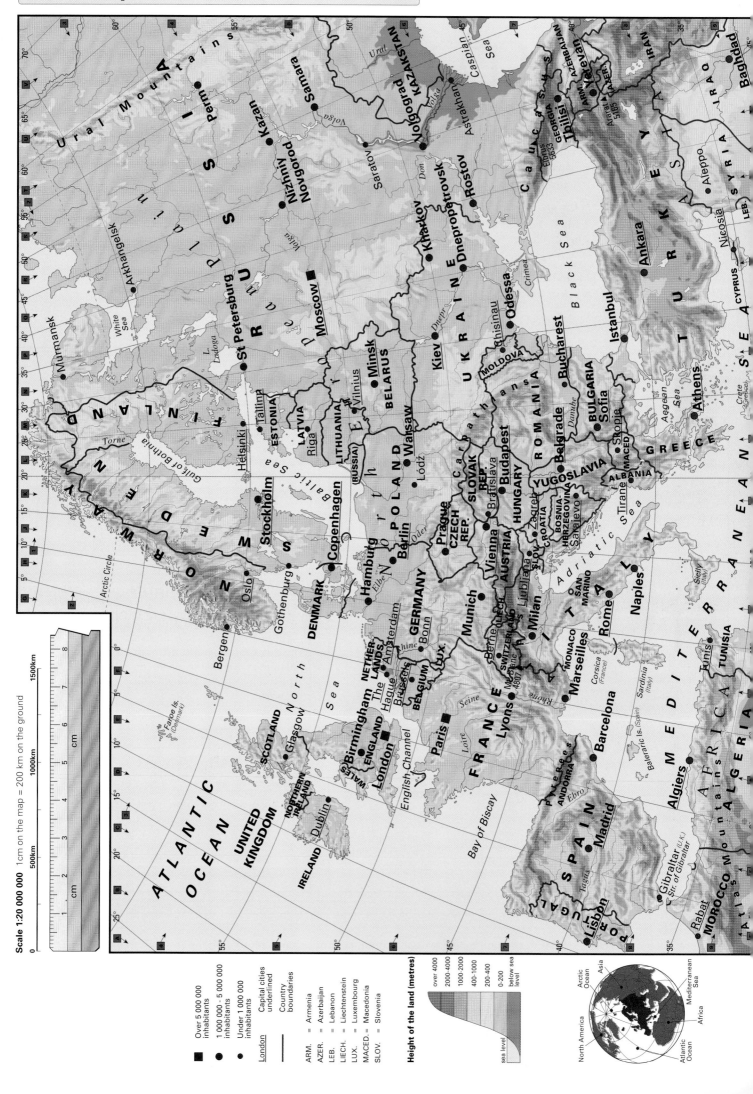

Scale 1:20 000 000 1cm on the map = 200 km on the ground

1500km

1000km

500km

cm

cm

ATLANTIC OCEAN

Faroe Is. (Denmark)

UNITED KINGDOM

SCOTLAND

Glasgow

NORTHERN IRELAND

IRELAND

Dublin

WALES

Birmingham

ENGLAND

London

English Channel

Bay of Biscay

Bergen

NORWAY

Oslo

SWEDEN

Gothenburg

Stockholm

DENMARK

Copenhagen

North Sea

Hamburg

NETHER-LANDS

The Hague

Amsterdam

BELGIUM

Brussels

LUX.

Paris

FRANCE

Loire

Lyons

Seine

Rhine

Bonn

GERMANY

Munich

Berlin

Elbe

Oder

POLAND

Łódź

Warsaw

CZECH REP.

Prague

SLOVAK REP.

Bratislava

Vienna

AUSTRIA

SWITZERLAND

Berne

Mont Blanc 4807

Rhône

Milan

Ljubljana

SLOV.

Zagreb

CROATIA

HUNGARY

Budapest

Carpathians

Transilvania

ROMANIA

Belgrade

YUGOSLAVIA

BOSNIA-HERZEGOVINA

Sarajevo

Danube

SAN MARINO

ITALY

Rome

Naples

Corsica (France)

Sardinia (Italy)

MONACO

Marseilles

Tunis

TUNISIA

ALGERIA

Algiers

Atlas Mountains

MOROCCO

Rabat

Gibraltar (U.K.) Str. of Gibraltar

Lisbon

PORTUGAL

SPAIN

Madrid

Tagus

Ebro

PYRENEES

ANDORRA

Barcelona

Balearic Is. (Spain)

MEDITERRANEAN SEA

AFRICA

ALBANIA

Tirane

MACED.

Skopje

BULGARIA

Sofia

GREECE

Athens

Crete (Greece)

Aegean Sea

Ionian Sea

Adriatic Sea

Bucharest

MOLDOVA

Chisinau

Odessa

Black Sea

Crimea

Istanbul

Ankara

TURKEY

Nicosia

CYPRUS

LEB.

Aleppo

SYRIA

Baghdad

IRAQ

IRAN

Yerevan

ARM.

AZER.

AZERBAIJAN

Ararat 5165

GEORGIA

Tbilisi

Elbrus 5633

CAUCASUS

Caspian Sea

Astrakhan

Volgograd

KAZAKSTAN

Ural

Volga

Saratov

Samara

Perm

Kazan

Nizhniy Novgorod

Don

Rostov

Dnepropetrovsk

Kharkov

UKRAINE

Kiev

Dnepr

BELARUS

Minsk

Moscow

RUSSIA

St Petersburg

Volga

Arkhangelsk

Murmansk

White Sea

L. Ladoga

FINLAND

Helsinki

Torne

Gulf of Bothnia

Tallina

ESTONIA

Riga

LATVIA

LITHUANIA

Vilnius

(RUSSIA)

Baltic Sea

Ural Mountains

Russian Plain

N o r t h   E u r o p e a n   P l a i n

Arctic Circle

Height of the land (metres)

over 4000
2000-4000
1000-2000
400-1000
200-400
0-200
below sea level

sea level

Over 5 000 000 inhabitants

1 000 000 - 5 000 000 inhabitants

Under 1 000 000 inhabitants

London   Capital cities underlined

Country boundaries

ARM. = Armenia
AZER. = Azerbaijan
LEB. = Lebanon
LIECH. = Liechtenstein
LUX. = Luxembourg
MACED. = Macedonia
SLOV. = Slovenia

Arctic Ocean

Asia

Mediterranean Sea

Africa

Atlantic Ocean

North America

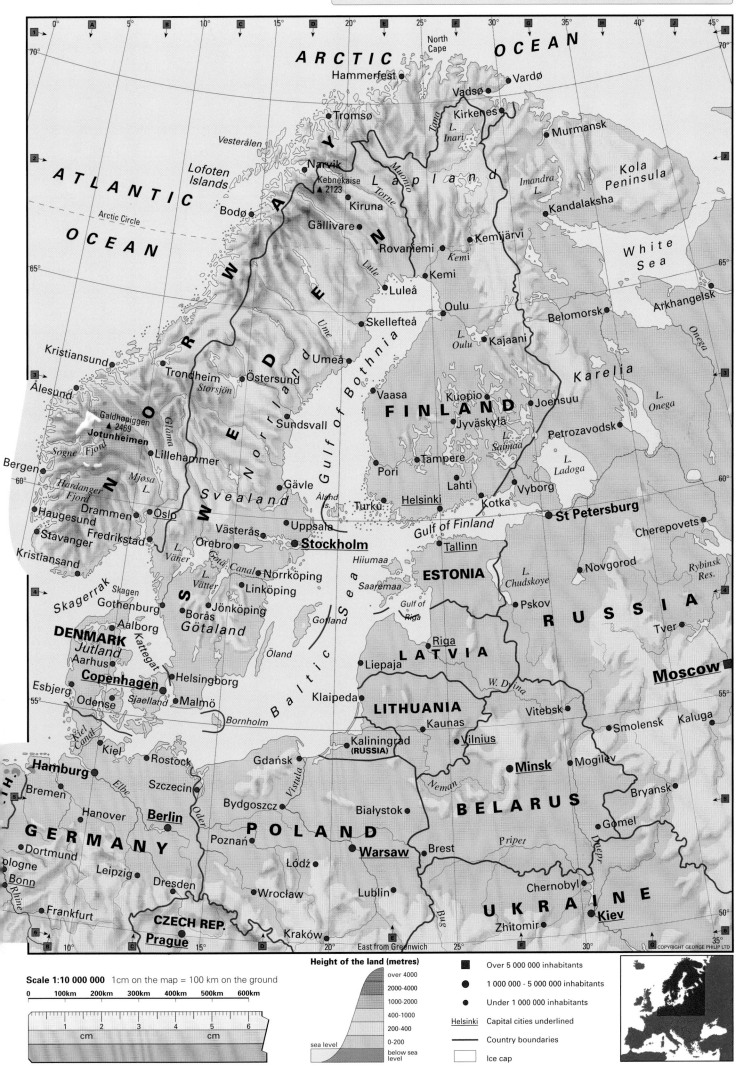

ARCTIC OCEAN

North Cape

Hammerfest
Vardø
Vadsø
Tromsø
Kirkenes
Murmansk
L. Inari
Tana
Vesterålen
Lofoten Islands
Narvik
Kebnekaise ▲ 2123
Bodø
Kiruna
Gällivare
L. Torne
Lapland
Imandra L.
Kola Peninsula
Kandalaksha

ATLANTIC OCEAN

Arctic Circle

Kemijärvi
Rovaniemi
Kemi
White Sea

Kristiansund
Kemi
Luleå
Belomorsk
Arkhangelsk
Oulu
Skellefteå
L. Oulu
Kajaani
Karelia
L. Onega

Ålesund
Trondheim
Östersund
Umeå
Storsjön
Ume
Vaasa
Kuopio
Joensuu
L. Onega

Galdhøpiggen ▲ 2469
Jotunheimen
Glåma
Sundsvall
FINLAND
Jyväskylä
Petrozavodsk
L. Saimaa

Bergen
Lillehammer
Svealand
Gävle
Pori
Tampere
Lahti
L. Ladoga
Vyborg

Sogne Fjord
Hardanger Fjord
Mjøsa L.
Åland Is.
Turku
Helsinki
Kotka
St Petersburg

Haugesund
Drammen
Oslo
Fredrikstad
Uppsala
Gulf of Finland
Cherepovets

Stavanger
Västerås
Stockholm
Hiiumaa
Tallinn
Novgorod
Rybinsk Res.

Kristiansand
Örebro
L. Väner
Norrköping
Saaremaa
ESTONIA
L. Chudskoye

Skagerrak
Skagen
Götaland
Linköping
Gotland
Gulf of Riga
Pskov
RUSSIA
Tver

Göta Canal
L. Vätter
Jönköping
Göteborg
Öland
Riga
Moscow

Gothenburg
Borås
LATVIA
Liepaja

DENMARK
Aalborg
Kattegat
Götaland
Klaipeda
W. Drina
Vitebsk
Smolensk
Kaluga

Jutland
Aarhus
Helsingborg
LITHUANIA
Kaunas

Esbjerg
Copenhagen
Sjælland
Malmö
Kaliningrad (RUSSIA)
Vilnius
Minsk
Mogilev

Odense
Bornholm
Gdańsk
Neman
Bryansk

Kiel Canal
Kiel
Rostock
Szczecin
Vistula
BELARUS
Gomel

Hamburg
Bremen
Hanover
Berlin
Oder
Bydgoszcz
Białystok
Pripet
Dnepr

GERMANY
Dortmund
Leipzig
Dresden
POLAND
Poznań
Warsaw
Brest

Bonn
Rhine
Frankfurt
CZECH REP.
Prague
Wrocław
Łódź
Lublin
Chernobyl
Kiev

Cologne
Kraków
Zhitomir
UKRAINE

East from Greenwich
COPYRIGHT GEORGE PHILIP LTD

Scale 1:10 000 000   1cm on the map = 100 km on the ground

0   100km   200km   300km   400km   500km   600km

cm

Height of the land (metres)

over 4000
2000-4000
1000-2000
400-1000
200-400
0-200
sea level
below sea level

■ Over 5 000 000 inhabitants

● 1 000 000 - 5 000 000 inhabitants

• Under 1 000 000 inhabitants

<u>Helsinki</u>   Capital cities underlined

——   Country boundaries

☐   Ice cap

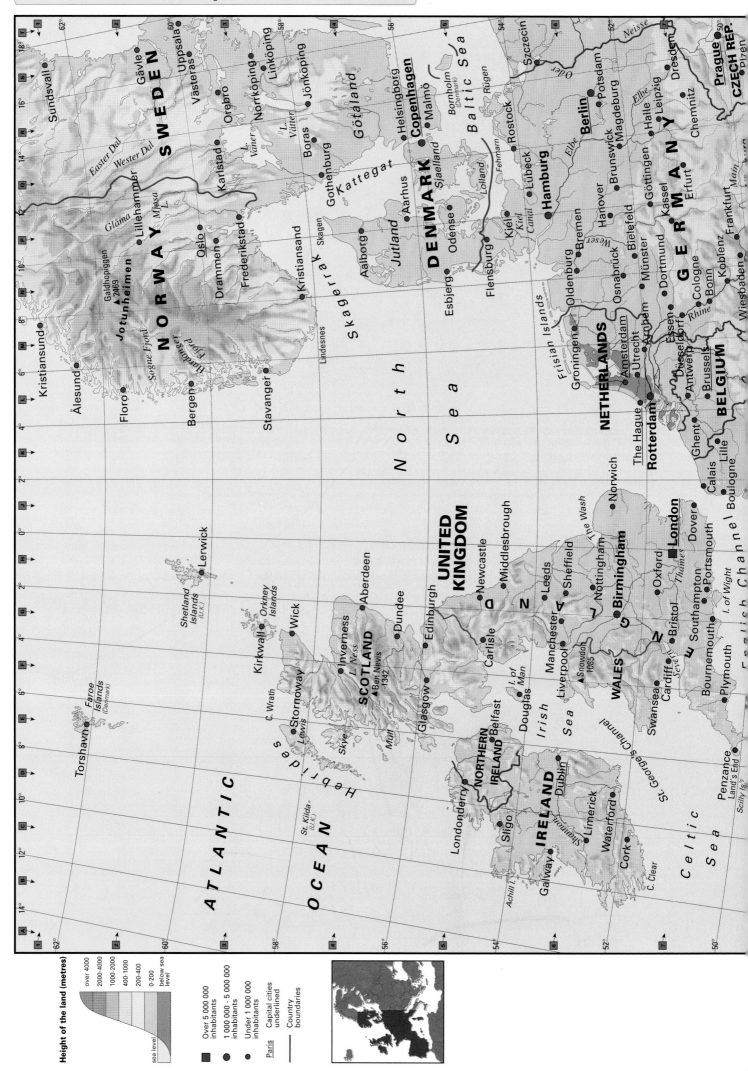

Height of the land (metres)

over 4000
2000-4000
1000-2000
400-1000
200-400
0-200
below sea level

sea level

■ Over 5 000 000 inhabitants
● 1 000 000 - 5 000 000 inhabitants
• Under 1 000 000 inhabitants

Paris Capital cities underlined

Country boundaries

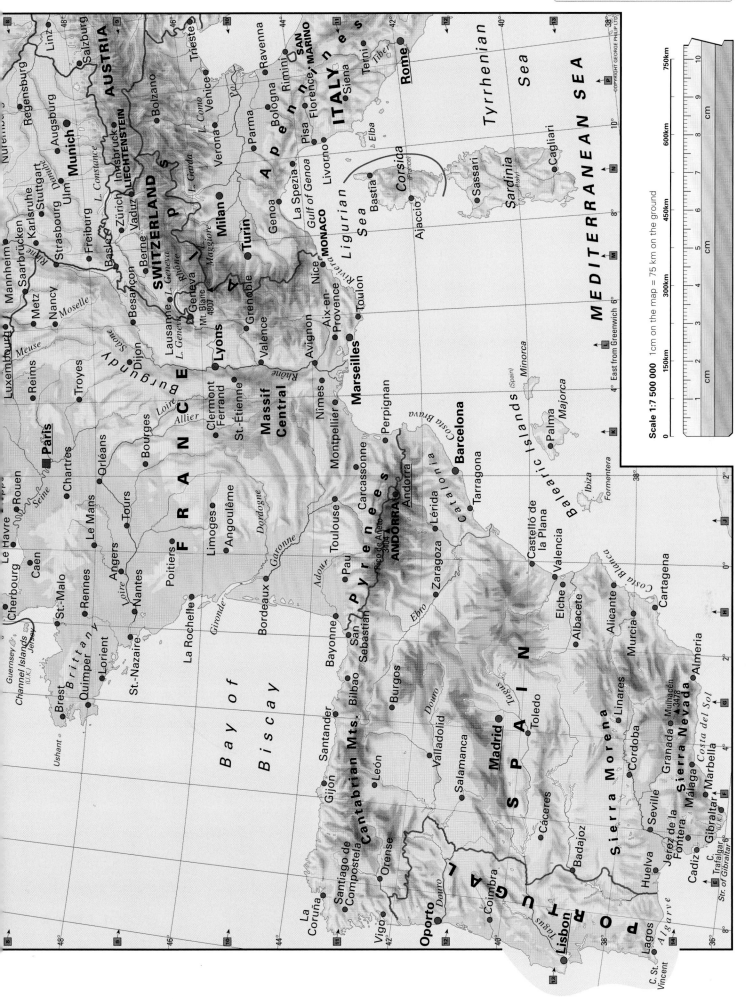

Scale 1:7 500 000 1cm on the map = 75 km on the ground

0   150km   300km   450km   600km   750km

MEDITERRANEAN SEA

Tyrrhenian Sea

ITALY

Rome

Corsica (France)

Sardinia (Italy)

Ligurian Sea

Gulf of Genoa

SAN MARINO

AUSTRIA

SWITZERLAND
LIECHTENSTEIN

A l p s

Munich

MONACO

Turin
Milan

Genoa

Florence
Siena
Terni

Bologna
Parma
Verona
Venice
L. Garda
L. Como

Ravenna
Rimini

Pisa
La Spezia
Livorno
Elba

Bastia
Ajaccio

Cagliari

Sassari

Linz
Salzburg
Regensburg
Augsburg
Nürnberg
Ulm
Stuttgart
Karlsruhe
Mannheim
Saarbrücken
Strasbourg
Metz
Nancy
Luxembourg
Reims
Troyes

Freiburg
Basle
Zürich
Innsbruck
Vaduz
Berne
Besançon
Geneva
Lausanne
L. Geneva
L. Neuch.
Mt. Blanc
4807

Bolzano

Grenoble
Valence
Lyons

Nice
Aix-en-Provence
Avignon
Toulon
Marseilles
Nîmes
Montpellier

FRANCE

Burgundy

Massif Central

Dijon
Bourges
Clermont Ferrand
St-Étienne
Orléans
Chartres
Paris

Rouen
Le Havre
Caen
Cherbourg
St-Malo
Rennes
Le Mans
Tours
Angers
Nantes
St-Nazaire
Lorient
Quimper
Brest
Brittany
Channel Islands (U.K.)
Jersey
Guernsey
Ushant

Angoulême
Limoges
Poitiers
La Rochelle

Bay of Biscay

Bordeaux

Dordogne
Garonne
Gironde

Toulouse
Carcassonne
Pau
Bayonne
Adour

Pyrenees
Pic de Aneto
3404
ANDORRA
Andorra

Perpignan
Costa Brava
Barcelona
Tarragona
Lérida
Zaragoza
Catalonia
Ebro
Castelló de la Plana
Valencia
Elche
Albacete
Alicante
Murcia
Cartagena

Balearic Islands
Minorca (Spain)
Majorca
Palma
Ibiza
Formentera

San Sebastián
Bilbao
Burgos
Santander
Gijón
La Coruña
Santiago de Compostela
Orense
Vigo
Oporto
Douro
Cantabrian Mts.
León
Valladolid
Salamanca

SPAIN

Madrid
Toledo
Tagus
Cáceres
Badajoz

Sierra Morena
Linares
Córdoba
Granada
Sierra Nevada
Mulhacén
3478
Jaén
Seville
Huelva
Jerez de la Frontera
Cádiz
C. Trafalgar
Gibraltar (U.K.)
Str. of Gibraltar
Málaga
Marbella
Costa del Sol
Almería
Costa Blanca

PORTUGAL
Coimbra
Douro
Tagus
Lisbon
Algarve
Lagos
C. St. Vincent

Apennines
Tiber

Rhône
Saône
Loire
Allier
Seine
Meuse
Moselle
Rhine
Danube
Po
Riviera

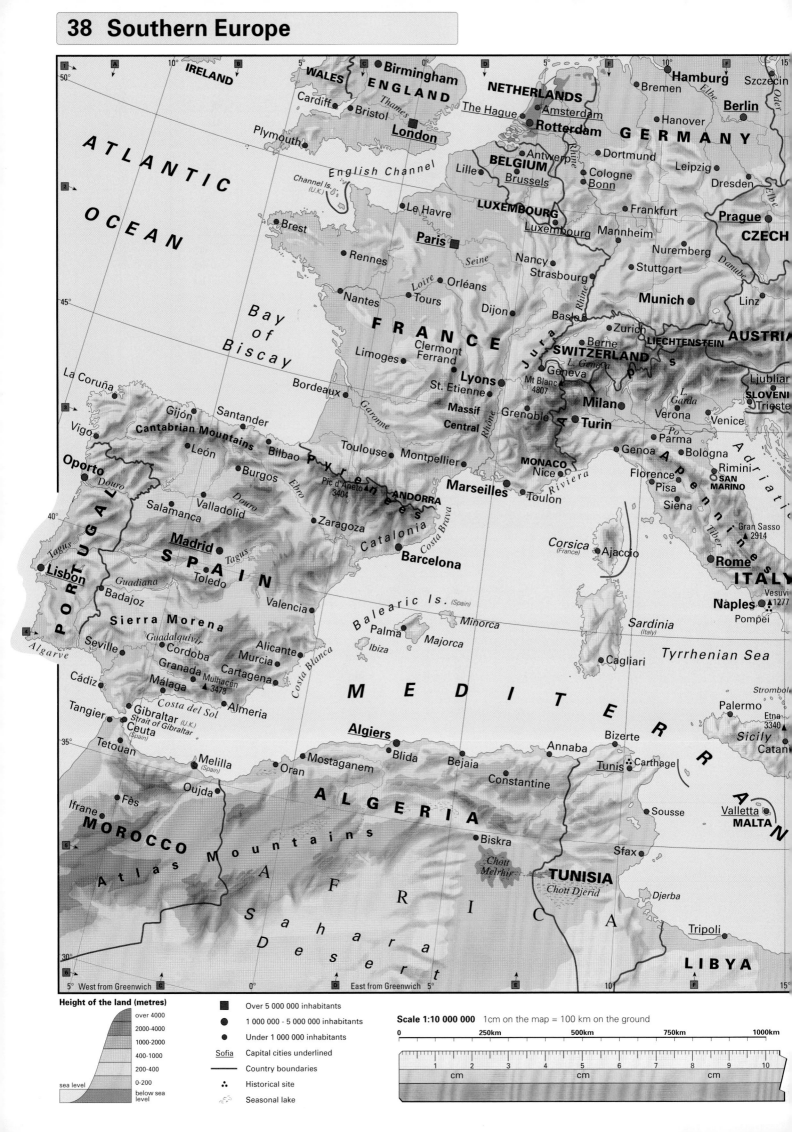

ATLANTIC
OCEAN

IRELAND

WALES
ENGLAND
Birmingham
Cardiff
Bristol
Plymouth
Thames
London

NETHERLANDS
The Hague
Amsterdam
Rotterdam

Hamburg
Szczecin
Bremen
Hanover
Berlin
GERMANY
Elbe
Oder

English Channel
Channel Is.
(U.K.)

Le Havre
BELGIUM
Lille
Antwerp
Brussels
Bonn
LUXEMBOURG
Luxembourg
Dortmund
Cologne
Rhine

Frankfurt
Mannheim
Nancy
Strasbourg
Leipzig
Dresden
Nuremberg
Prague
CZECH
Danube

Brest
Paris
Rennes
Seine
Nantes
Loire
Orléans
Tours

Bay
of
Biscay

FRANCE
Dijon
Limoges
Clermont
Ferrand
Lyons
St. Etienne
Massif
Central
Grenoble
Basle
Munich
Linz
AUSTRIA
Stuttgart
Zurich
Berne
SWITZERLAND
Geneva
L. Geneva
Mt Blanc
4807
Jura
LIECHTENSTEIN

La Coruña
Vigo
Gijón
Santander
Cantabrian Mountains
León
Burgos
Bilbao
Pyrenees
Pic d'Aneto
3404
Toulouse
Montpellier
Marseilles
Toulon
MONACO
Nice
Riviera
Milan
Turin
Genoa
Parma
Verona
Venice
Po
Bologna
Apennines
L. Garda
Ljubliana
SLOVENI
Trieste

Oporto
Douro
Salamanca
Valladolid
Douro
Zaragoza
Ebro
ANDORRA
Catalonia
Costa Brava
Barcelona

Madrid
SPAIN
Toledo
Tagus
Tagus
Guadiana
Badajoz
Valencia

Rimini
SAN
MARINO
Florence
Pisa
Siena
Gran Sasso
2914
Rome
ITALY
Adriatic
Tiber

Lisbon
PORTUGAL
Guadiana
Sierra Morena
Guadalquivir
Seville
Cádiz
Córdoba
Granada
Málaga
Mulhacén
3478
Almería
Costa del Sol
Murcia
Alicante
Cartagena
Costa Blanca

Balearic Is. (Spain)
Palma
Ibiza
Majorca
Minorca

Corsica
(France)
Ajaccio

Sardinia
(Italy)

Naples
Vesuvius
1277
Pompei

MEDITER
Tyrrhenian Sea
Cagliari

Stromboli
Palermo
Etna
3340
Sicily
Catani

Algarve
Tangier
Gibraltar (U.K.)
Strait of Gibraltar
Ceuta
(Spain)
Tetouan
Melilla
(Spain)
Oran
Mostaganem

Algiers
Blida
Bejaia
Annaba
Constantine

Bizerte
Tunis
Carthage
Sousse

Valletta
MALTA
R
R
A
N

Ifrane
Fès
Oujda
MOROCCO
Atlas Mountains
Biskra
Chott
Melrhir
TUNISIA
Chott Djerid
Sfax
Djerba

A
F
R
I
C
A

Sahara Desert

Tripoli
LIBYA

Height of the land (metres)

over 4000
2000-4000
1000-2000
400-1000
200-400
0-200
sea level
below sea level

■ Over 5 000 000 inhabitants
● 1 000 000 - 5 000 000 inhabitants
• Under 1 000 000 inhabitants
<u>Sofia</u> Capital cities underlined
— Country boundaries
∴ Historical site
Seasonal lake

Scale 1:10 000 000   1cm on the map = 100 km on the ground

0   250km   500km   750km   1000km

1 2 3 4 5 6 7 8 9 10
cm   cm   cm

POLAND

dgoszcz

BELARUS

Vistula

20° • Poznań

• Łódź

• Warsaw • Brest

Gomel

Chernigov

Kursk • Voronezh 40°

Pripet

25° 30° • Lublin

• Wrocław

Bug

Chernobyl

Kiev

Kharkov

Sumy

50°

Katowice

Zhitomir

Dnepr

Lugansk

deten Highlands • Kraków

Vistula

Lvov

Vinnitsa

U K R A I N E

Donetsk

REP.

C
a
r
p
a
t
h
i
a
n
s

Chernovtsy

Dnestr

Dnepropetrovsk

Krivoy
Rog

Zaporozhye

Rostov

RUSSIA

• Brno

SLOVAK
REP.

Košice

MOLDOVA

Prut

Mariupol

enna

Debrecen

Iaşi

Chişinău

Bug

Nikolayev

2

• Bratislava

Bacau

Stavropol

Budapest

HUNGARY

Cluj-
Napoca

ROMANIA

Galaţi

Odessa

Sea of Azov

Krasnodar

45°

L. Balaton

Danube

Tisza

Braşov

Crimea

Caucasus

Drava

Timişoara

Transylvanian Alps

Ploieşti

Sevastopol

Yalta

Sochi

Sukhumi

Zagreb

ROATIA

YUGOSLAVIA

Morava

Bucharest

Danube

Constanţa

Black Sea

Batumi

Belgrade

BOSNIA-
HERZEGOVINA

Sarajevo

Varna

3

olit

Dinaric Alps

MONTE-
NEGRO

Balkan Mts.

Burgas

Samsun

Pontine Mts

Trabzon

Dubrovnik

KOSOVO

Sofia

BULGARIA

Zonguldak

40°

Sea

Skopje

Plovdiv

Rhodope Mts

Bosporus

Sivas

Bari

MACEDONIA

Istanbul

Izmit

Ankara

Tirane

Thasos

Bursa

TURKEY

A S I A

Kayseri

Euphrates

Taranto

ALBANIA

Thessaloniki

Troy

Balıkeşir

Eskişehir

4

Dardanelles

Tuz Gölü

Gaziantep

Mt. Olympus
2917

Aegean

Lesbos

Manisa

Konya

Taurus Mountains

Adana

Aleppo

Corfu
(Greece)

Pindus Mts.

Khios

Izmir

Denizli

Isparta

Mersin

SYRIA

Ionian Islands

GREECE

Delphi

Sea

Samos

Antalya

35°

Messina

Ionian Sea

Gulf of Corinth

Marathon

Dodecanese

Latakia

Patrai

Athens

Homs

ait of Messina

Olympia

Peloponnese

Sparta

Rhodes
(Greece)

CYPRUS

Nicosia

Tripoli

LEBANON

Limassol

Beirut

Damascus

Iráklion

Knossos

Crete
(Greece)

Haifa

WEST
BANK

E A N

S E A

ISRAEL

Tel Aviv-Jaffa

Jerusalem

Amman

GAZA STRIP

Dead
Sea

JORDAN

30°

Benghazi

Port Said

Suez
Canal

Gulf of Sidra

LIBYA

Alexandria

EGYPT

Cairo

Ismailiya

Sinai

35°

COPYRIGHT GEORGE PHILIP LTD

20°

25°

30°

Cross section

FRANCE

ITALY

YUGOSLAVIA

ROMANIA

Bay of Biscay

Mont Dore
1886

Massif Central

Rhone
Valley

Alps

Po

Adriatic
Sea

Dinaric Alps

Sava

Danube

Transylvanian
Alps

Danube

Black Sea

45°N

45°N

Height of the land (metres)

- over 6000
- 4000-6000
- 2000-4000
- 1000-2000
- 400-1000
- 200-400
- 0-200
- below sea level

sea level

■ Over 5 000 000 inhabitants

● 1 000 000 - 5 000 000 inhabitants

• Under 1 000 000 inhabitants

Kiev Capital cities underlined

— Country boundaries

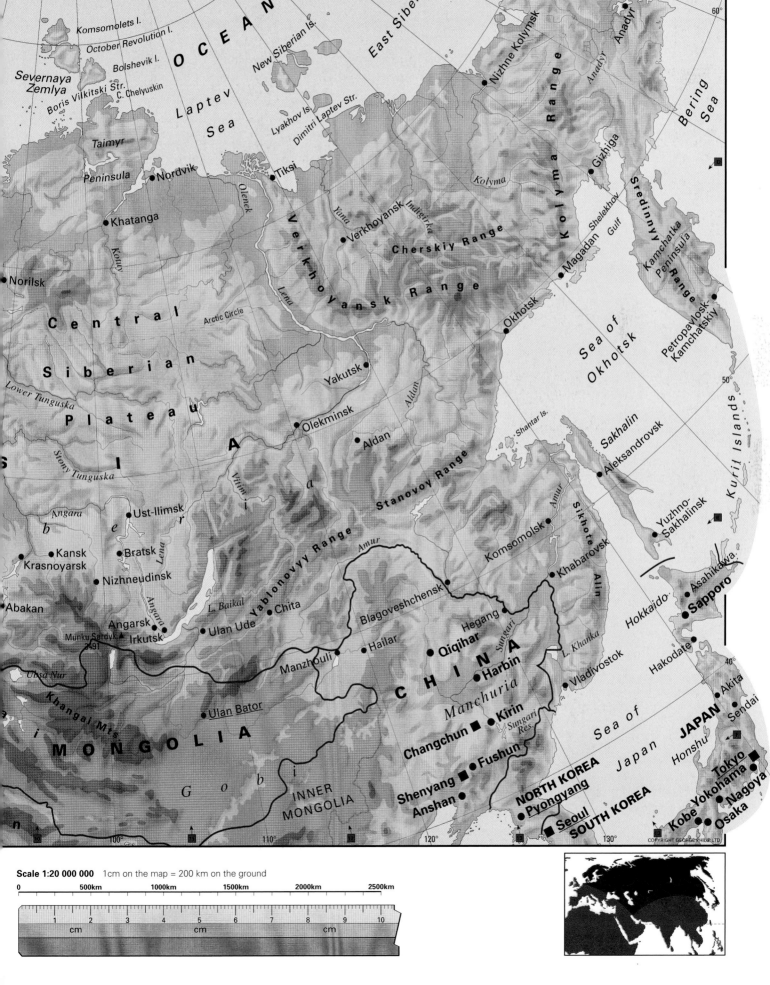

OCEAN

Komsomolets I.
Octoben Revolution I.
Bolshevik I.
Severnaya
Zemlya
Boris Vilkitski Str.
C. Chelyuskin

Laptev
Sea

New Siberian Is.

East Siberian Sea

Lyakhov Is.
Dimitri Laptev Str.

Wrangel I.

Gulf of Anadyr

Anadyr Range

Nizhne Kolymsk

Anadyr

Taimyr
Peninsula
Nordvik
Tiksi

Olenek

Yana

Verkhoyansk

Indigirka

Kolyma

Gizhiga

Bering
Sea

Khatanga

Kotuy

Lena

Verkhoyansk Range

Cherskiy Range

Kolyma Range

Shelekhov
Magadan   Gulf

Sredinnyy Range

Kamchatka
Peninsula

Norilsk

Central

Siberian

Arctic Circle

Cherskiy Range

Okhotsk

Sea of
Okhotsk

Petropavlovsk-
Kamchatskiy

Lower Tunguska

Plateau

S I A

Yakutsk

Aldan

Shantar Is.

Sakhalin
Aleksandrovsk

Stony Tunguska

Olekminsk

Aldan

Kuril Islands

Angara

Ust-Ilimsk

Vilimi

Lena

Stanovoy Range

Amur

Sikhote Alin

Yuzhno-
Sakhalinsk

Kansk
Krasnoyarsk

Bratsk

Yablonovyy Range

Komsomolsk

Khabarovsk

Nizhneudinsk

Abakan

Angarsk

Angara

L. Baikal

Chita

Amur

Blagoveshchensk

Hegang

Sungari

L. Khanka

Hokkaido

Asahikawa
Sapporo

Munku Sardyk
3491

Irkutsk

Ulan Ude

Hailar

Qiqihar

Harbin

Vladivostok

Hakodate

Ubsa Nur

Manzhouli

C H I N A

Manchuria

Sungari
Res.

Sea of

Akita

Khangai Mts

Ulan Bator

Kirin

Sungari

Japan

Honshu

Sendai

JAPAN

M O N G O L I A

Changchun

Fushun

NORTH KOREA

Tokyo

G   o   b   i

INNER
MONGOLIA

Shenyang
Anshan

Pyongyang

Seoul   SOUTH KOREA

Yokohama
Kobe   Nagoya
Osaka

COPYRIGHT GEORGE PHILIP LTD

Scale 1:20 000 000   1cm on the map = 200 km on the ground

0   500km   1000km   1500km   2000km   2500km

1   2   3   4   5   6   7   8   9   10
cm   cm   cm

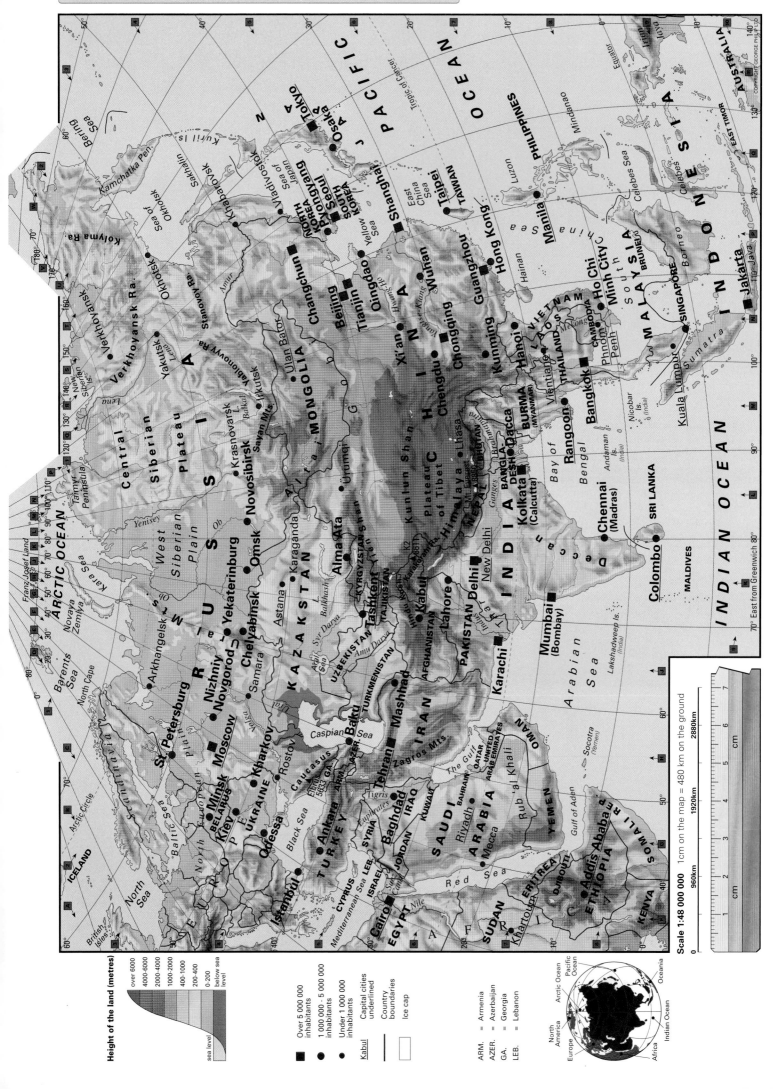

Height of the land (metres)

over 6000
4000-6000
2000-4000
1000-2000
400-1000
200-400
0-200
below sea level

sea level

Over 5 000 000 inhabitants

1 000 000 - 5 000 000 inhabitants

Under 1 000 000 inhabitants

Kabul Capital cities underlined

Country boundaries

Ice cap

ARM. = Armenia
AZER. = Azerbaijan
GA. = Georgia
LEB. = Lebanon

Scale 1:48 000 000 1cm on the map = 480 km on the ground

0   960km   1920km   2880km

COPYRIGHT GEORGE PHILIP LTD

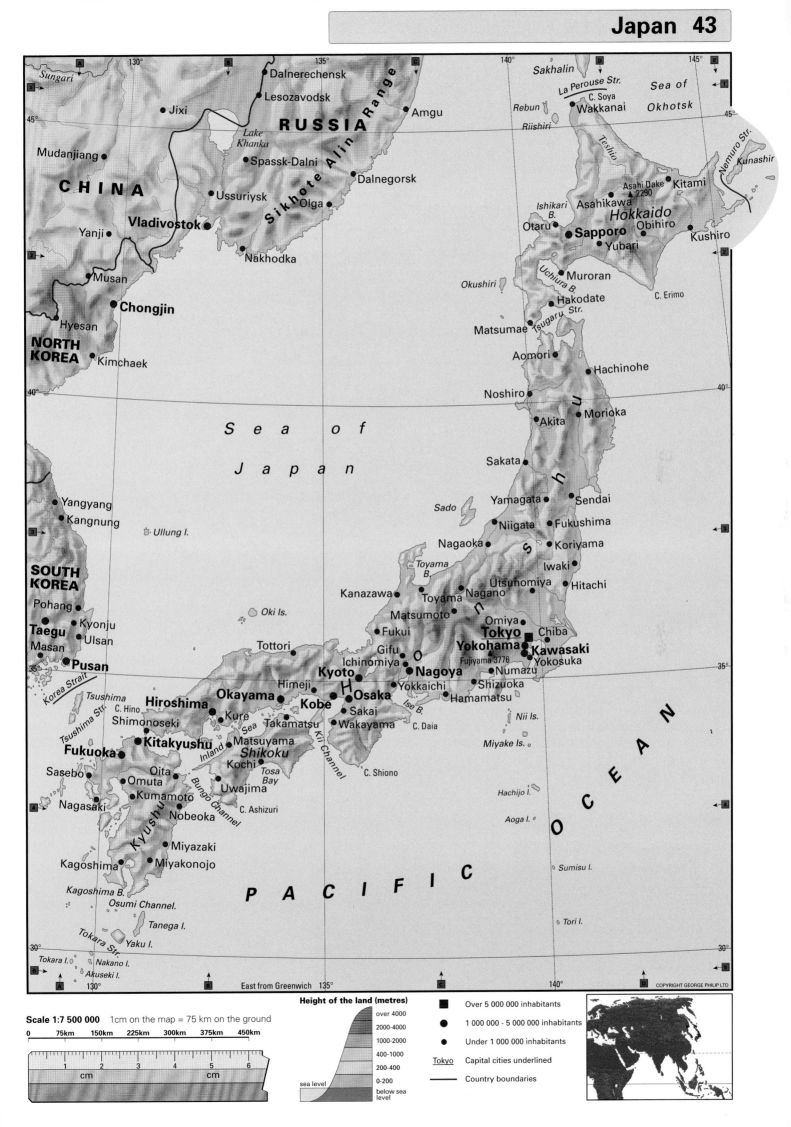

Scale 1:7 500 000   1cm on the map = 75 km on the ground

0   75km   150km   225km   300km   375km   450km

cm   cm

Height of the land (metres)

over 4000
2000-4000
1000-2000
400-1000
200-400
0-200
sea level
below sea level

■ Over 5 000 000 inhabitants

● 1 000 000 - 5 000 000 inhabitants

• Under 1 000 000 inhabitants

Tokyo   Capital cities underlined

——   Country boundaries

COPYRIGHT GEORGE PHILIP LTD

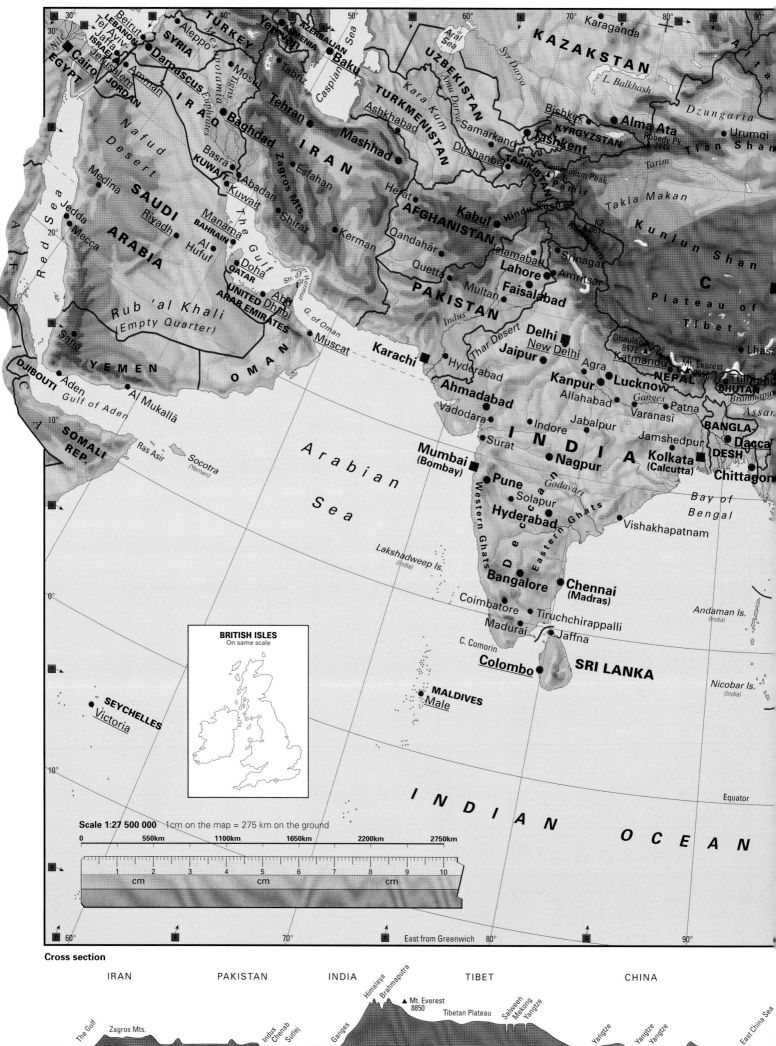

Cross section

IRAN PAKISTAN INDIA TIBET CHINA

MONGOLIA

Plateau of
Mongolia

Ulan Bator

Gobi

•Qiqihar
Manchuria
•Harbin

Great Khingan Mts.

Inner Mongolia

RUSSIA

•Vladivostok

Sea of
Japan

Hokkaido

•Sapporo

Changchun

Shenyang •Fushun
Anshan

NORTH
KOREA
•Pyongyang

Sendai

JAPAN
•Tokyo
Yokohama

Honshu

•Seoul
SOUTH
KOREA

Kyoto
Kobe Nagoya
Osaka

Beijing

WALL

GREAT

•Dalian

Tianjin

Taiyuan

Yellow
Sea

Pusan

Hiroshima
Kitakyushu

Shikoku
Kyushu

Nan Shan

•Lanzhou

Hwang-Ho

Grand
Canal

Qingdao

PACIFIC

I   N   A

Xi'an

Nanjing

•Shanghai

East China
Sea

Ryukyu Is.

Bonin Is.
(Japan)

OCEAN

Wuhan
Hangzhou

Chengdu

Yangtze-Kiang

Chongqing

Nanchang

Changsha

Tropic of Cancer

NORTHERN
MARIANAS
(U.S.A.)

Guiyang

Fuzhou

Taipei
TAIWAN
Kaohsiung

Mekong

Kunming

Nanning

Guangzhou

Macau Hong Kong

Guam
(U.S.A.)

URMA
•Mandalay
IYANMAR)

Hanoi

Haiphong

Gulf of
Tonkin

Hainan

Luzon

Quezon City

FEDERATED STATES
OF
MICRONESIA

Chiengmai

Vientiane

Da Nang

Manila

PHILIPPINES

angoon

THAILAND

Bangkok
CAMBODIA

Chao Phraya

Mekong

Moulmein

Phnom Penh

Ho Chi Minh
City

Gulf of
Thailand

South China Sea

Palawan

Cebu

Sulu Sea

Mindanao
Davao

PALAU

Zamboanga

Sulu Arch.

Songkhla

Kota
Kinabalu

Sabah

Celebes Sea

Halmahera

Irian Jaya

George
Town

Malay Peninsula

MALAYSIA

BRUNEI
Bandar Seri
Begawan

Sarawak

Manado

Moluccas

Medan

Str. of Malacca

Kuala Lumpur

Kucing

Borneo

Buru

Seram

East   Indies

Aru Is.

Padang

Sumatra

SINGAPORE

Pontianak

Celebes

Banda Sea

Tanimbar

Arafura
Sea

Palembang

Bangka

Banjarmasin

Ujung
Pandang

Flores
Sea

EAST
TIMOR

Jakarta

Semarang Surabaya

Lombok

Timor

Timor Sea

Bandung Java

Bali
Sumbawa

Sumba

AUSTRALIA

COPYRIGHT GEORGE PHILIP LTD

**Height of the land
(metres)**

over 6000
4000-6000
2000-4000
1000-2000
400-1000
200-400
0-200
sea level below sea
level

■ Over 5 000 000 inhabitants

● 1 000 000 - 5 000 000 inhabitants

• Under 1 000 000 inhabitants

Beijing Capital cities underlined

—— Country boundaries

〜 Seasonal lakes

☐ Ice

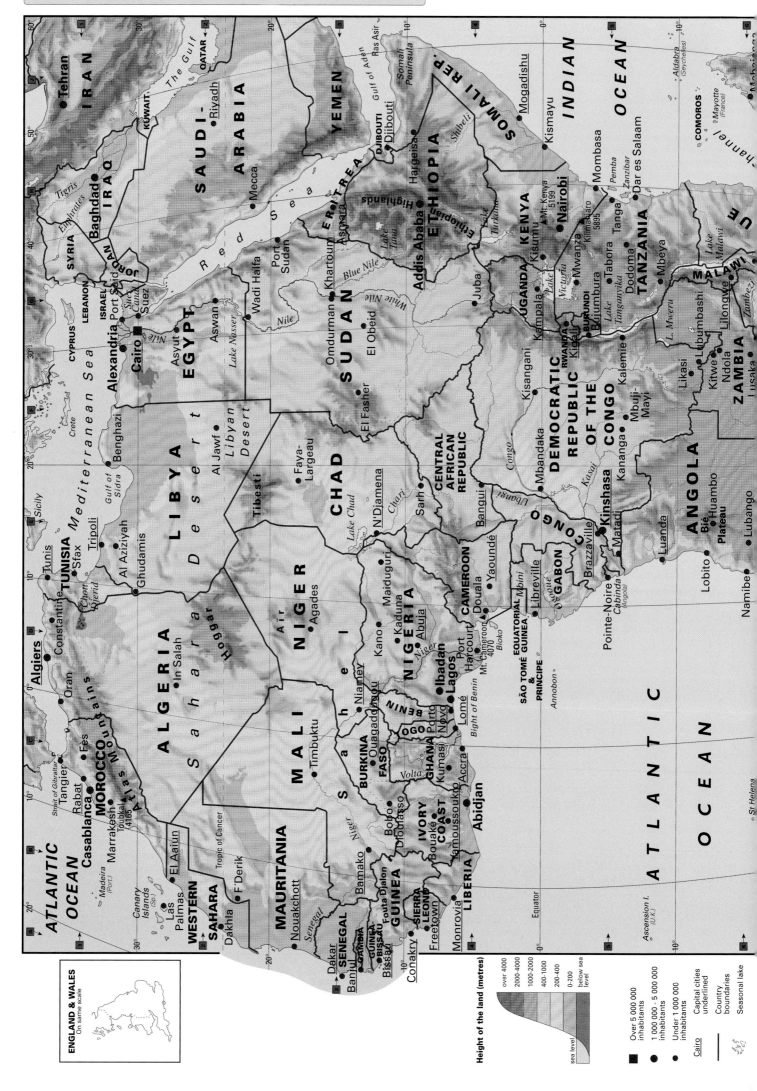

ENGLAND & WALES
On same scale

Height of the land (metres)

| over 4000 |
| 2000-4000 |
| 1000-2000 |
| 400-1000 |
| 200-400 |
| 0-200 |
| below sea level |

sea level

■ Over 5 000 000 inhabitants

● 1 000 000 - 5 000 000 inhabitants

• Under 1 000 000 inhabitants

Cairo   Capital cities underlined

——— Country boundaries

Seasonal lake

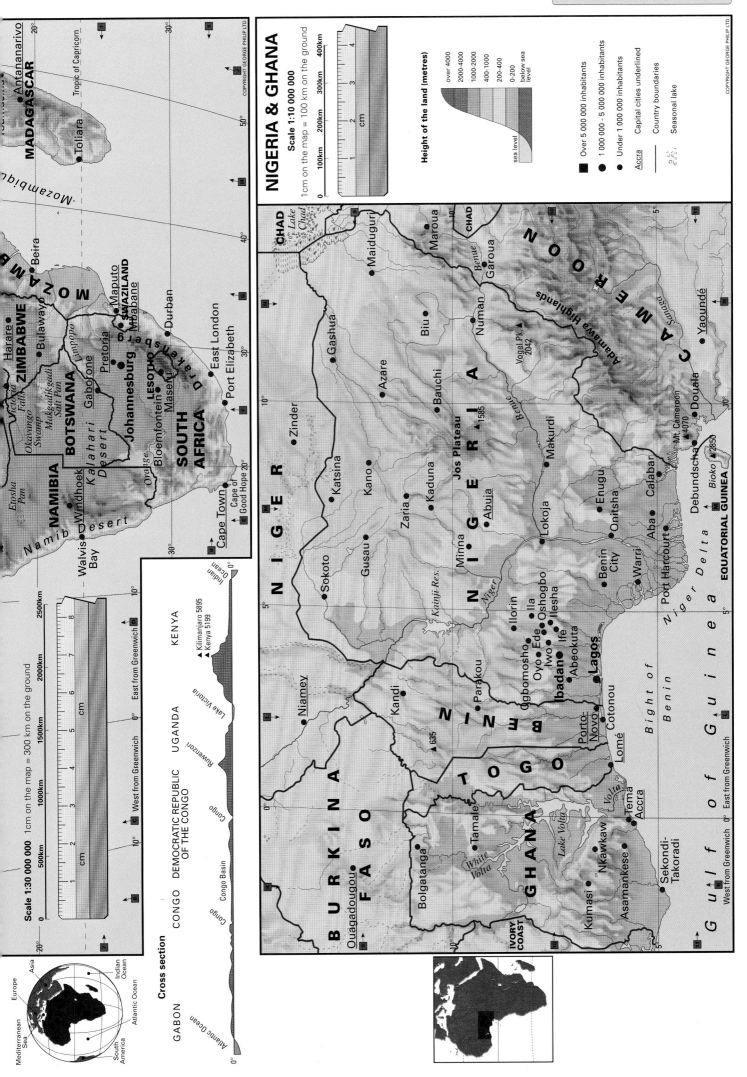

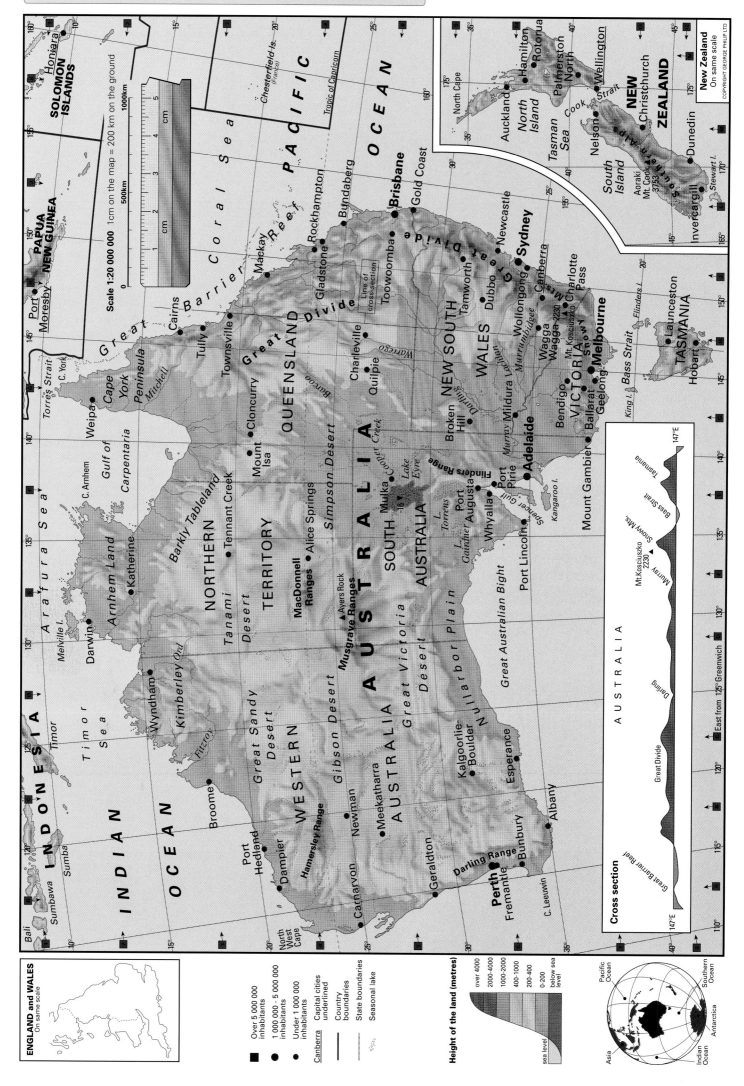

SOLOMON ISLANDS

Honiara

PACIFIC OCEAN

PAPUA NEW GUINEA

Port Moresby

Chesterfield Is. (France)

Tropic of Capricorn

Coral Sea

Great Barrier Reef

Cairns
Tully
Townsville
Mackay
Rockhampton
Gladstone
Bundaberg
Brisbane
Gold Coast

Torres Strait
C. York
Cape York Peninsula
Mitchell
Weipa
Gulf of Carpentaria

C. Arnhem
Arnhem Land
Melville I.
Katherine
Darwin

Arafura Sea

Timor Sea

Timor

INDONESIA
Bali
Sumba
Sumbawa

INDIAN OCEAN

Wyndham
Kimberley
Ord
Fitzroy
Broome
Port Hedland
Dampier
Hamersley Range
Carnarvon
Geraldton
North West Cape

NORTHERN TERRITORY
Barkly Tableland
Tennant Creek
Tanami Desert
Great Sandy Desert
Gibson Desert
WESTERN AUSTRALIA
Newman
Meekatharra
Kalgoorlie-Boulder
Esperance

QUEENSLAND
Great Dividing
Mount Isa
Cloncurry
Simpson Desert
MacDonnell Ranges
Alice Springs
Ayers Rock
Musgrave Ranges
Great Victoria Desert
Nullarbor Plain
Great Australian Bight

Charleville
Quilpie
Barcoo
Warrego
Cooper Creek

Toowoomba
Line of cross-section

NEW SOUTH WALES
Newcastle
Sydney
Wollongong
Canberra
Tamworth
Dubbo
Murrumbidgee
Wagga Wagga
Mt. Kosciuszko 2230
Charlotte Pass
Snowy Mts
Melbourne
Geelong
Ballarat
Bendigo
VICTORIA
Mildura
Murray
Lachlan
Darling
Broken Hill

SOUTH AUSTRALIA
Mulka -16
Lake Eyre
Flinders Range
L. Torrens
Port Augusta
L. Gairdner
Whyalla
Port Pirie
Adelaide
Spencer Gulf
Port Lincoln
Kangaroo I.
Mount Gambier

AUSTRALIA

Esperance
Albany
Bunbury
Darling Range
Perth
Fremantle
C. Leeuwin

Bass Strait
King I.
Flinders I.
Launceston
TASMANIA
Hobart

New Zealand
On same scale

North Cape
Auckland
Hamilton
Rotorua
North Island
Tasman Sea
Nelson
Palmerston North
Wellington
Cook Strait
NEW ZEALAND
South Island
Southern Alps
Aoraki Mt. Cook 3753
Christchurch
Dunedin
Invercargill
Stewart I.

COPYRIGHT GEORGE PHILIP LTD

Scale 1:20 000 000 1cm on the map = 200 km on the ground
1cm on the map = 200 km on the ground
1000km
500km

Cross section
Great Barrier Reef
Great Divide
Mt. Kosciuszko 2230
Snowy Mts
Murray
Darling
Bass Strait
Tasmania
147°E
East from 125° Greenwich
AUSTRALIA

Height of the land (metres)
over 4000
2000-4000
1000-2000
400-1000
200-400
0-200
below sea level
sea level

Over 5 000 000 inhabitants
1 000 000 - 5 000 000 inhabitants
Under 1 000 000 inhabitants
Capital cities underlined
Canberra
Country boundaries
State boundaries
Seasonal lake

Pacific Ocean
Asia
Indian Ocean
Antarctica
Southern Ocean

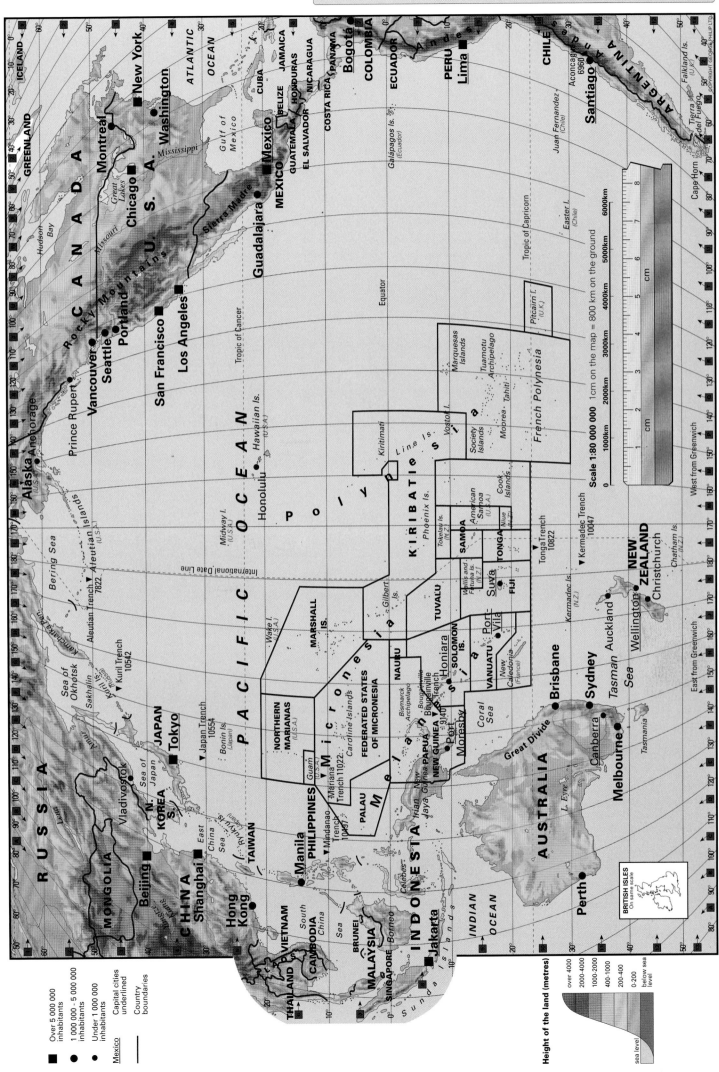

COPYRIGHT GEORGE PHILIP LTD.

ATLANTIC OCEAN

GREENLAND

ICELAND

CANADA

Montreal
New York
Washington
U. S. A.
Chicago
Portland
Seattle
Vancouver
Prince Rupert
Anchorage
Alaska
Rocky Mountains
Hudson Bay
Great Lakes
Missouri
Mississippi

San Francisco
Los Angeles
Sierra Madre
Guadalajara
MEXICO
Mexico
Gulf of Mexico
BELIZE
GUATEMALA
HONDURAS
EL SALVADOR
NICARAGUA
COSTA RICA
PANAMA
JAMAICA
CUBA

COLOMBIA
Bogotá
ECUADOR
Galápagos Is.
(Ecuador)
PERU
Lima
CHILE
Aconcagua 6960
Santiago
ARGENTINA
Andes
Juan Fernandez (Chile)
Easter I. (Chile)
Falkland Is. (U.K.)
Tierra del Fuego
Cape Horn

Tropic of Cancer

Equator

Tropic of Capricorn

Pitcairn I. (U.K.)

French Polynesia
Tuamotu Archipelago
Marquesas Islands
Society Islands
Tahiti
Moorea
Cook Islands
Vostok I.
Line Is.
Kiritimati

KIRIBATI

PACIFIC OCEAN

Polynesia

Hawaiian Is. (U.S.A.)
Honolulu
Midway I. (U.S.A.)

American Samoa (U.S.A.)
SAMOA
Niue (N.Z.)
TONGA
Tonga Trench 10822
Kermadec Trench 10047
Phoenix Is.
Tokelau Is. (N.Z.)
Wallis and Futuna (France)
Suva
FIJI
Kermadec Is. (N.Z.)

TUVALU

Gilbert Is.

Micronesia

MARSHALL IS.
Wake I. (U.S.A.)

NAURU
SOLOMON IS.
Honiara
VANUATU
Port Vila
New Caledonia (France)
Coral Sea

NEW ZEALAND
Auckland
Wellington
Christchurch
Chatham Is. (N.Z.)
Tasman Sea

Brisbane
Sydney
Canberra
Melbourne
Perth
AUSTRALIA
Great Divide
L. Eyre
Tasmania

PAPUA NEW GUINEA
Port Moresby
New Guinea Trench 9140
Bismarck Archipelago
Bougainville

NORTHERN MARIANAS (U.S.A.)
Guam (U.S.A.)
Mariana Trench 11022
FEDERATED STATES OF MICRONESIA
Caroline Islands
Bonin Is. (Japan)
PALAU

Melanesia

JAPAN
Tokyo
Japan Trench 10554
Sea of Japan

PHILIPPINES
Manila
Mindanao Trench 10047
TAIWAN

Aleutian Trench 7822
Aleutian Islands (U.S.A.)
Bering Sea
Kuril Trench 10542
Kuril Is. (Japan)
Sakhalin
Sea of Okhotsk
Kamchatka Peninsula
Amur

RUSSIA
Vladivostok
MONGOLIA
Beijing
CHINA
Shanghai
Hong Kong
N. KOREA
S. KOREA
East China Sea
Ryukyu Is. (Japan)
South China Sea
VIETNAM
CAMBODIA
THAILAND
MALAYSIA
SINGAPORE
BRUNEI
Borneo
INDONESIA
Jakarta
Java
Sumatra
Celebes
Irian Jaya
Sunda Islands
INDIAN OCEAN

International Date Line
West from Greenwich
East from Greenwich

Scale 1:80 000 000   1cm on the map = 800 km on the ground
0   1000km   2000km   3000km   4000km   5000km   6000km
cm   1   2   3   4   5   6   7   8   cm

BRITISH ISLES
On same scale

Height of the land (metres)
over 4000
2000-4000
1000-2000
400-1000
200-400
0-200
below sea level
sea level

■ Over 5 000 000 inhabitants
● 1 000 000 - 5 000 000 inhabitants
• Under 1 000 000 inhabitants
Mexico Capital cities underlined
—— Country boundaries

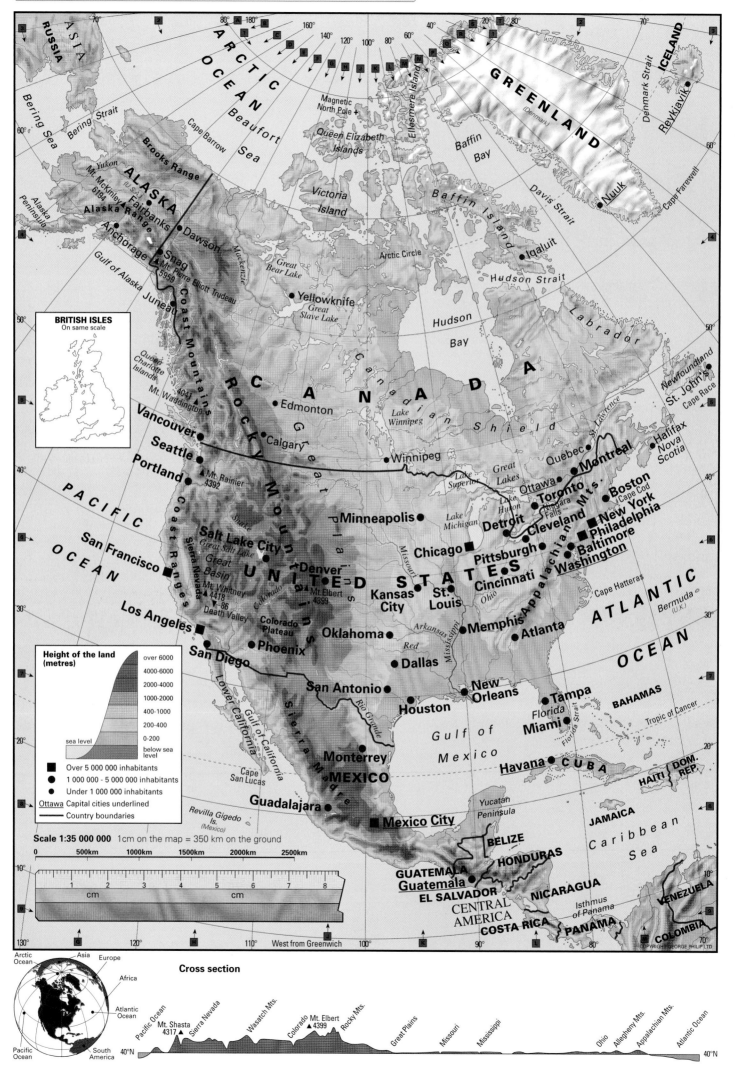

BRITISH ISLES
On same scale

Height of the land (metres)

over 6000	
4000-6000	
2000-4000	
1000-2000	
400-1000	
200-400	
0-200	
sea level	below sea level

■ Over 5 000 000 inhabitants
● 1 000 000 - 5 000 000 inhabitants
• Under 1 000 000 inhabitants
Ottawa Capital cities underlined
── Country boundaries

Scale 1:35 000 000 1cm on the map = 350 km on the ground

0	500km	1000km	1500km	2000km	2500km

cm

cm

Cross section

Arctic Ocean Asia Europe
Africa
Atlantic Ocean
Pacific Ocean
South America

Pacific Ocean Mt. Shasta 4317▲ Sierra Nevada Wasatch Mts. Colorado Mt. Elbert 4399▲ Rocky Mts. Great Plains Missouri Mississippi Ohio Allegheny Mts. Appalachian Mts. Atlantic Ocean
40°N   40°N

RUSSIA
ASIA
Bering Sea
Bering Strait
Alaska Peninsula
ARCTIC OCEAN
Beaufort Sea
Cape Barrow
Magnetic North Pole +
Queen Elizabeth Islands
Ellesmere Island
GREENLAND (Denmark)
Nuuk
Denmark Strait
ICELAND
Reykjavik
Cape Farewell

Yukon
Mt. McKinley (U.S.A.) 6194
Fairbanks
ALASKA
Brooks Range
Anchorage
Snag
Mt. Pierre Elliott Trudeau 5959
Gulf of Alaska
Juneau
Dawson
Mackenzie
Great Bear Lake
Victoria Island
Baffin Island
Baffin Bay
Davis Strait
Iqaluit
Hudson Strait

Coast Mountains
Queen Charlotte Islands
Mt. Waddington 4041▲
Vancouver
Seattle
Portland
Mt. Rainier 4392▲
Edmonton
Calgary
Yellowknife
Great Slave Lake
CANADA
Great Plains
Canadian Shield
Winnipeg
Lake Winnipeg
Hudson Bay
Labrador
Newfoundland
St. John's
Cape Race

PACIFIC OCEAN
San Francisco
Los Angeles
San Diego
Coast Ranges
Sierra Nevada
Great Basin
Great Salt Lake
Salt Lake City
Mt. Whitney 4418▲
Death Valley -86
Denver
Mt. Elbert 4399▲
UNITED STATES
Colorado
Colorado Plateau
Phoenix
Snake
Minneapolis
Lake Superior
Lake Michigan
Lake Huron
Great Lakes
Chicago
Detroit
Missouri
Kansas City
St. Louis
Ohio
Cincinnati
Pittsburgh
Cleveland
Niagara Falls
Toronto
Ottawa
Quebec
Montreal
Boston
Cape Cod
New York
Philadelphia
Baltimore
Washington
Halifax
Nova Scotia
Appalachian Mts.
ATLANTIC OCEAN
Cape Hatteras
Bermuda (U.K.)

Oklahoma
Dallas
San Antonio
Houston
Arkansas
Red
Mississippi
Memphis
Atlanta
New Orleans
Tampa
Florida
Miami
Florida Strait
BAHAMAS
Tropic of Cancer

Lower California
Gulf of California
Sierra Madre
Cape San Lucas
Monterrey
MEXICO
Guadalajara
Revilla Gigedo Is. (Mexico)
Mexico City
Rio Grande
Gulf of Mexico
Yucatan Peninsula
Havana CUBA
HAITI DOM. REP.
JAMAICA
Caribbean Sea

BELIZE
GUATEMALA
Guatemala
EL SALVADOR
HONDURAS
NICARAGUA
CENTRAL AMERICA
COSTA RICA
PANAMA
Isthmus of Panama
VENEZUELA
COLOMBIA

West from Greenwich

COPYRIGHT GEORGE PHILIP LTD

BAHAMAS
Havana
CUBA
Port au Prince
Santo Domingo
San Juan
Milwaukee Deep 9200
HAITI
DOM. REP.
Puerto Rico (U.S.A.)
ST KITTS & NEVIS
ANTIGUA & BARBUDA
Guadeloupe (France)
JAMAICA
Kingston
Leeward Is.
DOMINICA
Martinique (France)

MEXICO
BELIZE
GUATEMALA
San Salvador
HONDURAS
Tegucigalpa
EL SALVADOR
NICARAGUA
Managua

Greater Antilles

Caribbean Sea

Curaçao (Neth.)
ST LUCIA
ST VINCENT & THE GRENADINES
BARBADOS
Windward Is.
GRENADA
Lesser Antilles
Port of Spain
TRINIDAD & TOBAGO

A T L A N T I C

San José
COSTA RICA
PANAMA
Panama Canal
Gulf of Panama

Barranquilla
Maracaibo
Barquisimeto
Caracas
VENEZUELA
Orinoco
Ciudad Guayana
Angel Falls
Georgetown
GUYANA
Paramaribo
Cayenne
SURINAM
FRENCH GUIANA

O C E A N

Bucaramanga
Medellín
Bogotá
Calí
COLOMBIA

Guiana Highlands

Negro
Amazon
Manaus
Santarém
Amazon
Belém
São Luis

Equator

Galápagos Islands (Ecuador)
Quito
ECUADOR
Guayaquil
Cuenca
Iquitos
Ucayali

Fortaleza
Natal

BRITISH ISLES
On same scale

Trujillo
Selvas
Tapajós
Madeira
Pôrto Velho
Imperatrix
Teresina
Recife
Aracaju

P E R U
Machu Picchu
Cuzco
Xingu
São Francisco
Salvador

Lima
Lake Titicaca
La Paz
BOLIVIA
Plateau of Mato Grosso
Cuiabá
Brasília
Brazilian Highlands

Arequipa
Arica
Lake Poopó
Sucre
Santa Cruz
Goiânia
Campo Grande
Belo Horizonte

Antofagasta
Atacama Desert
PARAGUAY
Gran Chaco
Paraná
Campinas
Novo Iguaçu
Rio de Janeiro
São Paulo

Tropic of Capricorn

O C E A N

Asunción
Iguaçu Falls
Curitiba

Tucumán
Paraná

San Juan
Córdoba
Santa Fé
Pôrto Alegre

Aconcagua 6990
Mendoza
Rosario
URUGUAY
A T L A N T I C

Juan Fernández (Chile)
Valparaiso
Santiago
Buenos Aires
Montevideo
La Plata
Rivadavia
Rio de la Plata

CHILE
Concepción
ARGENTINA
Mar del Plata
O C E A N

Temuco
Bahía Blanca

Height of the land (metres)
	over 6000
	4000-6000
	2000-4000
	1000-2000
	400-1000
	200-400
	0-200
sea level	
	below sea level

■ Over 5 000 000 inhabitants
● 1 000 000 - 5 000 000 inhabitants
• Under 1 000 000 inhabitants
Lima Capital cities underlined
— Country boundaries
DOM. REP. = Dominican Rep.

P A C I F I C
O C E A N

Pampas
Patagonia
Andes

Sacramento

Scale 1:35 000 000   1cm on the map = 350 km on the ground
0	500km	1000km	1500km	2000km	2500km

cm   cm

Falkland Islands (U.K.)
Stanley
Strait of Magellan
Tierra del Fuego
Cape Horn
South Georgia (U.K.)

110° West from Greenwich 100°

North America
Atlantic Ocean
Africa
Pacific Ocean
Antarctica

Cross section
CHILE   BOLIVIA   PARAGUAY   BRAZIL

▲ Ojos del Salado 6863
▲ Ancohuma & Illampu 6550

Pacific Ocean
Andes
Pilcomayo
Gran Chaco
Paraguay
Verde
Paraná
Brazilian Highlands
São Francisco
Doce
Atlantic Ocean

20°S   20°S

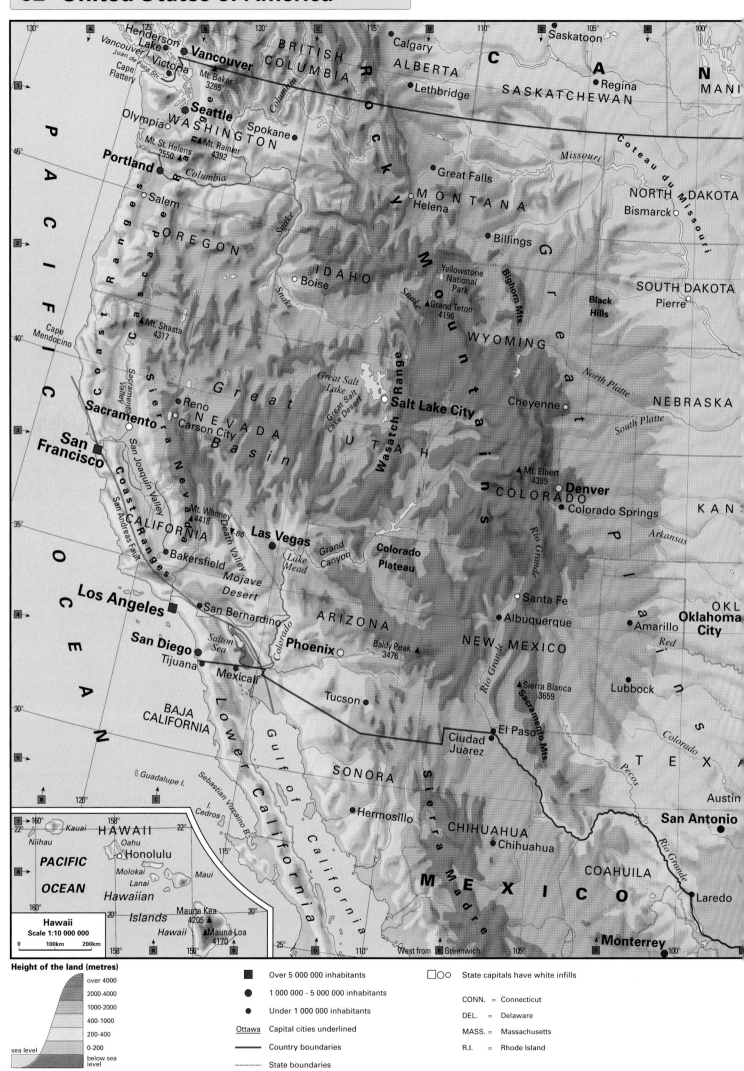

Height of the land (metres)

over 4000
2000-4000
1000-2000
400-1000
200-400
0-200
sea level
below sea
level

■ Over 5 000 000 inhabitants

● 1 000 000 - 5 000 000 inhabitants

● Under 1 000 000 inhabitants

Ottawa Capital cities underlined

——— Country boundaries

- - - - State boundaries

□○○ State capitals have white infills

CONN. = Connecticut

DEL. = Delaware

MASS. = Massachusetts

R.I. = Rhode Island

95° H 90° J 85° K 80° L 75° M 70° N 65°

Lake Winnipeg

BA
Winnipeg

A D A

O N T A R I O

Q U E B E C

St. Lawrence

NEW BRUNSWICK

1

45°

Quebec

Thunder Bay

Lake Superior

Ottawa

Montreal

MAINE

Fargo

Duluth

Sault Ste.Marie

Sudbury

Georgian Bay

Ottawa

VERMONT

Mt. Washington 1917

Augusta

Mississippi

MINNESOTA

Great Lakes

Montpelier

NEW HAMPSHIRE

Portland

2

Minneapolis

St. Paul

WISCONSIN

MICHIGAN

Lake Huron

Toronto

Lake Ontario

Rochester

Albany

Hudson

Concord

New England

MASS.

Boston

C. Cod

Hamilton

Buffalo

NEW YORK

Hartford

CONN.

R.I.

Providence

Madison

Lansing

Lake Erie

Long I.

40°

Milwaukee

Lake Michigan

Detroit

Cleveland

PENNSYLVANIA

NEW

New York

IOWA

Chicago

Toledo

Trenton

Philadelphia

Des Moines

Midwest

OHIO

Pittsburgh

Harrisburg

JERSEY

Baltimore

Dover

ATLANTIC OCEAN

3

Omaha

ILLINOIS

INDIANA

Columbus

Potomac

MARYLAND

Annapolis

DEL.

Dayton

Allegheny Mts.

Washington

Delaware Bay

ncoln

Springfield

Indianapolis

Cincinatti

Ohio

WEST

D.C.

Chesapeake Bay

Missouri

Charleston

VIRGINIA

VIRGINIA

Topeka

Kansas City

St. Louis

Louisville

Frankfort

Richmond

Norfolk

35°

Jefferson City

MISSOURI

Lake of the Ozarks

Ozark Plateau

Ohio

KENTUCKY

Cumberland

Appalachian Plateau

Blue Ridge

Raleigh

Pamlico Sd.

C. Hatteras

S

Cumberland Plateau

NORTH CAROLINA

OMA

Arkansas

Nashville

Charlotte

C. Fear

4

Memphis

TENNESSEE

Tennessee

SOUTH

Columbia

ARKANSAS

Little Rock

Birmingham

Atlanta

CAROLINA

Red

Savannah

GEORGIA

Columbus

Savannah

30°

Dallas

Sabine

MISSISSIPPI

ALABAMA

ort Worth

Jackson

Montgomery

Chattahoochee

Tombigbee

Alabama

LOUISIANA

Mississippi

Trinity

Jacksonville

S

Brazos

Baton Rouge

L. Pontchartrain

Tallahassee

Cape San Blas

5

Houston

New Orleans

Orlando

C. Canaveral

Delta of the Mississippi

Tampa

Indian River

FLORIDA

Grand Bahama I.

Great Abaco

Tampa B.

L. Okeechobee

Gulf of Mexico

Everglades

Miami

BAHAMAS

Str.

Nassau

Eleuthera I.

25°

aguna Madre

Florida Keys

Florida

Andros I.

Long I.

Cat I.

6

COPYRIGHT GEORGE PHILIP LTD

95° H 90° J 85° K 80° L 75° M

Scale 1:12 000 000   1cm on the map = 120 km on the ground

0   200km   400km   600km   800km   1000km   1200km

1 2 3 4 5 6 7 8 9 10
cm   cm   cm

ENGLAND and WALES
On same scale

Height of the land (metres)

over 4000
2000-4000
1000-2000
400-1000
200-400
0-200
sea level
below sea
level

■ Over 5 000 000 inhabitants

● 1 000 000 - 5 000 000 inhabitants

• Under 1 000 000 inhabitants

<u>Mexico</u> Capital cities underlined

——— Country boundaries

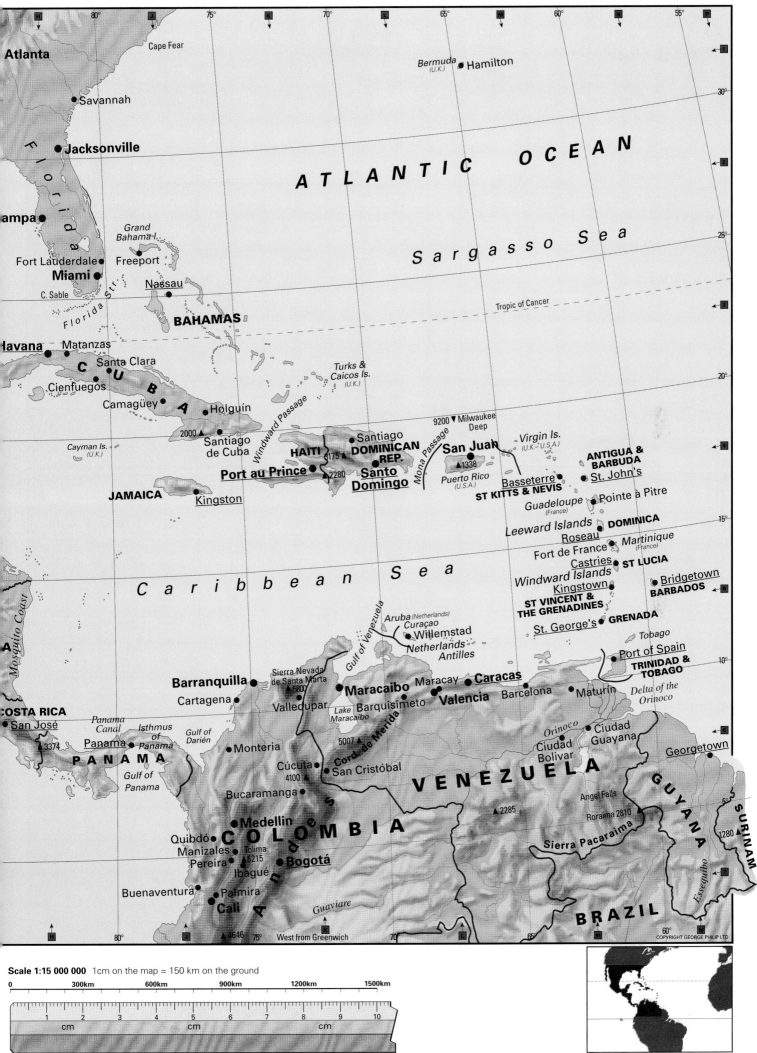

Atlanta

• Savannah

Cape Fear

Bermuda
(U.K.) ● Hamilton

ATLANTIC OCEAN

● **Jacksonville**

Florida

30°

S a r g a s s o   S e a

ampa ●

25°

Grand
Bahama I.

Fort Lauderdale ●
● Freeport
Miami

C. Sable

● Nassau

Tropic of Cancer

Florida Str.

BAHAMAS

20°

Havana ● Matanzas

● Santa Clara

C

Turks &
Caicos Is.
(U.K.)

● Cienfuegos

U

● Camagüey ● Holguín

B

Windward Passage

2000 ▲

Cayman Is.
(U.K.)

Santiago
de Cuba ▲

9200 ▼ Milwaukee
Deep

Santiago
● ● **DOMINICAN
REP.**

Virgin Is.
(U.K.–U.S.A.)

● **San Juan**

A

HAITI ▲3175

Mona Passage

Port au Prince
▲2280

**ANTIGUA &
BARBUDA**

▲1338

**Santo
Domingo**

Puerto Rico
(U.S.A.)

● **St. John's**

Basseterre ●

JAMAICA

● **ST KITTS & NEVIS**

● Kingston

Guadeloupe ● Pointe à Pitre
(France)

15°

Leeward Islands ● **DOMINICA**

Roseau ●

Martinique
(France)

Fort de France ●

C a r i b b e a n   S e a

Castries ● **ST LUCIA**

Windward Islands

● **Bridgetown**

Kingstown ●

BARBADOS

**ST VINCENT &
THE GRENADINES**

Aruba (Netherlands)
Curaçao

St. George's ● **GRENADA**

Willemstad ●

● *Tobago*

*Netherlands
Antilles*

● **Port of Spain**

10°

Gulf of Venezuela

**TRINIDAD &
TOBAGO**

● **Barranquilla**

Sierra Nevada
de Santa Marta

Maracay ● **Caracas**

*Delta of the
Orinoco*

▲5800

● **Maracaibo**

Barcelona ● ● Maturín

Cartagena ●

Valledupar ● Barquisimeto ● ● **Valencia**

Mosquito Coast

Lake
Maracaibo

COSTA RICA

*Panama
Canal*

*Isthmus
of
Panama*

*Gulf of
Darién*

● Monteria

5007 ▲

Cord. de Mérida

Orinoco ● Ciudad
Guayana

● San José

● **Panama**

Ciudad
Bolívar ●

● Georgetown

▲3374

*Gulf of
Panama*

● Bucaramanga

Cúcuta ●
4100 ▲

VENEZUELA

PANAMA

● San Cristóbal

Angel Falls

**G
U
Y
A
N
A**

● **Medellín**

Quibdó ●

C O L O M B I A

▲2285

Roraima 2810

SURINAM

Manizales ●

Tolima

Sierra Pacaraima

1280

Pereira ● ▲5215

● **Bogotá**

● Ibagué

Buenaventura ●

● Palmira

Guaviare

B R A Z I L

Cali

Andes

▲4646

West from Greenwich

COPYRIGHT GEORGE PHILIP LTD.

5°

Scale 1:15 000 000 1cm on the map = 150 km on the ground

0   300km   600km   900km   1200km   1500km

1   2   3   4   5   6   7   8   9   10
cm   cm   cm

1

PACIFIC
OCEAN
Anchorage
Yukon
Alaska
Vancouver
Mackenzie
Great Bear L.
Banks Island (Canada)
Yellowknife
Edmonton
Great Slave L.
Victoria Island (Canada)
NORTH AMERICA
Nelson
Churchill
Hudson Bay
L. Michigan
Chicago
L. Superior
L. Huron
Toronto
Iqaluit
Baffin Island (Canada)
Hudson Strait
Labrador
Davis Strait
Nuuk (Godthåb)
C. Farewell 60°N
Bering Strait
Wrangel I. (Russia)
New Siberian Is. (Russia)
Cape Barrow
Beaufort Sea
Queen Elizabeth Islands (Canada)
North Magnetic Pole
Ellesmere Island (Canada)
ARCTIC OCEAN
North Pole
Thule
Baffin Bay
1000
Greenland (Denmark) 4000
2000
Denmark Strait
Iceland
Reykjavík
70°N
80°N
C. Morris Jesup
Nizhne Kolymsk
Tiksi
Laptev Sea
Taimyr Peninsula
C. Chelyuskin
Severnaya Zemlya (Russia)
Franz Josef Land (Russia)
Novaya Zemlya (Russia)
Barents Sea
Svalbard (Norway)
Greenland Sea
Jan Mayen I. (Norway)
Arctic Circle
Faroe Is. (Denmark)
British Isles
Edinburgh
North Sea
West from Greenwich 0° East from Greenwich
ASIA
Novosibirsk
Siberia
Yenisei
Norilsk
Ob
Kara Sea
Vorkuta
Ural Mts.
N. Dvina
Arkhangelsk
North Cape
Murmansk
Tromsø
Scandinavia
Oslo
Baltic Sea
Moscow
St. Petersburg
EUROPE
Black Sea
150° 180° 150° 120° 90°
120° 60°
90° 30°
60° 30°

2

ATLANTIC OCEAN
South Sandwich Island Trench ▼ 8265
South Sandwich Is. (U.K.)
South Georgia (U.K.)
South Orkney Is.
Scotia Sea
Falkland Is. (U.K.)
Strait of Magellan
Punta Arenas
SOUTH AMERICA
Drake Passage
C. Horn
Tierra del Fuego
Bellingshausen Sea
South Shetland Is.
O'Higgins (Chile)
Esperanza (Arg.)
Palmer (U.S.A.)
Rothera (U.K.)
Alexander I.
Antarctic Peninsula
Ellsworth Land
Marie Byrd Land
Sanae (S. Africa)
Antarctic Circle
Halley (U.K.)
Weddell Sea
Berkner I.
Ronne Ice Shelf
Coats Land
Queen Maud Land
ANTARCTICA
South Pole
Vinson Massif 5140
Queen Maud Ra.
Beardmore Glacier
Mt Markham ▲ 4349
Ross Ice Shelf
Scott (N.Z.)
McMurdo (U.S.A.)
Vanda (N.Z.)
Ross Sea
C. Adare
Victoria Land
Balleny Is.
Enderby Land
1000
2000
Mawson (Austr.)
C. Darnley
Prince Charles Mts.
American Highland
Davis (Austr.)
4000
Vostok (Russia)
Casey (Austr.)
Wilkes Land
South Magnetic Pole
Adélie Land
Dumont d'Urville (France)
70°S
80°S
INDIAN OCEAN
SOUTHERN OCEAN
Antarctic Circle
Tasmania
Hobart
AUSTRALIA
Macquarie I. (Australia)
Campbell I. (N.Z.)
Auckland I.
West from Greenwich 180° East from Greenwich
COPYRIGHT GEORGE PHILIP LTD
30° 0° 30° 60° 90°
120°
90° 120° 150° 150° 60°

Scale 1:50 000 000 1cm on the map = 500 km on the ground

0 500km 1000km 1500km 2000km 2500km 3000km

1 2 3 4 5 6
cm   cm

Height of the land (metres)

over 4000
2000-4000
1000-2000
400-1000
200-400
0-200
sea level
below sea level

■ Over 5 000 000 inhabitants
● 1 000 000 - 5 000 000 inhabitants
• Under 1 000 000 inhabitants
Oslo Capital cities underlined
■ Davis (Austr.) Research station and the country which runs it

Limit of permanently frozen sea
Icebergs
Furthest extent of icebergs
Land permanently covered with ice
─100─ Height of ice (in metres)

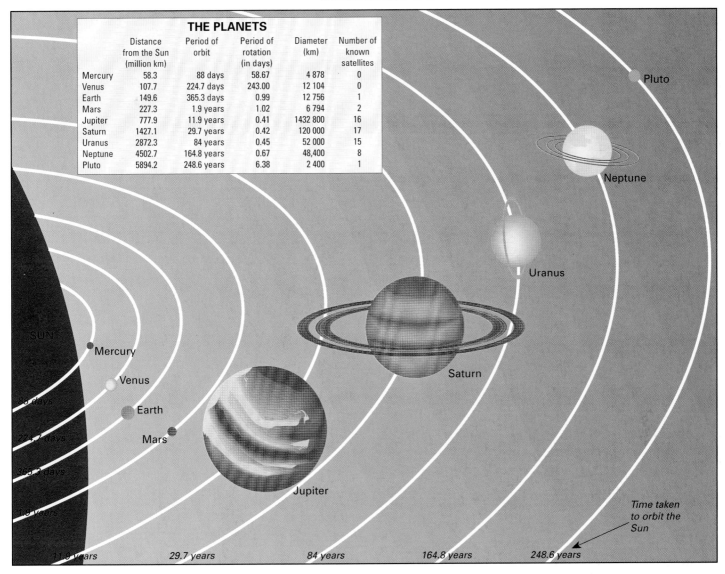

THE PLANETS				
	Distance from the Sun (million km)	Period of orbit	Period of rotation (in days)	Diameter (km)	Number of known satellites
Mercury	58.3	88 days	58.67	4 878	0
Venus	107.7	224.7 days	243.00	12 104	0
Earth	149.6	365.3 days	0.99	12 756	1
Mars	227.3	1.9 years	1.02	6 794	2
Jupiter	777.9	11.9 years	0.41	1432 800	16
Saturn	1427.1	29.7 years	0.42	120 000	17
Uranus	2872.3	84 years	0.45	52 000	15
Neptune	4502.7	164.8 years	0.67	48,400	8
Pluto	5894.2	248.6 years	6.38	2 400	1

Time taken to orbit the Sun

THE SOLAR SYSTEM

The universe is made up of many galaxies, or collections of stars. Our galaxy is called the Milky Way. It is made of about 100 000 stars. The Sun is one of these stars. Around it revolve nine planets, one of which is the Earth. The Sun, its planets and their satellites are known as the Solar System.
The Sun is the only source of light and heat in the Solar System. The other planets are visible from the Earth because of the sunlight which they reflect. The planets move in two ways at once. They revolve round, or orbit the Sun in an anti-clockwise direction, each planet keeping a fixed distance from the Sun. They also rotate anti-clockwise on their own axes. The planets remain in orbit because they are attracted by the Sun's pull of gravity.

THE MOON

Some of the planets have satellites revolving around them. The Earth has one satellite called the Moon, which takes approximately 29½ days, or one month, to rotate on its own axis as well as to revolve around the Earth. As a result, the Moon always faces us with the same side.
The diagrams and pictures on the left show how the Moon appears to have different shapes at different times of the month. These are known as the phases of the Moon. The Earth is nearly always between the Sun's rays and the Moon and casts a shadow on it. The apparent changes in the shape of the Moon are caused by its changing position in relation to both the Earth and the rays of the Sun.

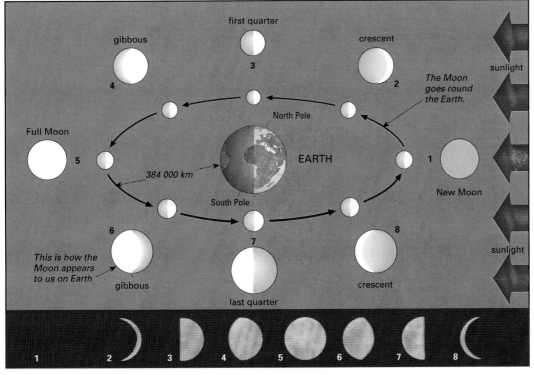

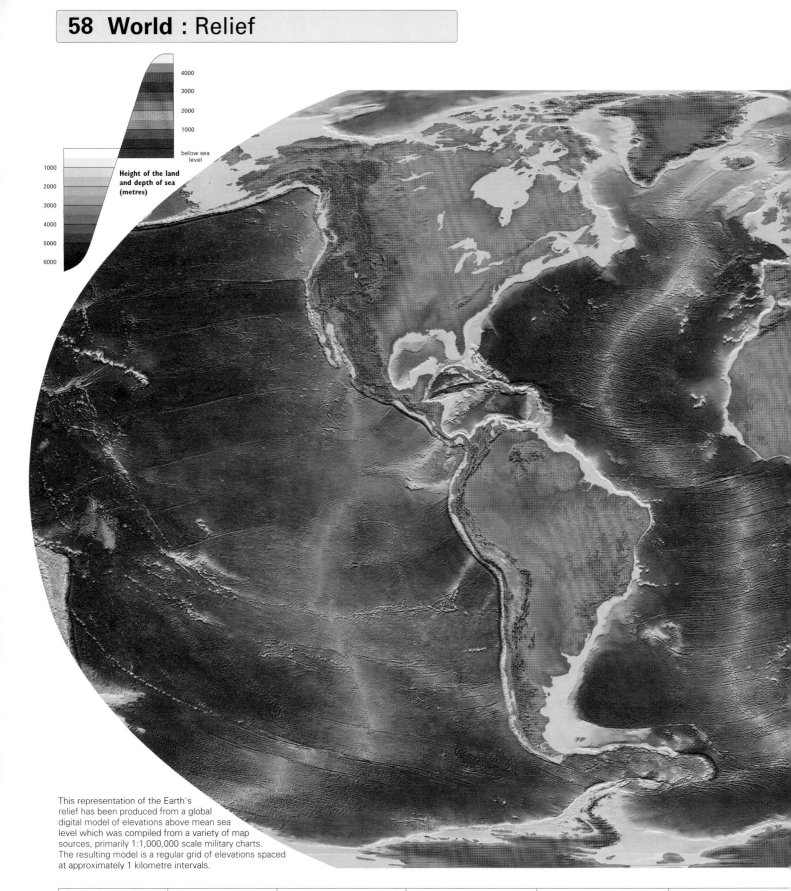

4000
3000
2000
1000
below sea
level

**Height of the land
and depth of sea
(metres)**

1000
2000
3000
4000
5000
6000

This representation of the Earth's
relief has been produced from a global
digital model of elevations above mean sea
level which was compiled from a variety of map
sources, primarily 1:1 000 000 scale military charts.
The resulting model is a regular grid of elevations spaced
at approximately 1 kilometre intervals.

Continent	Area, '000 km²	Coldest place, °C	Hottest place, °C	Wettest place (average annual rainfall, mm)	Driest place (average annual rainfall, mm)
Asia	44 500	Verkhoyansk, Russia -68°C	Tirat Zevi, Israel 54°C	Cherrapunji, India 11 430	Aden, Yemen 46
Africa	30 302	Ifrane, Morocco -24°C	El Azizia, Libya 58°C	Debundscha, Cameroon 10 290	Wadi Halfa, Sudan 2
North America	24 241	Snag, Yukon -63°C	Death Valley, California 57°C	Henderson Lake, Canada 6 500	Bataques, Mexico 30
South America	17 793	Sarmiento, Argentina -33°C	Rivadavia, Argentina 49°C	Quibdó, Colombia 8 990	Arica, Chile 0.8
Antarctica	14 000	Vostok -89°C	Vanda Station 15°C		
Europe	9 957	Ust'Shchugor, Russia -55°C	Seville, Spain 50°C	Crkvice, Yugoslavia 4 650	Astrakhan, Russia 160
Oceania	8 557	Charlotte Pass, Australia -22°C	Cloncurry, Australia 53°C	Tully, Australia 4 550	Mulka, Australia 100

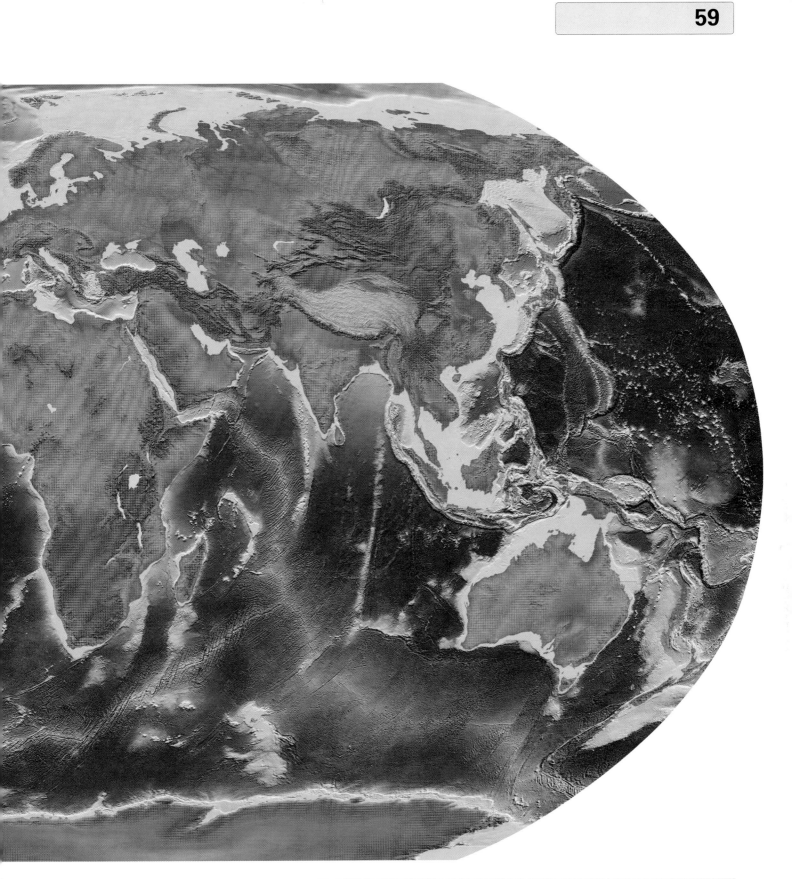

World - largest seas, '000 km²	World - largest lakes, '000 km²	World - longest rivers, km	World - largest islands, '000 km²	World - highest peaks, m	World - deepest trenches, m
Pacific Ocean 165 721	Caspian Sea 424	Nile 6 690	Greenland 2 176	Himalayas: Mt. Everest 8 850	Mariana Trench 11 022
Atlantic Ocean 81 660	Lake Superior 82	Amazon 6 280	New Guinea 777	Karakoram Ra: K2 8 611	Tonga Trench 10 822
Indian Ocean 73 442	Lake Victoria 69	Mississippi -Missouri 6 270	Borneo 725	Pamirs: Communism Pk. 7 495	Japan Trench 10 554
Arctic Ocean 14 351	Lake Huron 60	Yangtze-Kiang 4 990	Madagascar 590	Tien Shan: Pik Pobedy 7 444	Kuril Trench 10 542
Mediterranean Sea 2 966	Lake Michigan 58	Congo 4 670	Baffin Island 476	Andes: Aconcagua 6 960	Mindanao Trench 10 497
South China Sea 2 318	Aral Sea 36	Amur 4 410	Sumatra 474	Rocky Mts: Mt. McKinley 6 194	Kermadec Trench 10 047
Bering Sea 2 274	Lake Tanganyika 33	Hwang-Ho 4 350	Honshu 228	East Africa: Mt. Kilimanjaro 5 895	Milwaukee Deep 9 200
Caribbean Sea 1 942	Lake Baikal 31	Lena 4 260	Great Britain 217	Caucasus: Elbrus 5 633	Bougainville Trench 9 140
Gulf of Mexico 1 813	Great Bear Lake 31	Mekong 4 180	Victoria Island 212	Antarctica: Vinson Massif 5 139	South Sandwich Island Trench 8 428
Sea of Okhotsk 1 528	Lake Malawi 31	Niger 4 180	Ellesmere Island 197	Alps: Mt. Blanc 4 807	Aleutian Trench 7 822

Country	Population in thousands 1998 estimate	Area in thous' km²	Country	Population in thousands 1998 estimate	Area in thous' km²	Country	Population in thousands 1998 estimate	Area in thous' km²	Country	Population in thousands 1998 estimate	Area in thous' km²	Country	Population in thousands 1998 estimate	Area in thous' km²
China	1 255 698	9 597	Mexico	95 831	924	United Kingdom	58 649	301	Argentina	36 123	2 767	Venezuela	23 242	
India	982 223	3 288	Germany	82 113	357	Italy	57 369	604	Tanzania	32 102	2 506	Nepal	22 847	
United States	274 028	9 373	Vietnam	77 562	332	Ukraine	50 861	1 128	Canada	30 563	9 976	Romania	22 474	
Indonesia	206 338	1 905	Philippines	72 944	1 648	Congo, Dem. Rep.	49 139	677	Algeria	30 081	945	Iraq	21 800	
Brazil	165 851	8 512	Egypt	65 978	300	Korea, South	46 109	99	Kenya	29 008	580	Malaysia	21 410	
Pakistan	148 166	796	Iran	65 758	1 001	Burma	44 497	2 345	Sudan	28 292	2 382	Afghanistan	21 354	
Russia	147 434	17 075	Turkey	64 479	779	Colombia	40 803	1 220	Morocco	27 377	447	Taiwan*	21 100	
Japan	126 281	378	Thailand	60 300	513	Spain	39 628	505	Peru	24 797	121	Uganda	20 554	
Bangladesh	124 774	144	Ethiopia	59 649	243	South Africa	39 357	313	Uzbekistan	23 574	1 285	Saudi Arabia	20 181	2
Nigeria	106 409	1 958	France	58 683	552	Poland	38 718	1 139	Korea, North	23 348	238	Ghana	19 162	

* figures for Taiwan obtained from 1995 esti

untry	Population in thousands 1998 estimate	Area in thous' km²	Country	Population in thousands 1998 estimate	Area in thous' km²	Country	Population in thousands 1998 estimate	Area in thous' km²	Country	Population in thousands 1998 estimate	Area in thous' km²	Country	Population in thousands 1998 estimate	Area in thous' km²
ozambique	18 880	7 687	Ivory Coast	14 292	475	Greece	10 600	208	Senegal	9 003	164	Switzerland	7 299	28
ustralia	18 520	802	Ecuador	12 175	391	Malawi	10 346	79	Sweden	8 875	450	Chad	7 270	246
Lanka	18 455	239	Angola	12 092	284	Belarus	10 315	93	Zambia	8 781	111	Hong Kong SAR**	6 660	28
men	16 887	2 717	Zimbabwe	11 377	111	Czech Republic	10 282	181	Bulgaria	8 336	197	Rwanda	6 604	1 284
zakstan	16 319	42	Burkina Faso	11 305	102	Belgium	10 141	274	Dominican Republic	8 232	84	Burundi	6 457	143
etherlands	15 678	587	Cuba	11 116	1 247	Hungary	10 116	31	Austria	8 140	1 099	Jordan	6 304	1
ria	15 333	185	Guatemala	10 801	1 240	Niger	10 078	118	Bolivia	7 957	26	Honduras	6 147	112
adagascar	15 057	528	Cambodia	10 716	109	Portugal	9 869	753	Haiti	7 952	49	El Salvador	6 032	21
ile	14 824	757	Mali	10 694	92	Tunisia	9 335	638	Azerbaijan	7 669	87	Tajikistan	6 015	27
meroon	14 305	322	Yugoslavia	10 635	132	Somalia	9 237	1 267	Guinea	7 337	41	Israel	5 984	89

** now part of China

CLIMATE REGIONS

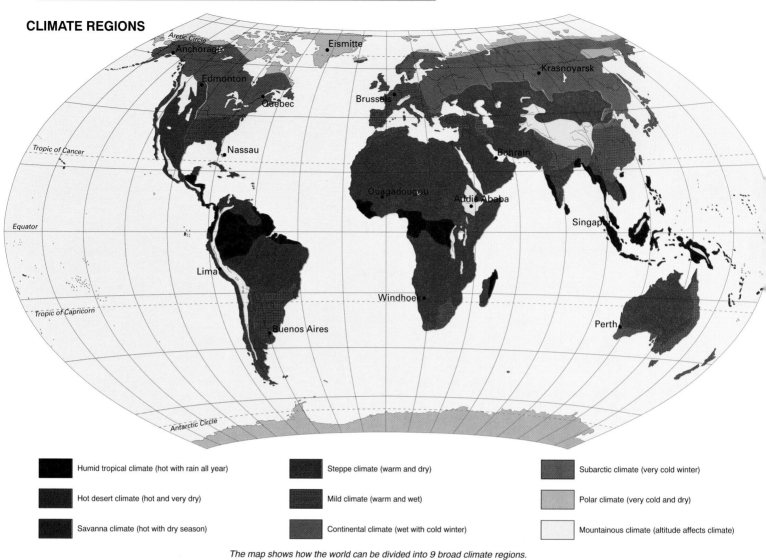

■	Humid tropical climate (hot with rain all year)	■	Steppe climate (warm and dry)	■	Subarctic climate (very cold winter)
■	Hot desert climate (hot and very dry)	■	Mild climate (warm and wet)	■	Polar climate (very cold and dry)
■	Savanna climate (hot with dry season)	■	Continental climate (wet with cold winter)	■	Mountainous climate (altitude affects climate)

The map shows how the world can be divided into 9 broad climate regions.

CLIMATE GRAPHS

The graphs below give examples of places within each climate region, showing how temperature and rainfall vary from month to month.

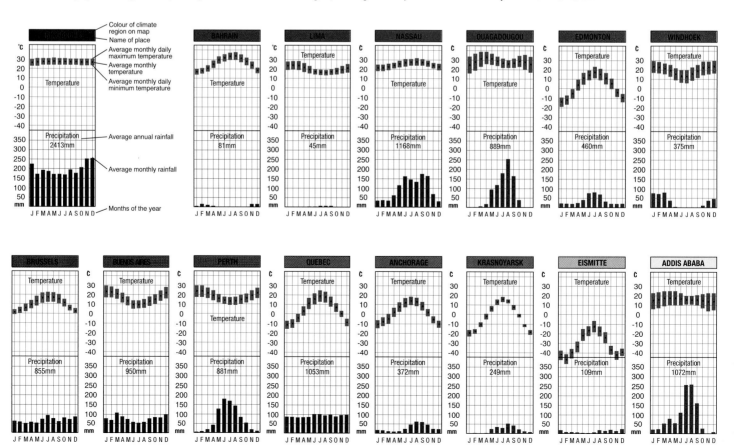

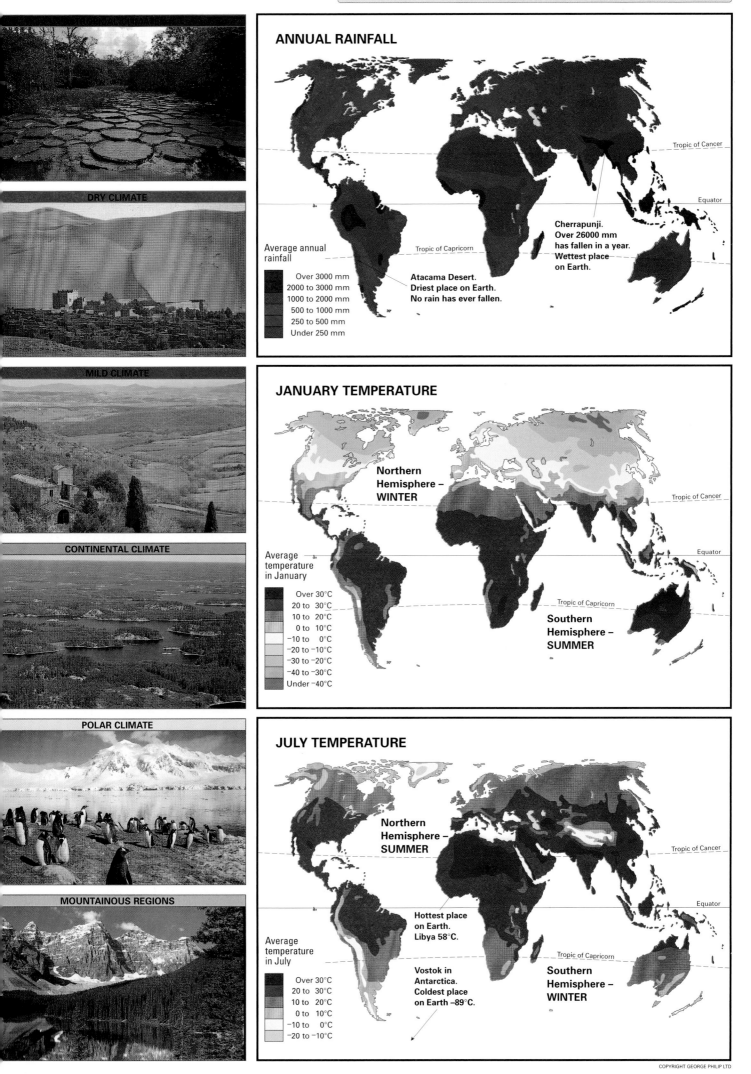

TROPICAL CLIMATE

DRY CLIMATE

MILD CLIMATE

CONTINENTAL CLIMATE

POLAR CLIMATE

MOUNTAINOUS REGIONS

ANNUAL RAINFALL

Tropic of Cancer

Equator

Cherrapunji.
Over 26000 mm
has fallen in a year.
Wettest place
on Earth.

Average annual
rainfall

Tropic of Capricorn

Atacama Desert.
Driest place on Earth.
No rain has ever fallen.

Over 3000 mm
2000 to 3000 mm
1000 to 2000 mm
500 to 1000 mm
250 to 500 mm
Under 250 mm

JANUARY TEMPERATURE

Northern
Hemisphere –
WINTER

Tropic of Cancer

Average
temperature
in January

Equator

Over 30°C
20 to 30°C
10 to 20°C
0 to 10°C
−10 to 0°C
−20 to −10°C
−30 to −20°C
−40 to −30°C
Under −40°C

Tropic of Capricorn

Southern
Hemisphere –
SUMMER

JULY TEMPERATURE

Northern
Hemisphere –
SUMMER

Tropic of Cancer

Hottest place
on Earth.
Libya 58°C.

Equator

Average
temperature
in July

Vostok in
Antarctica.
Coldest place
on Earth −89°C.

Tropic of Capricorn

Southern
Hemisphere –
WINTER

Over 30°C
20 to 30°C
10 to 20°C
0 to 10°C
−10 to 0°C
−20 to −10°C

NATURAL VEGETATION

The map shows the type of vegetation that would grow if people were not there. People have cleared forests and natural grasslands for thousands of years. Most of the broadleaf deciduous woodland that would naturally cover the British Isles has been cleared for farming and for building. In more recent years, much of the tropical broadleaf rainforest and monsoon forests have been felled.

Tundra and mountain vegetation

Needleleaf evergreen forest

Mixed forest of needleleaf evergreen and broadleaf deciduous trees

Broadleaf deciduous woodland

Mid-latitude grassland

Evergreen broadleaf and deciduous trees, shrubs and herbs

Semi-desert scrub

Desert

Tropical grassland (savanna)

Tropical broadleaf rainforest and needleleaf forest

Sub-tropical broadleaf and needleleaf forest

NATURAL DISASTERS

Locust invasion area

■ Major famines

■ Major storms and floo

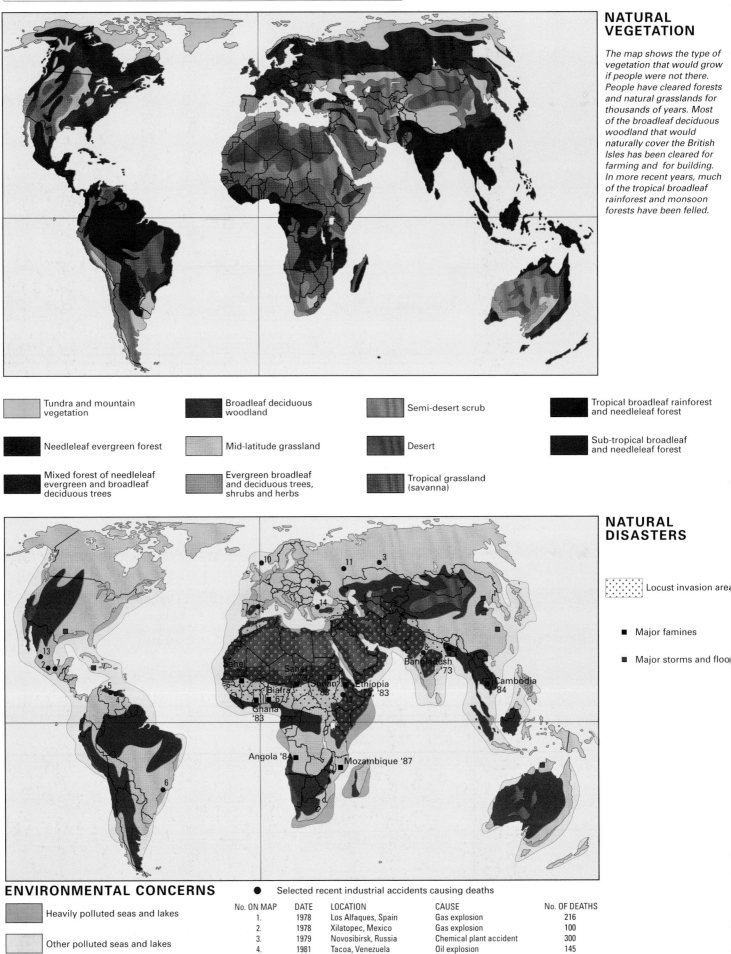

ENVIRONMENTAL CONCERNS

Heavily polluted seas and lakes

Other polluted seas and lakes

Areas where the forest is being rapidly cut down (deforestation)

Areas of continuous drought (deserts)

Areas which are turning into desert due to soil erosion plus low rainfall (desertification)

● Selected recent industrial accidents causing deaths

No. ON MAP	DATE	LOCATION	CAUSE	No. OF DEATHS
1.	1978	Los Alfaques, Spain	Gas explosion	216
2.	1978	Xilatopec, Mexico	Gas explosion	100
3.	1979	Novosibirsk, Russia	Chemical plant accident	300
4.	1981	Tacoa, Venezuela	Oil explosion	145
5.	1982	Caracas, Venezuela	Explosives accident	101
6.	1984	São Paulo, Brazil	Gas explosion	508
7.	1984	Ixhuatepec, Mexico	Gas explosion	452
8.	1984	Bhopal, India	Chemical leakage	2500
9.	1986	Chernobyl, Ukraine	Nuclear reactor explosion	31
10.	1988	Piper Alpha, North Sea	Gas explosion	166
11.	1989	Ufa, Russia	Gas explosion	650
12.	1991	Addis Ababa, Ethiopia	Explosives accident	100
13.	1992	Guadalajara, Mexico	Gas explosion	206
14.	1992	Kozlu, Turkey	Gas explosion	272

CARTOGRAPHY BY PHILIP'S.

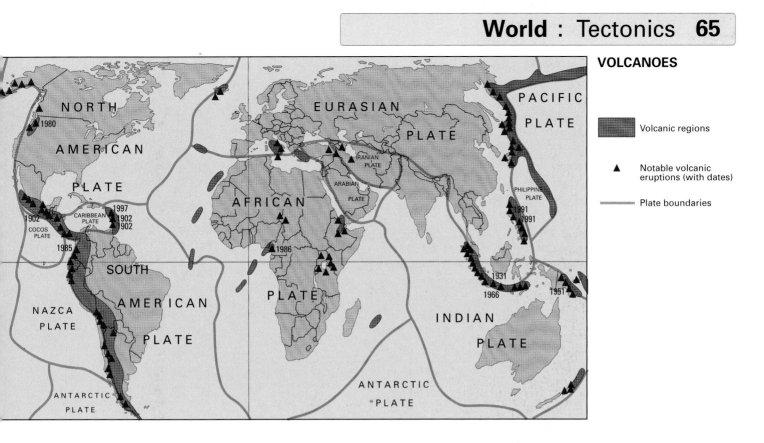

VOLCANOES

▨	Volcanic regions
▲	Notable volcanic eruptions (with dates)
——	Plate boundaries

OTABLE VOLCANIC ERUPTIONS

ar	Volcano	Deaths					
			1792	Unzen-Dake, Japan	15,000	1951	Mount Lamington, Papua New Guinea	6,000

ar	Volcano	Deaths
79	Vesuvius, Italy	16,000
69	Mount Etna, Italy	20,000
72	Papandajan, Java	3,000
83	Skaptar Jökull, Iceland	10,000

Year	Volcano	Deaths
1792	Unzen-Dake, Japan	15,000
1793	Miyi-Yama, Indonesia	50,000
1815	Tambora, Java	12,000
1883	Krakatoa, Indonesia	50,000
1902	Mount Pelée, Martinique	40,000
1902	Santa Maria, Guatemala	6,000
1902	Mount Taal, Philippines	1,400
1931	Merapi, Java	1,000

Year	Volcano	Deaths
1951	Mount Lamington, Papua New Guinea	6,000
1966	Mount Kelud, Java	1,000
1980	Mount St. Helens, USA	100
1985	Nevado del Ruiz, Colombia	22,940
1986	Wum, Cameroon	1,700
1991	Mount Pinatubo, Philippines	300
1993	Mount Mayon, Philippines	77
1997	Soufrière Hills, Montserrat	23

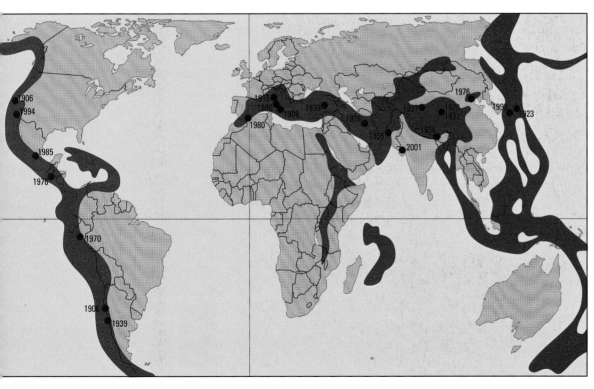

EARTHQUAKES

▬	Earthquake regions
●	Notable earthquakes (with dates)

OTABLE EARTHQUAKES SINCE 1900

ar	Location	Mag.	Deaths
06	San Francisco, USA	8.3	503
06	Valparaiso, Chile	8.6	22,000
08	Messina, Italy	7.5	83,000
15	Avezzano, Italy	7.5	30,000
20	Gansu (Kansu), China	8.6	180,000
23	Yokohama, Japan	8.3	143,000
27	Nan Shan, China	8.3	200,000
32	Gansu (Kansu), China	7.6	70,000
34	Bihar, India/Nepal	8.4	10,700

Year	Location	Mag.	Deaths
1939	Quetta, India	7.5	60,000
1939	Chillan, Chile	8.3	28,000
1939	Erzincan, Turkey	7.9	30,000
1960	Agadir, Morocco	5.8	12,000
1962	Khorasan, Iran	7.1	12,230
1964	Anchorage, Alaska	8.4	131
1970	Northern Peru	7.7	66,794
1972	Managua, Nicaragua	6.2	5,000
1974	Northern Pakistan	6.3	5,000
1976	Guatemala	7.5	22,778
1976	Tangshan, China	8.2	650,000
1978	Tabas, Iran	7.7	25,000
1980	El Asnam, Algeria	7.3	20,000

Year	Location	Mag.	Deaths
1980	Southern Italy	7.2	4,800
1985	Mexico City, Mexico	8.1	4,200
1988	Armenia	6.8	55,000
1990	Northern Iran	7.7	36,000
1993	Maharashtra, India	6.4	36,000
1994	Los Angeles, USA	6.6	57
1995	Kobe, Japan	7.2	5,000
1995	Sakhalin, Russia	7.5	2,000
1998	Takhar, Afghanistan	6.1	4,200
1998	Rostaq, Afghanistan	7.0	5,000
1999	Izmit, Turkey	7.4	15,000
1999	Taipei, Taiwan	7.6	1,700
2001	Gujarat, India	7.7	16,800

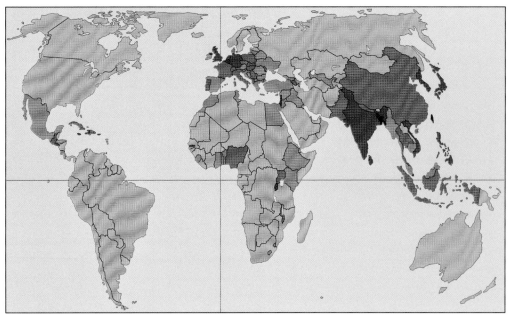

POPULATION DENSITY BY COUNTRY

The density of people per square kilometre 1997

- Over 500 people per km²
- 200 – 500 people per km²
- 100 – 200 people per km²
- 50 – 100 people per km²
- 10 – 50 people per km²
- Under 10 people per km²

Top 5 countries		Bottom 5 countries	
Macau	22 111 per km²	Namibia	1.9 per km²
Monaco	20 805 per km²	French Guiana	1.5 per km²
Singapore	5 246 per km²	Mongolia	1.4 per km²
Malta	1 172 per km²	W. Sahara	0.8 per km²
Bangladesh	953 per km²	Greenland	0.2 per km²

U.K.   243 per km²

POPULATION CHANGE 1990–2000

The population change for the years 1990–2000

- Over 40% population gain
- 30 – 40% population gain
- 20 – 30% population gain
- 10 – 20% population gain
- 0 – 10% population gain
- No change or population loss

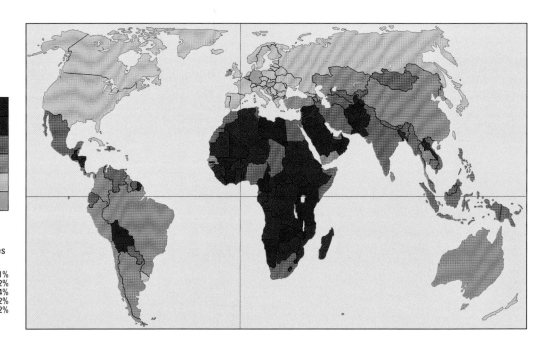

Top 5 countries		Bottom 5 countries	
Kuwait	+75.9%	Belgium	-0.1%
Namibia	+62.5%	Hungary	-0.2%
Afghanistan	+60.1%	Grenada	-2.4%
Mali	+55.5%	Germany	-3.2%
Tanzania	+54.6%	Tonga	-3.2%

U.K.   +2.0%

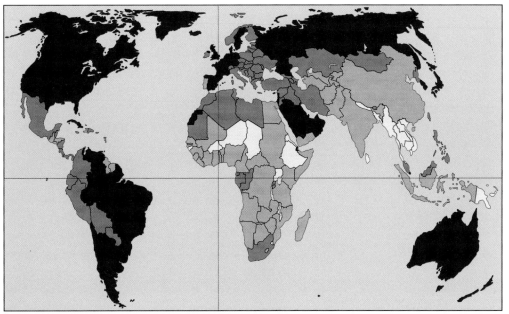

URBAN POPULATION

Percentage of total population living in towns and cities 1997

- Over 75%
- 50 – 75%
- 25 – 50%
- 10 – 25%
- Under 10%

Most urbanized		Least urbanized	
Singapore	100%	Rwanda	6%
Belgium	97%	Burundi	8%
Israel	91%	Bhutan	8%
Uruguay	91%	Nepal	11%
Netherlands	89%	Swaziland	12%

U.K.   89%

Projection: *Modified Hammer Equal Area*

POPULATION BY CONTINENTS

In this diagram the size of each continent is in proportion to its population. Each square represents 1% of the projected world population of 6 122 000 000 in 2000.

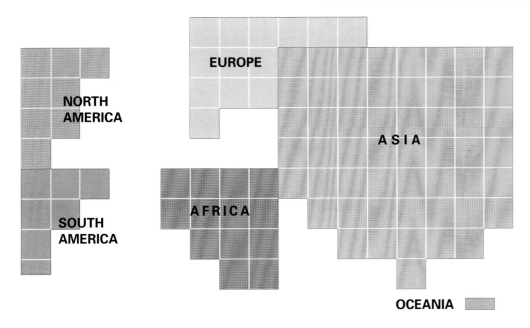

EUROPE

NORTH
AMERICA

ASIA

AFRICA

SOUTH
AMERICA

OCEANIA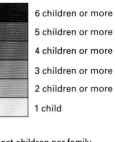

Population of countries 1998
Top 20 countries (thousands)

China	1 255 698
India	982 223
U.S.A.	274 028
Indonesia	206 338
Brazil	165 851
Pakistan	148 166
Russia	147 434
Japan	126 281
Bangladesh	124 774
Nigeria	106 409
Mexico	95 831
Germany	82 113
Vietnam	77 562
Philippines	72 944
Egypt	65 978
Iran	65 758
Turkey	64 479
Thailand	60 300
Ethiopia	59 649
France	58 683
United Kingdom	58 649

LIFE EXPECTANCY

The average expected lifespan of babies born in 1997

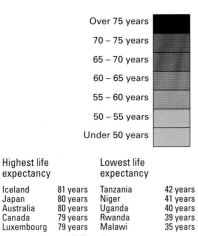

Over 75 years	
70 – 75 years	
65 – 70 years	
60 – 65 years	
55 – 60 years	
50 – 55 years	
Under 50 years	

Highest life expectancy		Lowest life expectancy	
Iceland	81 years	Tanzania	42 years
Japan	80 years	Niger	41 years
Australia	80 years	Uganda	40 years
Canada	79 years	Rwanda	39 years
Luxembourg	79 years	Malawi	35 years
	U.K.	77 years	

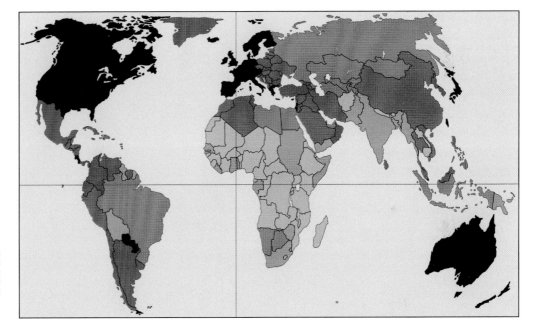

FAMILY SIZE

The average number of children a woman can expect to bear during her lifetime 1999

6 children or more	
5 children or more	
4 children or more	
3 children or more	
2 children or more	
1 child	

Most children per family

Yemen	7.4
Niger	7.4
Somalia	7.0
Oman	7.0
Ethiopia	7.0
U.K.	1.7

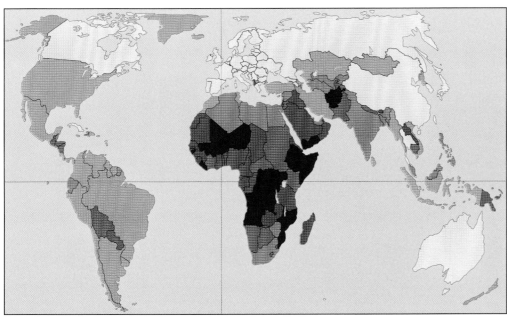

Projection: *Modified Hammer Equal Area*

WEALTH

The value of total production in 1998
divided by the population.
(The Gross National Product per capita)

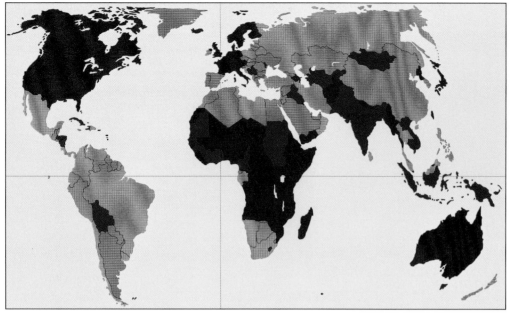

Over 400% of world average

200 – 400% of world average

100 – 200% of world average

World average wealth per person $4 890

50 – 100% of world average

25 – 50% of world average

10 – 25% of world average

Top 5 countries		Bottom 5 countries	
Luxembourg	$36 703	Ethiopia	$566
U.S.A.	$29 240	Burundi	$561
Switzerland	$26 876	Malawi	$551
Norway	$26 196	Tanzania	$483
Singapore	$25 295	Sierra Leone	$445
		U.K.	$18 700

WATER SUPPLY

The percentage of total population with
access to safe drinking water
(average 1990 – 1996)

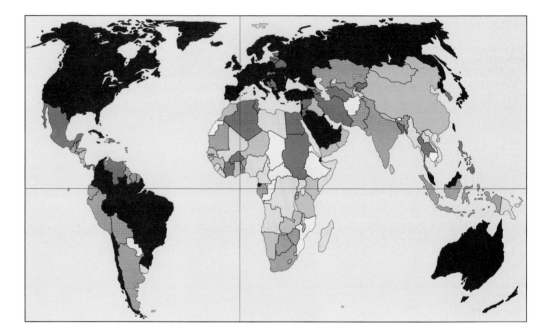

Over 90% with safe water

75 – 90% with safe water

60 – 75% with safe water

45 – 60% with safe water

30 – 45% with safe water

Under 30% with safe water

Least well-provided countries

Paraguay	8 %
Afghanistan	10 %
Cambodia	13 %
South Africa	18 %
Bhutan	21 %

ILLITERACY

The percentage of total population
unable to read or write 1998

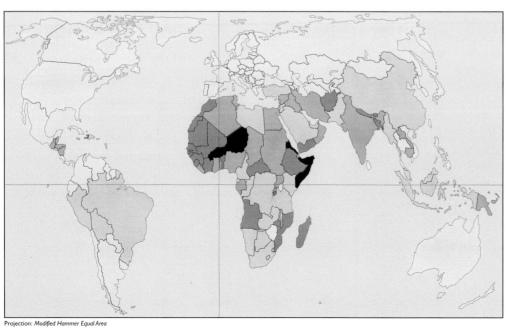

Over 75% of population illiterate

50 – 75% of population illiterate

25 – 50% of population illiterate

10 – 25% of population illiterate

Under 10% of population illiterate

Educational expenditure per person
(latest available year)

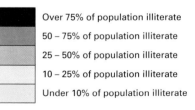

Top five countries		Bottom five countries	
Norway	$2 820	Congo (Dem. Rep.)	$1
Denmark	$2 450	Somalia	$2
Switzerland	$2 256	Sierra Leone	$2
Japan	$1 853	Nigeria	$3
Finland	$1 706	Haiti	$3
		U.K.	$1 009

Projection: Modified Hammer Equal Area

EMPLOYMENT

The number of workers employed in
manufacturing for every 100 workers
engaged in agriculture (1997)

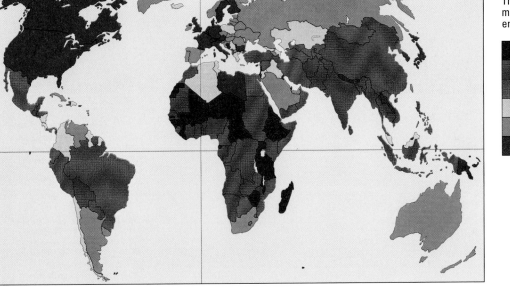

Under 10	Mainly
10 – 50	agricultural
50 – 100	countries
100 – 200	Mainly
200 – 500	industrial
Over 500	countries

DAILY FOOD CONSUMPTION

Average daily food intake
in calories per person 1995

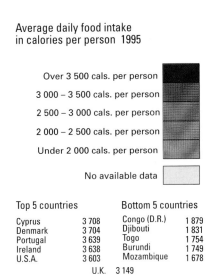

Over 3 500 cals. per person

3 000 – 3 500 cals. per person

2 500 – 3 000 cals. per person

2 000 – 2 500 cals. per person

Under 2 000 cals. per person

No available data

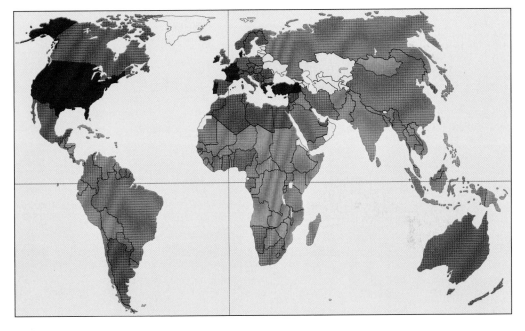

Top 5 countries		Bottom 5 countries	
Cyprus	3 708	Congo (D.R.)	1 879
Denmark	3 704	Djibouti	1 831
Portugal	3 639	Togo	1 754
Ireland	3 638	Burundi	1 749
U.S.A.	3 603	Mozambique	1 678
U.K.	3 149		

HEALTH CARE

Number of doctors per 100 000 persons 1997

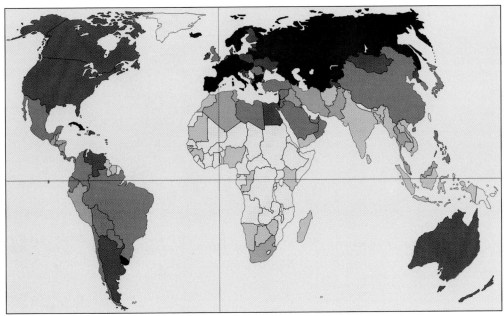

Over 300 doctors per 100 000 persons

200 – 300 doctors per 100 000 persons

100 – 200 doctors per 100 000 persons

50 – 100 doctors per 100 000 persons

10 – 50 doctors per 100 000 persons

Under 10 doctors per 100 000 persons

Most doctors per 100 000 persons 1997		Least doctors per 100 000 persons 1997	
Monaco	664.0	Ethiopia	0.05
Italy	554.0	Malawi	0.05
Cuba	530.4	Mozambique	0.05
Belarus	443.0	Rwanda	0.05
Georgia	436.0	Uganda	0.05
U.K.	164.0		

Projection: *Modified Hammer Equal Area*

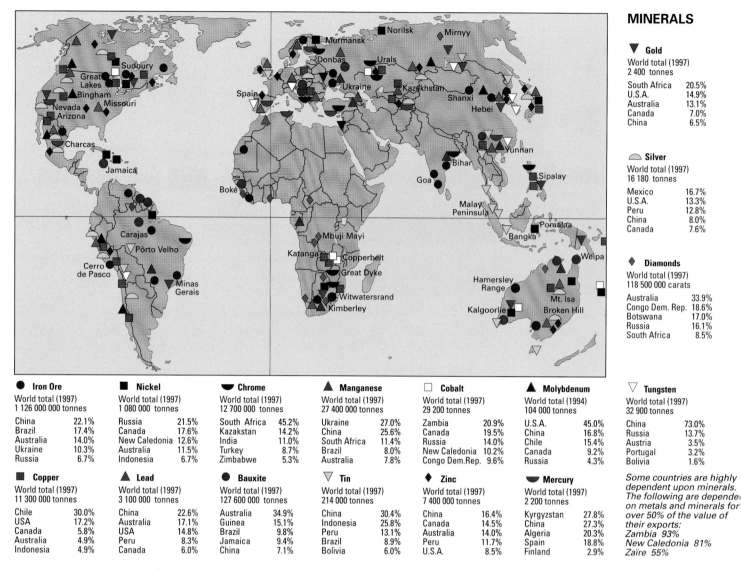

MINERALS

▼ Gold
World total (1997)
2 400 tonnes

South Africa	20.5%
U.S.A.	14.9%
Australia	13.1%
Canada	7.0%
China	6.5%

◖ Silver
World total (1997)
16 180 tonnes

Mexico	16.7%
U.S.A.	13.3%
Peru	12.8%
China	8.0%
Canada	7.6%

◆ Diamonds
World total (1997)
118 500 000 carats

Australia	33.9%
Congo Dem. Rep.	18.6%
Botswana	17.0%
Russia	16.1%
South Africa	8.5%

Map labels: Norilsk, Mirnyy, Murmansk, Donbas, Urals, Spain, Ukraine, Kazakhstan, Shanxi, Hebei, Sudbury, Great Lakes, Bingham, Nevada, Arizona, Missouri, Charcas, Jamaica, Boké, Yunnan, Bihar, Goa, Sipalay, Malay Peninsula, Pomalaa, Bangka, Weipa, Carajas, Pôrto Velho, Cerro de Pasco, Minas Gerais, Mbuji Mayi, Katanga, Copperbelt, Great Dyke, Witwatersrand, Kimberley, Hamersley Range, Mt. Isa, Broken Hill, Kalgoorlie

---

● Iron Ore
World total (1997)
1 126 000 000 tonnes

China	22.1%
Brazil	17.4%
Australia	14.0%
Ukraine	10.3%
Russia	6.7%

■ Copper
World total (1997)
11 300 000 tonnes

Chile	30.0%
USA	17.2%
Canada	5.8%
Australia	4.9%
Indonesia	4.9%

■ Nickel
World total (1997)
1 080 000 tonnes

Russia	21.5%
Canada	17.6%
New Caledonia	12.6%
Australia	11.5%
Indonesia	6.7%

▲ Lead
World total (1997)
3 100 000 tonnes

China	22.6%
Australia	17.1%
USA	14.8%
Peru	8.3%
Canada	6.0%

◗ Chrome
World total (1997)
12 700 000 tonnes

South Africa	45.2%
Kazakstan	14.2%
India	11.0%
Turkey	8.7%
Zimbabwe	5.3%

● Bauxite
World total (1997)
127 600 000 tonnes

Australia	34.9%
Guinea	15.1%
Brazil	9.8%
Jamaica	9.4%
China	7.1%

▲ Manganese
World total (1997)
27 400 000 tonnes

Ukraine	27.0%
China	25.6%
South Africa	11.4%
Brazil	8.0%
Australia	7.8%

▽ Tin
World total (1997)
214 000 tonnes

China	30.4%
Indonesia	25.8%
Peru	13.1%
Brazil	8.9%
Bolivia	6.0%

□ Cobalt
World total (1997)
29 200 tonnes

Zambia	20.9%
Canada	19.5%
Russia	14.0%
New Caledonia	10.2%
Congo Dem.Rep.	9.6%

◆ Zinc
World total (1997)
7 400 000 tonnes

China	16.4%
Canada	14.5%
Australia	14.0%
Peru	11.7%
U.S.A.	8.5%

▲ Molybdenum
World total (1994)
104 000 tonnes

U.S.A.	45.0%
China	16.8%
Chile	15.4%
Canada	9.2%
Russia	4.3%

◗ Mercury
World total (1997)
2 200 tonnes

Kyrgyzstan	27.8%
China	27.3%
Algeria	20.3%
Spain	18.8%
Finland	2.9%

▽ Tungsten
World total (1997)
32 900 tonnes

China	73.0%
Russia	13.7%
Austria	3.5%
Portugal	3.2%
Bolivia	1.6%

Some countries are highly dependent upon minerals. The following are depende on metals and minerals for over 50% of the value of their exports:
Zambia 93%
New Caledonia 81%
Zaïre 55%

FISHING AND LAND USE

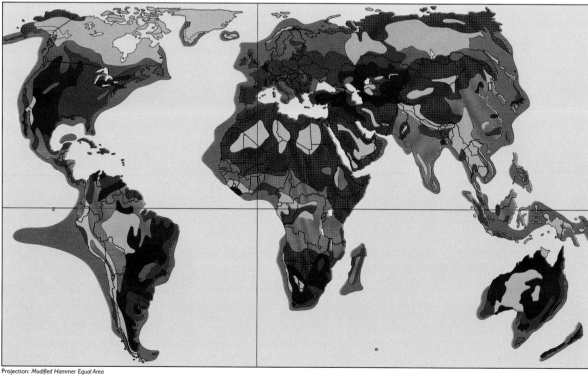

Projection: Modified Hammer Equal Area

  Principal fishing areas

Nomadic herding

Forestry

 Hunting, fishing and gathering

Subsistence agriculture (growing food to feed the family)

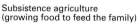 Livestock ranching (large scale breeding and rearing of animals for sale)

 Commercial farming (arable land, dairying, and small scale grazing to produce food for sale)

Urban areas (commercial, industrial and residential land use)

Unproductive land

ENERGY PRODUCTION

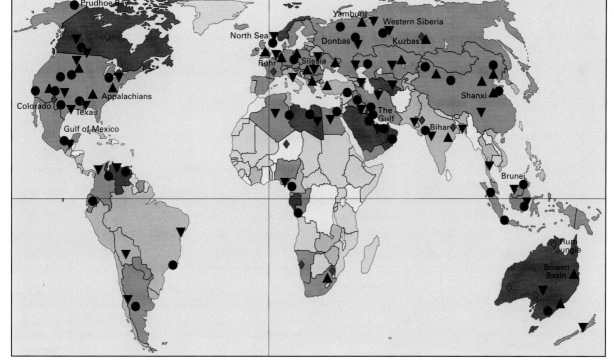

Primary energy production expressed in kilograms of coal equivalent per person 1996

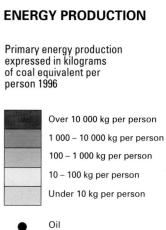

- Over 10 000 kg per person
- 1 000 – 10 000 kg per person
- 100 – 1 000 kg per person
- 10 – 100 kg per person
- Under 10 kg per person

- ● Oil
- ▼ Natural gas
- ▲ Coal and lignite
- ◆ Uranium *(the fuel used to generate nuclear power)*

In developing countries traditional fuels are still very important. Sometimes called biomass fuels, they include wood, charcoal and dried dung. The pie graph for Nigeria at the foot of the page shows their importance.

Oil		Natural Gas		Coal (bituminous)		Coal (lignite)		Uranium		Nuclear Power		Hydro-Electric Power	
World total (1996) 3 108 094 000 tonnes		World total (1996) 3 059 970 000 tonnes of coal equivalent		World total (1996) 3 798 880 000 tonnes		World total (1996) 955 964 000 tonnes		World total (1996) 33 748 tonnes (metal content)		World total (1996) 867 151 000 tonnes of coal equivalent		World total (1996) 318 364 000 tonnes of coal equivalent	
Saudi Arabia	13.0%	Russia	24.7%	China	36.8%	Germany	19.6%	Canada	34.7%	U.S.A.	29.0%	Canada	13.6%
U.S.A.	10.3%	U.S.A.	23.8%	U.S.A.	23.3%	Russia	9.8%	Australia	14.7%	France	17.1%	U.S.A.	13.3%
Russia	9.7%	Canada	6.9%	India	7.5%	U.S.A.	8.5%	Niger	9.8%	Japan	13.0%	Brazil	10.3%
Iran	5.8%	U.K.	3.8%	South Africa	5.5%	Poland	6.7%	Russia	7.7%	Germany	6.9%	China	7.3%
China	5.1%	Netherlands	3.5%	Australia	5.1%	Greece	6.3%	U.S.A.	7.2%	Russia	4.3%	Russia	6.4%

ENERGY CONSUMPTION

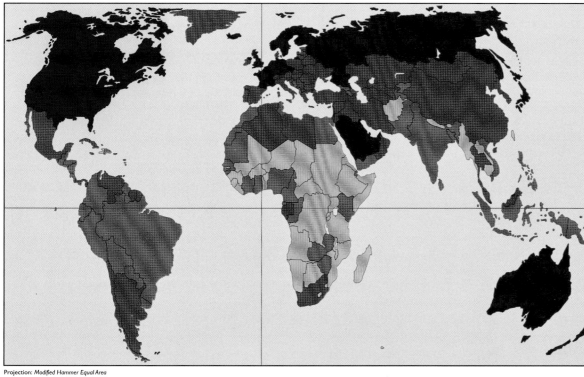

Primary energy consumption expressed in kilograms of coal equivalent per person 1996

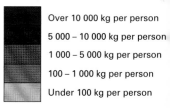

- Over 10 000 kg per person
- 5 000 – 10 000 kg per person
- 1 000 – 5 000 kg per person
- 100 – 1 000 kg per person
- Under 100 kg per person

Energy consumption by Continent 1996

		Change 1995–96
Asia	31.9%	*(+4.7%)*
North America	30.7%	*(+2.3%)*
Europe	29.8%	*(+0.4%)*
South America	3.5%	*(+3.0%)*
Africa	2.6%	*(+2.5%)*
Australia	1.5%	*(+7.8%)*

Projection: *Modified Hammer Equal Area*

TYPE OF ENERGY CONSUMED BY SELECTED COUNTRIES 1997

- Coal & Lignite
- Oil
- Natural gas
- Hydro-electricity
- Nuclear electricity
- Traditional Fuels

NIGERIA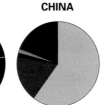

CHINA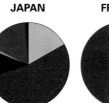

JAPAN

FRANCE

USA

NORWAY

THE SEASONS

The Earth revolves around the Sun once a year in an anti-clockwise direction. It is tilted at an angle of 66½°. In June, the northern hemisphere is tilted towards the Sun. As a result it receives more hours of sunshine in a day and therefore has its warmest season, summer. By December, the Earth has rotated halfway round the Sun so that the southern hemisphere is tilted towards the Sun and it has its summer. The hemisphere that is tilted away from the Sun has winter. On 21 June the Sun is directly overhead at the Tropic of Cancer, 23½°N, and this is midsummer in the northern hemisphere. Midsummer in the southern hemisphere occurs on 21 December, when the Sun is overhead at the Tropic of Capricorn.

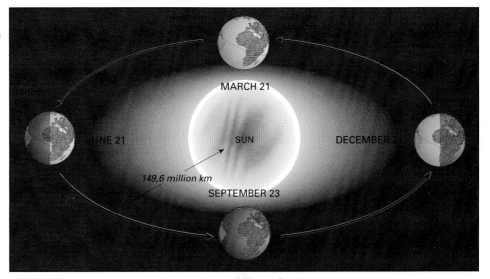

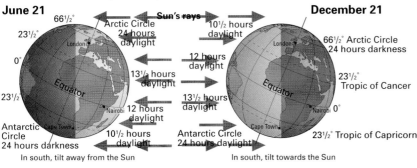

DAY AND NIGHT

The Sun appears to rise in the east, reach its highest point at noon, and then set in the west. In reality it is not the Sun that is moving but the Earth revolving from west to east. Due to the tilting of the Earth the length of day and night varies from place to place and month to month. In June the Arctic has constant daylight and the Antarctic has constant darkness. The situations are reversed in December. In the Tropics the length of day and night varies little throughout the year. The table below gives day and night lengths for three cities at different times of the year.

City	March (Northern Spring / Southern Autumn)			June (Northern Summer / Southern Winter)			September (Northern Autumn / Southern Spring)			December (Northern Winter / Southern Summer)		
	London	Nairobi	Cape Town	London	Nairobi	Cape Town	London	Nairobi	Cape Town	London	Nairobi	Cape Town
Latitude	51°N	1°S	34°S	51°N	1°S	34°S	51°N	1°S	34°S	51°N	1°S	34°S
Day length	12 hrs	12 hrs	12 hrs	16 hrs	12 hrs	10 hrs	12 hrs	12 hrs	12 hrs	8 hrs	12 hrs	14 hrs
Night length	12 hrs	12 hrs	12 hrs	8 hrs	12 hrs	14 hrs	12 hrs	12 hrs	12 hrs	16 hrs	12 hrs	10 hrs
Temperature	7°C	21°C	21°C	16°C	18°C	13°C	15°C	19°C	14°C	5°C	19°C	20°C

The Earth rotates through 360° in 24 hours, and so moves 15° every hour. The World is divided into 24 standard time zones, each centred on lines of longitude at 15° intervals. The Greenwich Meridian lies on the centre of the first zone. All places to the west of Greenwich are one hour behind for every 15° of longitude; places to the east are ahead by one hour for every 15°.

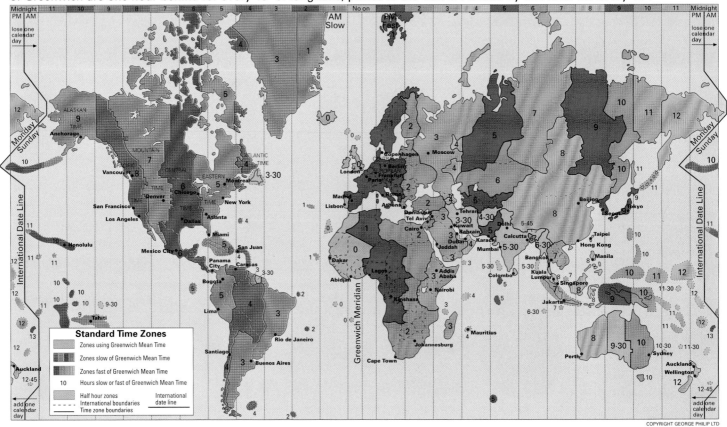

This index is a list of all the names on the maps in the atlas. They are listed in alphabetical order. If a name has a description with it, for example, Bay of Biscay, the name is in alphabetical order, followed by the description:

Biscay, Bay of ....

Sometimes, the same name occurs in more than one country. In these cases, the country names are added after each place name, and they are indexed alphabetically by country.
For example:

Cordoba, Argentina ...
Cordoba, Spain ......

All rivers are indexed to their mouths or confluences and are followed by the symbol →.

Each name in the index is followed by a number in **bold** type which refers to the number of the page the map appears on.

The figure and letter which follow the page number give the grid rectangle on the map within which the feature appears. The grid is formed by the lines of latitude and longitude. The columns are labelled at the top and bottom with a letter and the rows at the sides with a number. Wrocław for example, is in the grid square where row 5 crosses column D.

For more precise location on small scale maps the latitude and longitude are given after the figure/letter reference. The first set of figures represent the latitude, the second set of figures represent the longitude.

The unit of measurement for latitude and longitude is the degree (°), which is subdivided into minutes ('). Here only full degree figures are given. The Latitude is followed by N(orth) or S(outh) of the Equator and the longitude by East or West of the prime meridian.
For example:

Wrocław..... **35** **5 D** 51°N 17°E

Aalborg	**36**	**4 P**	57°N	9° E
Aarhus	**36**	**4 P**	56°N	10° E
Abadan	**44**	**3 C**	30°N	48° E
Abaetetuba	**30**	**3 F**	1°S	48°W
Abakan	**41**	**10 D**	53°N	91° E
Abeokuta	**47**	**10 L**	7°N	3° E
Aberdare	**5**	**5 C**	51°N	3°W
Aberdare Range	**26**	**3 B**	0°S	36° E
Aberdeen	**6**	**2 F**	57°N	2°W
Aberystwyth	**5**	**4 B**	52°N	4°W
Abidjan	**46**	**4 C**	5°N	3°W
Abu Dhabi	**44**	**4 D**	24°N	54° E
Abuja	**47**	**10 M**	9°N	7° E
Acapulco	**54**	**4 D**	16°N	99°W
Accra	**47**	**10 K**	5°N	0°W
Accrington	**4**	**3 D**	53°N	2°W
Achill Island	**7**	**3 A**	53°N	10°W
Aconcagua	**51**	**7 E**	32°S	70°W
Acre	**30**	**4 A**	9°S	71°W
Adamawa Highlands	**47**	**10 N**	7°N	12° E
Adana	**39**	**4 L**	37°N	35° E
Addis Ababa	**46**	**4 G**	9°N	38° E
Adelaide	**48**	**6 F**	34°S	138° E
Aden	**44**	**5 C**	12°N	45° E
Aden, Gulf of	**44**	**5 C**	12°N	47° E
Adriatic Sea	**22**	**3 F**	43°N	16° E
Aegean Sea	**39**	**4 J**	38°N	25° E
Afghanistan	**44**	**3 E**	33°N	65° E
Africa	**46**	**5 F**	10°N	20° E
Agades	**46**	**3 D**	16°N	7° E
Agra	**44**	**4 F**	27°N	77° E
Aguanaval →	**54**	**3 D**	25°N	102°W
Aguascalientes	**54**	**3 D**	21°N	102°W
Agulhas, Cape	**28**	**3 C**	34°S	20° E
Ahmadabad	**44**	**4 F**	23°N	72° E
Ai-Ais and Fish River Canyon	**28**	**2 B**	27°S	17° E
Aïr	**46**	**3 D**	18°N	8° E
Airdrie	**6**	**4 E**	55°N	3°W
Aire →	**14**	**5 F**	53°N	0°W
Aix-en-Provence	**37**	**11 L**	43°N	5° E
Ajaccio	**37**	**12 N**	41°N	8° E
Akita	**43**	**3 D**	39°N	140° E
Al Aziziyah	**46**	**1 E**	32°N	13° E
Al Hufuf	**44**	**4 C**	25°N	49° E
Al Jawf	**46**	**2 F**	24°N	23° E
Alabama	**53**	**4 J**	33°N	87°W
Alabama →	**53**	**4 J**	31°N	87°W
Alagoas	**30**	**4 H**	9°S	36°W
Åland Islands	**35**	**3 D**	60°N	20° E
Alaska	**50**	**3 D**	65°N	150°W
Alaska Peninsula	**50**	**4 C**	56°N	160°W
Alaska Range	**50**	**3 D**	62°N	151°W
Alaska, Gulf of	**50**	**4 E**	58°N	145°W
Albacete	**37**	**13 H**	39°N	1°W
Albania	**39**	**3 G**	41°N	20° E
Albany	**48**	**6 B**	35°S	117° E
Albert Nile →	**26**	**2 A**	3°N	32° E
Albuquerque	**52**	**3 E**	35°N	106°W
Aldabra Islands	**46**	**5 H**	9°S	46° E
Aldeburgh	**5**	**4 H**	52°N	1° E
Alderney	**5**	**7 D**	49°N	2°W
Ålesund	**35**	**3 B**	62°N	6° E
Aleutian Islands	**49**	**2 K**	52°N	175°W
Aleutian Trench	**49**	**2 K**	48°N	180° E
Alexandria	**46**	**1 G**	31°N	30° E
Algarve	**37**	**14 D**	36°N	8°W
Algeria	**46**	**2 D**	28°N	2° E
Algiers	**46**	**1 D**	36°N	3° E
Alicante	**37**	**13 H**	38°N	0°W
Alice Springs	**48**	**4 E**	23°S	133° E
Allahabad	**44**	**4 G**	25°N	81° E
Allegheny Mountains	**53**	**3 L**	38°N	80°W
Allen, Bog of	**7**	**3 D**	53°N	7°W
Allen, Lough	**7**	**2 C**	54°N	8°W
Alma Ata	**40**	**8 E**	43°N	76° E
Almeria	**37**	**14 G**	36°N	2°W
Alnwick	**4**	**1 E**	55°N	1°W
Alps	**37**	**9 N**	46°N	9° E
Altai	**40**	**9 D**	46°N	92° E
Altamira	**30**	**3 E**	3°S	52°W
Amagasaki	**24**	**2 D**	34°N	135° E
Amapá	**30**	**2 E**	2°N	50°W
Amazon →	**30**	**3 E**	0°S	50°W
Amazonas	**30**	**4 B**	5°S	65°W
America, North	**50**	**5 K**	45°N	100°W
America, South	**51**	**5 F**	10°S	60°W
Amiens	**37**	**8 J**	49°N	2° E
Amlwch	**4**	**3 B**	53°N	4°W
Amritsar	**44**	**3 F**	31°N	74° E
Amsterdam	**36**	**6 L**	52°N	4° E
Amu Darya →	**40**	**6 E**	43°N	59° E
Amur →	**41**	**15 D**	52°N	141° E
An Uaimh	**7**	**3 E**	53°N	6°W
Anadyr Range	**41**	**18 C**	68°N	175° E
Anápolis	**30**	**6 F**	16°S	48°W
Anchorage	**50**	**3 E**	61°N	149°W
Ancona	**22**	**3 D**	43°N	13° E
Andaman Islands	**44**	**5 H**	12°N	92° E
Andes	**51**	**5 D**	10°S	75°W
Andizhan	**40**	**8 E**	41°N	72° E
Andorra	**37**	**11 J**	42°N	1° E
Andover	**5**	**5 E**	51°N	1°W
Aneto, Pico de	**37**	**11 J**	42°N	0° E
Angara →	**41**	**10 D**	58°N	94° E
Angel Falls	**51**	**3 E**	5°N	62°W
Angers	**37**	**9 H**	47°N	0°W
Anglesey	**4**	**3 B**	53°N	4°W
Angola	**46**	**6 E**	12°S	18° E
Angoulême	**37**	**10 J**	45°N	0° E
Angus	**9**	**3 E**	56°N	2°W
Ankara	**39**	**4 K**	39°N	32° E
Annaba	**38**	**4 E**	36°N	7° E
Annan	**6**	**5 E**	54°N	3°W
Annan →	**6**	**4 E**	54°N	3°W
Annapolis	**53**	**3 L**	38°N	76°W
Anshan	**45**	**2 L**	41°N	122° E
Antalya	**39**	**4 K**	36°N	30° E
Antananarivo	**47**	**6 H**	18°S	47° E
Antarctic Peninsula	**56**	**2 L**	67°S	60°W
Antarctica	**56**	**2 D**	90°S	0°W
Antigua	**55**	**4 M**	17°N	61°W
Antofagasta	**51**	**6 D**	23°S	70°W
Antrim	**7**	**2 E**	54°N	6°W
Antrim, Mountains of	**7**	**2 E**	54°N	6°W
Antwerp	**36**	**7 L**	51°N	4° E
Aomori	**43**	**2 D**	40°N	140° E
Apennines	**22**	**3 D**	44°N	10° E
Appalachian Mountains	**53**	**3 K**	38°N	80°W
Appleby	**4**	**2 D**	54°N	2°W
Arabian Sea	**44**	**5 E**	16°N	65° E
Aracaju	**30**	**5 H**	10°S	37°W
Araçatuba	**30**	**7 E**	21°S	50°W
Arafura Sea	**48**	**2 E**	9°S	135° E
Araguaia →	**30**	**4 F**	5°S	48°W
Aral Sea	**40**	**6 E**	44°N	60° E
Aran Island	**7**	**2 C**	55°N	8°W
Ararat, Mount	**34**	**8 Q**	39°N	44° E
Arbroath	**6**	**3 F**	56°N	2°W
Arctic Ocean	**56**	**B**	78°N	160°W
Ardnamurchan, Point of	**6**	**3 B**	56°N	6°W
Ardrossan	**6**	**4 D**	55°N	4°W
Ards Peninsula	**7**	**2 F**	54°N	5°W
Arequipa	**51**	**5 D**	16°S	71°W
Argentina	**51**	**7 E**	35°S	66°W
Argyll & Bute	**9**	**3 D**	56°N	5°W
Arica	**51**	**5 D**	18°S	70°W
Aripuanã →	**30**	**4 C**	5°S	60°W
Arizona	**52**	**4 D**	34°N	112°W
Arkaig, Loch	**6**	**3 C**	56°N	5°W
Arkansas	**53**	**4 H**	35°N	92°W
Arkansas →	**53**	**4 H**	33°N	91°W
Arkhangelsk	**35**	**3 J**	64°N	41° E
Arklow	**7**	**4 E**	52°N	6°W
Armagh	**7**	**2 E**	54°N	6°W
Armenia	**40**	**5 E**	40°N	45° E
Arnhem	**36**	**7 L**	51°N	5° E
Arnhem Land	**48**	**2 E**	13°S	134° E
Arran	**6**	**4 C**	55°N	5°W
Aru Islands	**45**	**7 M**	6°S	134° E
Arusha	**26**	**3 B**	3°S	36° E
Asamankese	**47**	**10 K**	5°N	0°W
Ascension Island	**60**	**4 J**	8°S	14°W
Ashford	**5**	**5 G**	51°N	0° E
Ashikaga	**24**	**1 F**	36°N	139° E
Ashington	**4**	**1 E**	55°N	1°W
Ashizuri, Cape	**24**	**3 C**	32°N	133° E
Ashkhabad	**40**	**6 F**	38°N	57° E
Ashton under Lyne	**4**	**3 D**	53°N	2°W
Asmara	**46**	**3 G**	15°N	38° E
Assam	**44**	**4 H**	26°N	93° E
Astana	**40**	**8 D**	51°N	71° E
Astrakhan	**40**	**5 D**	46°N	48° E
Asunción	**51**	**6 F**	25°S	57°W
Aswan	**46**	**2 G**	24°N	32° E
Asyût	**46**	**2 G**	27°N	31° E
Atacama Desert	**51**	**6 D**	24°S	69°W
Athens	**39**	**4 H**	37°N	23° E
Athlone	**7**	**3 D**	53°N	7°W
Athy	**7**	**4 E**	53°N	7°W
Atlanta	**53**	**4 K**	33°N	84°W
Atlantic Ocean	**60**	**3 G**	0°	20°W
Atlas Mountains	**46**	**1 C**	32°N	5°W
Auasberg	**28**	**1 B**	22°S	17° E
Auckland	**48**	**10 M**	36°S	174° E
Augsburg	**37**	**8 P**	48°N	10° E
Augusta	**53**	**2 N**	44°N	69°W
Auob →	**28**	**2 B**	25°S	19° E
Austin	**52**	**4 G**	30°N	97°W
Australia	**48**	**4 E**	23°S	135° E
Austria	**38**	**2 F**	47°N	14° E
Aviemore	**6**	**2 E**	57°N	3°W
Avignon	**37**	**11 L**	43°N	4° E
Avon →, Bristol	**5**	**5 D**	51°N	2°W
Avon →, Hampshire	**5**	**6 E**	50°N	1°W
Avon →, Warwickshire	**14**	**5 F**	51°N	2°W
Awe, Loch	**6**	**3 C**	56°N	5°W
Ayers Rock	**48**	**5 E**	25°S	131° E
Aylesbury	**5**	**5 F**	51°N	0°W
Ayr	**6**	**4 D**	55°N	4°W
Azerbaijan	**40**	**5 E**	40°N	48° E
Azores	**60**	**3 H**	38°N	29°W
Azov, Sea of	**39**	**2 L**	46°N	36° E
Bacabal	**30**	**3 G**	4°S	44°W
Bacău	**39**	**2 J**	46°N	26° E
Badajoz	**37**	**13 E**	38°N	6°W
Baffin Bay	**50**	**2 N**	72°N	64°W
Baffin Island	**50**	**2 M**	68°N	75°W
Bagé	**30**	**9 E**	31°S	54°W
Baghdad	**44**	**3 C**	33°N	44° E
Bahamas	**55**	**3 J**	24°N	75°W
Bahía	**30**	**5 G**	12°S	42°W
Bahía Blanca	**51**	**7 E**	38°S	62°W
Bahrain	**44**	**4 D**	26°N	50° E
Baikal, Lake	**41**	**11 D**	53°N	108° E
Baja California	**52**	**4 C**	31°N	115°W
Baku	**40**	**6 E**	40°N	49° E
Balearic Islands	**37**	**13 J**	39°N	3° E
Bali	**45**	**7 K**	8°S	115° E
Balikeşir	**39**	**4 J**	39°N	27° E
Balkan Mountains	**39**	**3 H**	43°N	23° E
Balkhash, Lake	**40**	**8 E**	46°N	74° E
Ballachulish	**6**	**3 C**	56°N	5°W
Ballarat	**48**	**7 G**	37°S	143° E

Ballater	6	2 E	57°N	3°W
Ballina	7	2 B	54°N	9°W
Ballinasloe	7	3 C	53°N	8°W
Ballycastle	7	1 E	55°N	6°W
Ballymena	7	2 E	54°N	6°W
Ballymoney	7	1 E	55°N	6°W
Balmoral	6	2 E	57°N	3°W
Balsas →	54	4 D	17°N	102°W
Baltic Sea	35	4 D	57°N	19° E
Baltimore	53	3 L	39°N	76°W
Bamako	46	3 C	12°N	7°W
Banbridge	7	2 E	54°N	6°W
Banbury	5	4 E	52°N	1°W
Banda Sea	45	7 L	6°S	130° E
Bandar Seri Begawan	45	6 K	4°N	115° E
Bandon	7	5 C	51°N	8°W
Bandung	45	7 J	6°S	107° E
Banff	6	2 F	57°N	2°W
Bangalore	44	5 F	12°N	77° E
Bangka	45	7 J	2°S	105° E
Bangkok	45	5 J	13°N	100° E
Bangladesh	44	4 G	24°N	90° E
Bangor, Caernarfon	4	3 B	53°N	4°W
Bangor, Down	7	2 F	54°N	5°W
Bangui	46	3 E	4°N	18° E
Banjarmasin	45	7 K	3°S	114° E
Banjul	46	3 B	13°N	16°W
Bann →	7	2 E	54°N	6°W
Bantry	7	5 B	51°N	9°W
Bantry Bay	7	5 B	51°N	9°W
Barbados	55	5 N	13°N	59°W
Barcelona, Spain	37	12 K	41°N	2° E
Barcelona, Venezuela	55	5 M	10°N	64°W
Barcoo →	48	4 G	25°S	142° E
Bardsey Island	4	4 B	52°N	4°W
Barents Sea	40	4 B	73°N	39° E
Bari	22	4 F	41°N	16° E
Barkly Tableland	48	3 F	17°S	136° E
Barnsley	4	3 E	53°N	1°W
Barnstaple	5	5 B	51°N	4°W
Barquisimeto	55	5 L	10°N	69°W
Barra	6	3 A	57°N	7°W
Barra Head	6	3 A	56°N	7°W
Barranquilla	55	5 K	11°N	74°W
Barrow-in-Furness	4	2 C	54°N	3°W
Barrow →	7	4 E	52°N	6°W
Barry	5	5 C	51°N	3°W
Basildon	5	5 G	51°N	0° E
Basingstoke	5	5 E	51°N	1°W
Basle	37	9 M	47°N	7° E
Basra	44	3 C	30°N	47° E
Bass Strait	48	7 H	39°S	146° E
Basseterre	55	4 M	17°N	62°W
Bataques	54	1 A	32°N	115°W
Bath	5	5 D	51°N	2°W
Batumi	39	3 M	41°N	41° E
Bauru	30	7 F	22°S	49°W
Bayonne	37	11 H	43°N	1°W
Beachy Head	5	6 G	50°N	0° E
Bear Island	7	5 B	51°N	9°W
Beaufort Sea	50	2 E	72°N	140°W
Beaufort West	28	3 C	32°S	22° E
Beauly →	6	2 D	57°N	4°W
Bebington	4	3 D	53°N	3°W
Bedford	5	4 F	52°N	0°W
Bedfordshire	9	5 F	52°N	0°W
Beijing	45	3 K	39°N	116° E
Beira	47	6 G	19°S	34° E
Bejaia	38	4 D	36°N	5° E
Belarus	35	5 F	53°N	27° E
Belém	30	3 F	1°S	48°W
Belfast	7	2 F	54°N	5°W
Belfast Lough	7	2 F	54°N	5°W
Belgium	36	7 K	50°N	5° E
Belgrade	39	3 H	44°N	20° E
Belize	54	4 G	17°N	88°W
Belize City	54	4 G	17°N	88°W
Bellingshausen Sea	56	2 L	66°S	80°W
Belmopan	54	4 G	17°N	88°W
Belo Horizonte	30	6 G	19°S	43°W
Belomorsk	35	3 G	64°N	34° E
Ben Cruachan	6	3 C	56°N	5°W
Ben Lawers	6	3 D	56°N	4°W
Ben Macdhui, South Africa	29	3 D	30°S	27° E
Ben Macdhui, U.K.	6	2 E	57°N	3°W
Ben Nevis	6	3 D	56°N	4°W
Benbecula	6	2 A	57°N	7°W
Bendigo	48	7 G	36°S	144° E
Bengal, Bay of	44	4 G	15°N	90° E
Benghazi	46	1 F	32°N	20° E
Benin	47	10 L	10°N	2° E
Benin City	47	10 M	6°N	5° E
Benin, Bight of	47	10 L	5°N	3° E
Benue →	47	10 M	7°N	6° E
Beppu	24	3 B	33°N	131° E
Berezniki	40	6 D	59°N	56° E
Bergen	35	3 B	60°N	5° E
Bering Sea	49	2 L	58°N	171° E
Bering Strait	50	2 C	66°N	170°W
Berlin	36	6 Q	52°N	13° E
Bermuda	55	1 M	32°N	65°W
Berne	37	9 M	46°N	7° E
Berwick-upon-Tweed	4	1 D	55°N	2°W
Besançon	37	9 M	47°N	6° E
Bethlehem	29	2 D	28°S	28° E
Beverley	4	3 F	53°N	0°W
Bexhill	5	6 G	50°N	0° E
Bhutan	44	4 G	27°N	90° E
Białystok	35	5 E	53°N	23° E
Bideford	5	5 B	51°N	4°W
Bié Plateau	46	6 E	12°S	16° E
Bielefeld	36	6 N	52°N	8° E
Bighorn Mountains	52	2 E	44°N	107°W
Bilbao	37	11 G	43°N	2°W
Billingham	4	2 E	54°N	1°W
Bioko	47	11 M	3°N	8° E
Birkenhead	4	3 C	53°N	3°W
Birmingham	5	4 E	52°N	1°W
Biscay, Bay of	37	10 F	45°N	2°W
Bishkek	40	8 E	42°N	74° E
Bisho	28	3 D	32°S	27° E
Bishop Auckland	4	2 E	54°N	1°W
Bishop's Stortford	5	5 G	51°N	0° E
Bismarck	52	1 F	46°N	100°W
Bismarck Archipelago	49	8 H	2°S	150° E
Bissau	46	3 B	11°N	15°W
Bitterfontein	28	3 B	31°S	18° E
Bizerte	38	4 E	37°N	9° E
Black Hills	52	2 F	44°N	103°W
Black Sea	39	3 K	43°N	35° E
Blackburn	4	3 D	53°N	2°W
Blackpool	4	3 C	53°N	3°W
Blackwater →	7	4 C	51°N	7°W
Blaenau Ffestiniog	4	4 C	52°N	3°W
Blaenau Gwent	9	6 E	51°N	3°W
Blairgowrie	6	3 E	56°N	3°W
Blanc, Mont	37	10 M	45°N	6° E
Blantyre	46	6 G	15°S	35° E
Blarney	7	5 C	51°N	8°W
Blida	38	4 D	36°N	2° E
Bloemfontein	28	2 D	29°S	26° E
Bloody Foreland	7	1 C	55°N	8°W
Blouberg	29	1 D	23°S	28° E
Blue Nile →	46	3 G	15°N	32° E
Blue Ridge Mountains	53	3 K	36°N	80°W
Blyth	4	1 E	55°N	1°W
Boa Vista	30	2 C	2°N	60°W
Bobo-Dioulasso	46	3 C	11°N	4°W
Bodmin Moor	5	6 B	50°N	4°W
Bodø	35	2 C	67°N	14° E
Bog of Allen	7	3 D	53°N	7°W
Boggeragh Mountains	7	4 C	52°N	8°W
Bognor Regis	5	6 F	50°N	0°W
Bogotá	55	7 K	4°N	74°W
Bolivia	51	5 E	17°S	64°W
Bologna	22	2 C	44°N	11° E
Bolton	4	3 D	53°N	2°W
Bolzano	22	1 C	46°N	11° E
Bombay = Mumbai	44	5 F	18°N	72° E
Bonifacio, Strait of	22	4 B	41°N	9° E
Bonin Islands	49	5 G	27°N	142° E
Bonn	36	7 M	50°N	7° E
Bootle	4	3 D	53°N	3°W
Bordeaux	37	10 H	44°N	0°W
Borneo	45	6 K	1°N	115° E
Bornholm	35	4 C	55°N	15° E
Bosnia-Herzegovina	39	3 G	44°N	17° E
Bosporus	39	3 J	41°N	29° E
Boston, U.K.	4	4 F	52°N	0°W
Boston, U.S.A.	53	2 M	42°N	71°W
Bothnia, Gulf of	35	3 E	63°N	20° E
Botswana	47	7 F	22°S	24° E
Bougainville	49	8 H	6°S	155° E
Bougainville Trench	49	8 H	6°S	155° E
Boulogne-sur-Mer	36	7 J	50°N	1° E
Bourges	37	9 K	47°N	2° E
Bournemouth	5	6 E	50°N	1°W
Boyne →	7	3 E	53°N	6°W
Bracknell Forest	9	6 F	51°N	0°W
Bradford	4	3 E	53°N	1°W
Bragança	30	3 F	1°S	47°W
Brahmaputra →	44	4 H	23°N	89° E
Branco →	30	3 C	1°S	61°W
Brandon Mountain	7	4 A	52°N	10°W
Brasília	30	6 F	15°S	47°W
Brasov	39	2 J	45°N	25° E
Bratislava	34	6 K	48°N	17° E
Bray	7	3 E	53°N	6°W
Brazil	30	5 E	12°S	50°W
Brazos →	53	5 G	28°N	95°W
Brazzaville	46	5 E	4°S	15° E
Brechin	6	3 F	56°N	2°W
Brecon	5	5 C	51°N	3°W
Brecon Beacons	5	5 C	51°N	3°W
Bremen	36	6 N	53°N	8° E
Brentwood	5	5 G	51°N	0° E
Bressay	6	8 J	60°N	1°W
Brest, Belarus	35	5 E	52°N	23° E
Brest, France	37	8 F	48°N	4°W
Bridgend	9	6 E	51°N	3°W
Bridgetown	55	5 N	13°N	59°W
Bridgwater	5	6 D	51°N	2°W
Bridlington	4	2 F	54°N	0°W
Brigg	4	3 F	53°N	0°W
Brighton	5	6 F	50°N	0°W
Brindisi	22	4 G	40°N	17° E
Brisbane	48	5 J	27°S	153° E
Bristol	5	5 D	51°N	2°W
Bristol Channel	5	5 B	51°N	4°W
British Isles	42	3 B	54°N	4°W
Brittany	37	8 G	48°N	3°W
Brno	39	2 G	49°N	16° E
Broad Law	6	4 E	55°N	3°W
Broken Hill	48	6 G	31°S	141° E
Brooks Range	50	3 D	68°N	147°W
Broome	48	3 C	18°S	122° E
Brown Willy	5	6 B	50°N	4°W
Brunei	45	6 K	4°N	115° E
Brunswick	36	6 P	52°N	10° E
Brussels	36	7 L	50°N	4° E
Bryansk	35	5 G	53°N	34° E
Bucaramanga	51	3 D	7°N	73°W
Buchan Ness	6	2 G	57°N	1°W
Bucharest	39	3 J	44°N	26° E
Buckie	6	2 F	57°N	2°W
Buckinghamshire	9	6 F	51°N	0°W
Budapest	39	2 G	47°N	19° E
Bude	5	6 B	50°N	4°W
Buenaventura	55	7 J	3°N	77°W
Buenos Aires	51	7 F	34°S	58°W
Buffalo	53	2 L	42°N	78°W
Bug →	39	2 K	46°N	31° E
Bujumbura	46	5 F	3°S	29° E
Bukoba	26	3 A	1°S	31° E
Bulawayo	47	7 F	20°S	28° E
Bulgaria	39	3 H	42°N	25° E
Buncrana	7	1 D	55°N	7°W
Bundaberg	48	4 J	24°S	152° E
Bundoran	7	2 C	54°N	8°W
Bungo Channel	24	3 C	33°N	132° E
Bure →	4	4 H	52°N	1° E
Burgas	39	2 J	42°N	27° E
Burgos	37	11 G	42°N	3°W
Burgundy	37	9 L	47°N	4° E
Burkina Faso	46	3 C	12°N	1°W
Burma	45	4 H	21°N	96° E
Burnley	4	3 D	53°N	2°W
Bursa	39	3 J	40°N	29° E
Burton upon Trent	4	4 E	52°N	1°W
Buru	45	7 L	3°S	126° E
Burundi	46	5 F	3°S	30° E
Bury	4	3 D	53°N	2°W
Bury Saint Edmunds	5	4 G	52°N	0° E
Busia	26	2 A	0°N	34° E
Bute	6	4 C	55°N	5°W
Buxton	4	3 E	53°N	1°W
Buzen	24	3 B	33°N	131° E
Bydgoszcz	35	5 D	53°N	18° E
Cabinda	46	5 E	5°S	12° E
Cáceres, Brazil	30	6 D	16°S	57°W
Cáceres, Spain	37	13 E	39°N	6°W
Cader Idris	4	4 C	52°N	3°W
Cádiz	37	14 E	36°N	6°W
Caen	37	8 H	49°N	0°W
Caernarfon	4	3 B	53°N	4°W
Caerphilly	9	6 E	51°N	3°W
Cagliari	22	5 B	39°N	9° E
Caha Mountains	7	5 B	51°N	9°W
Caher	7	4 D	52°N	7°W
Caherciveen	7	5 A	51°N	10°W
Cairn Gorm	6	2 E	57°N	3°W
Cairns	48	3 H	16°S	145° E
Cairo	46	1 G	30°N	31° E
Calabar	47	11 M	4°N	8° E
Calais	36	7 J	50°N	1° E
Calcutta = Kolkata	44	4 G	22°N	88° E
Calder →	4	3 E	53°N	1°W
Caledon →	28	3 D	30°S	26° E
Caledonian Canal	6	2 D	56°N	5°W
Calgary	50	4 H	51°N	114°W
Cali	55	7 J	3°N	76°W
California	52	3 B	37°N	119°W
California, Gulf of	54	2 B	27°N	111°W
Callander	6	3 D	56°N	4°W
Calvinia	28	3 B	31°S	19° E
Cam →	5	4 G	52°N	0° E
Camagüey	55	3 J	21°N	78°W
Cambodia	45	5 J	12°N	105° E
Cambrian Mountains	5	4 C	52°N	3°W
Cambridge	5	4 G	52°N	0° E
Cambridgeshire	9	5 F	52°N	0° E
Cameroon	46	4 E	6°N	12° E
Cameroon, Mount	47	11 M	4°N	9° E
Cametá	30	3 F	2°S	49°W
Campbeltown	6	4 C	55°N	5°W
Campeche	54	4 F	19°N	90°W
Campeche, Gulf of	54	3 F	19°N	93°W
Campina Grande	30	4 H	7°S	35°W
Campinas	30	7 F	22°S	47°W
Campo Grande	30	7 E	20°S	54°W
Campos	30	7 G	21°S	41°W
Canada	50	4 K	60°N	100°W
Canadian Shield	50	4 J	53°N	75°W
Canary Islands	46	2 B	28°N	16°W
Canaveral, Cape	53	5 K	28°N	80°W
Canberra	48	7 H	35°S	149° E
Cancún	54	3 G	21°N	86°W
Cannock	4	4 D	52°N	2°W
Cantabrian Mountains	37	11 F	43°N	5°W
Canterbury	5	5 H	51°N	1° E
Canton = Guangzhou	45	4 K	23°N	113° E
Cape Town	28	3 B	33°S	18° E
Cape Verde Islands	60	3 H	17°N	25°W
Cape York Peninsula	48	2 G	12°S	142° E
Capri	22	4 E	40°N	14° E
Caracas	55	5 L	10°N	66°W
Carcassonne	37	11 K	43°N	2° E
Cardiff	5	5 C	51°N	3°W
Cardigan	5	4 B	52°N	4°W
Cardigan Bay	5	4 B	52°N	4°W
Caribbean Sea	55	5 J	15°N	75°W
Carlisle	4	2 D	54°N	2°W
Carlow	7	4 E	52°N	6°W
Carmarthen	5	5 B	51°N	4°W
Carmarthen Bay	5	5 B	51°N	4°W
Carn Eige	6	2 C	57°N	5°W
Caroline Islands	49	7 H	8°N	150° E
Carpathians	39	2 H	49°N	21° E
Carpentaria, Gulf of	48	2 F	14°S	139° E
Carrauntoohill	7	4 B	52°N	9°W
Carrick-on-Shannon	7	3 C	53°N	8°W
Carrick-on-Suir	7	4 D	52°N	7°W
Carrickfergus	7	2 F	54°N	5°W
Carrickmacross	7	3 E	53°N	6°W
Carron, Loch	6	2 C	57°N	5°W
Carson City	52	3 C	39°N	119°W
Cartagena, Colombia	55	5 J	10°N	75°W
Cartagena, Spain	37	14 H	37°N	0°W
Casablanca	46	1 C	33°N	7°W
Cascade Range	52	1 B	47°N	121°W
Cashel	7	4 D	52°N	7°W
Caspian Sea	40	6 F	43°N	50° E
Castelló de la Plana	37	13 H	39°N	0°W
Castle Douglas	6	5 E	54°N	3°W
Castlebar	7	3 B	53°N	9°W
Castleford	4	3 E	53°N	1°W
Castletown Bearhaven	7	5 B	51°N	9°W
Castries	55	5 M	14°N	60°W
Catalonia	38	3 D	41°N	1° E
Catania	22	6 E	37°N	15° E
Caucasus	40	5 E	42°N	44° E
Cavan	7	3 D	54°N	7°W
Caxias do Sul	30	8 E	29°S	51°W
Cayenne	51	3 F	5°N	52°W
Cayman Islands	55	4 H	19°N	80°W
Ceará	30	4 G	5°S	40°W
Cebu	45	5 L	10°N	123° E
Celano	22	3 D	42°N	13° E
Celebes	45	7 L	2°S	120° E
Celebes Sea	45	6 L	3°N	123° E
Celtic Sea	14	6 B	50°N	8°W
Central African Republic	46	4 E	7°N	20° E
Central America	58	3 C	10°N	85°W
Central Kalahari Game Reserve	28	1 C	22°S	24° E
Central Province	26	3 B	0°S	37° E
Ceredigion	9	5 D	52°N	4°W
Ceuta	38	4 B	35°N	5°W
Chad	46	3 E	15°N	17° E
Chad, Lake	46	3 E	13°N	14° E
Changane →	29	1 E	24°S	33° E
Changchun	45	2 L	43°N	125° E
Changsha	45	4 K	28°N	113° E
Channel Islands	5	7 D	49°N	2°W
Chari →	46	3 E	12°N	14° E
Charleston	53	3 K	38°N	81°W
Charleville	48	5 H	26°S	146° E
Charlotte	53	3 K	35°N	80°W
Charlotte Pass	48	7 H	36°S	148° E
Chartres	37	8 J	48°N	1° E
Chatham	5	5 G	51°N	0° E
Chatham Islands	49	12 L	44°S	176°W
Chattahoochee →	53	4 K	30°N	84°W
Chelmsford	5	5 G	51°N	0° E
Cheltenham	5	5 D	51°N	2°W
Chelyabinsk	40	7 D	55°N	61° E
Chelyuskin, Cape	41	11 B	77°N	103° E
Chemnitz	36	7 Q	50°N	12° E
Chengdu	45	3 J	30°N	104° E
Chennai	44	5 G	13°N	80° E
Cherbourg	37	8 H	49°N	1°W
Cherepovets	35	4 H	59°N	37° E
Chernigov	39	1 K	51°N	31° E
Chernovtsy	39	2 J	48°N	25° E
Cherrapunji	45	4 H	25°N	91° E
Cherwell →	5	5 E	51°N	1°W
Chesapeake Bay	53	3 L	38°N	76°W
Cheshire	9	5 E	53°N	2°W
Chester	4	3 D	53°N	2°W
Chesterfield	4	3 E	53°N	1°W
Cheviot Hills	4	1 D	55°N	2°W
Cheviot, The	4	1 D	55°N	2°W
Chew Bahir	26	2 B	4°N	36° E
Cheyenne	52	2 F	41°N	104°W
Chiapa →	54	4 F	16°N	93°W
Chiba Choshi	24	2 G	35°N	140° E
Chicago	53	2 J	41°N	87°W
Chichester	5	6 F	50°N	0°W
Chiengmai	45	5 H	18°N	98° E
Chihuahua	54	2 C	28°N	106°W
Chile	51	7 D	35°S	72°W
Chiltern Hills	5	5 F	51°N	0°W
China	45	3 J	30°N	110° E
Chisinau	39	2 J	47°N	28° E
Chita	41	12 D	52°N	113° E
Chittagong	45	4 H	22°N	91° E
Chongqing	45	4 J	29°N	106° E
Chorley	4	3 D	53°N	2°W
Chott Melrhir	38	5 E	34°N	6° E
Christchurch	48	11 M	43°S	172° E
Chudskoye, Lake	35	4 F	58°N	27° E
Chungking = Chongqing	45	4 J	29°N	106° E
Cienfuegos	55	3 H	22°N	80°W
Cincinnati	53	3 K	39°N	84°W
Cirencester	5	5 E	51°N	1°W
Citlaltepetl	54	4 E	19°N	97°W
Ciudad Bolívar	55	6 M	8°N	63°W
Ciudad Guayana	51	3 E	8°N	62°W
Ciudad Juarez	54	1 C	31°N	106°W
Ciudad Obregón	54	2 C	27°N	109°W
Clackmannanshire	9	3 E	56°N	3°W
Clacton	5	5 H	51°N	1° E
Clare	9	5 B	52°N	9°W
Clare →	7	3 C	53°N	9°W
Claremorris	7	3 B	53°N	9°W
Clear Island	7	5 B	51°N	9°W
Clear, Cape	7	5 B	51°N	9°W
Cleethorpes	4	3 F	53°N	0°W
Clermont-Ferrand	37	10 K	45°N	3° E
Cleveland	53	2 K	41°N	81°W
Clew Bay	7	3 B	53°N	9°W
Clifden	7	3 A	53°N	10°W
Clonakilty	7	5 C	51°N	8°W
Cloncurry	48	4 G	20°S	140° E
Clonmel	7	4 D	52°N	7°W
Cluj-Napoca	39	2 H	46°N	23° E
Clwyd →	4	3 C	53°N	3°W
Clyde →	6	4 E	55°N	4°W
Clyde, Firth of	6	4 C	55°N	5°W
Clydebank	6	4 D	55°N	4°W
Coahuila	52	5 E	27°N	103°W
Coalville	4	4 E	52°N	1°W
Coast Province	26	2 B	2°N	39° E
Coast Ranges	52	3 B	39°N	123°W
Coatbridge	6	4 D	55°N	4°W

Cobh 7 5C 51°N 8°W
Cod, Cape 50 5M 42°N 70°W
Coimbatore 44 5F 11°N 76°E
Colchester 5 5G 51°N 0°E
Coldstream 6 4F 55°N 2°W
Coleraine 7 1E 55°N 6°W
Coll 6 3B 56°N 6°W
Cologne 36 7M 50°N 6°E
Colombia 51 3D 3°N 73°W
Colombo 44 6F 6°N 79°E
Colonsay 6 3B 56°N 6°W
Colorado 52 3E 39°N 105°W
Colorado Plateau 52 3D 36°N 110°W
Colorado Springs 52 3F 38°N 104°W
Colorado → 52 4D 28°N 95°W
Columbia 53 4K 34°N 81°W
Columbia → 52 1B 46°N 124°W
Columbus 53 3K 39°N 83°W
Colwyn Bay 4 3C 53°N 3°W
Communism Peak 40 8F 39°N 72°E
Como, Lake 22 1B 46°N 9°E
Comorin, Cape 44 6F 8°N 77°E
Comoros 46 6H 12°S 44°E
Conakry 46 4B 9°N 13°W
Concepción 51 7D 36°S 73°W
Conchos → 54 2C 29°N 105°W
Concord 53 2M 43°N 71°W
Congleton 4 3D 53°N 2°W
Congo 46 5E 1°S 16°E
Congo → 46 5E 6°S 12°E
Congo, Democratic Republic of the 46 5F 3°S 23°E
Conn, Lough 7 2B 54°N 9°W
Connacht 7 3B 53°N 9°W
Connecticut 53 2M 41°N 72°W
Consett 4 2E 54°N 1°W
Constance, Lake 37 9N 47°N 9°E
Constanţa 39 3J 44°N 28°E
Constantine 46 1D 36°N 6°E
Conwy → 4 3C 53°N 3°W
Cook Islands 49 10N 17°S 160°W
Cook Strait 48 11M 41°S 174°E
Cook, Mount 48 11M 43°S 170°E
Cookstown 7 2E 54°N 6°W
Cooper Creek → 48 5F 28°S 137°E
Copenhagen 36 5Q 55°N 12°E
Coral Sea 48 3J 15°S 150°E
Corby 5 4F 52°N 0°W
Córdoba, Argentina 51 7E 31°S 64°W
Córdoba, Spain 37 14F 37°N 4°W
Corfu 39 4G 39°N 19°E
Corinth, Gulf of 39 4H 38°N 22°E
Cork 7 5C 51°N 8°W
Cornwall 9 6D 50°N 4°W
Corrib, Lough 7 3B 53°N 9°W
Corrientes, Cape 54 3C 20°N 105°W
Corsica 37 11N 42°N 9°E
Cosenza 22 5F 39°N 16°E
Costa Blanca 37 14H 38°N 0°W
Costa Brava 38 3D 41°N 3°E
Costa del Sol 38 4C 36°N 4°W
Costa Rica 55 5H 10°N 84°W
Coteau du Missouri 52 1F 47°N 100°W
Cotonou 47 10L 6°N 2°E
Cotswolds 5 5D 51°N 2°W
Coventry 5 4E 52°N 1°W
Cradock 28 3D 32°S 25°E
Crawley 5 5F 51°N 0°W
Crete 39 4H 35°N 25°E
Crewe 4 3D 53°N 2°W
Crieff 6 3E 56°N 3°W
Crimea 39 2K 45°N 34°E
Croatia 39 2G 45°N 17°E
Cromarty 6 2D 57°N 4°W
Cromer 4 4H 52°N 1°E
Crosby 4 3C 53°N 3°W
Cross Fell 4 2D 54°N 2°W
Crow Head 7 5A 51°N 10°W
Croydon 5 5F 51°N 0°W
Cuba 55 3J 22°N 79°W
Cúcuta 55 6K 7°N 72°W
Cuenca 51 4D 2°S 79°W
Cuernavaca 54 4E 18°N 99°W
Cuiabá 30 6D 15°S 56°W
Culiacan 54 3C 24°N 107°W
Cumberland → 53 2J 36°N 87°W
Cumberland Plateau 53 3J 36°N 85°W
Cumbernauld 6 4E 55°N 3°W
Cumbria 9 4E 54°N 2°W
Cumbrian Mountains 4 2C 54°N 3°W
Cupar 6 3E 56°N 3°W
Curaçao 51 2E 12°N 69°W
Curitiba 30 8F 25°S 49°W
Cuzco 51 5D 13°S 72°W
Cwmbran 5 5C 51°N 3°W
Cyprus 39 4K 35°N 33°E
Czech Republic 38 2F 50°N 15°E

Da Nang 45 5J 16°N 108°E
Dacca 44 4H 23°N 90°E
Daio, Cape 24 2E 34°N 136°E
Dakar 46 3B 14°N 17°W
Dakhla 46 2B 23°N 15°W
Dalian 45 3L 38°N 121°E
Dallas 53 4G 32°N 96°W
Dampier 48 4B 20°S 116°E
Danube → 39 3J 45°N 29°E
Dar es Salaam 46 5G 6°S 39°E
Dardanelles 39 3J 40°N 26°E
Darién, Gulf of 55 6J 9°N 77°W
Darling Range 48 6B 32°S 116°E
Darling → 48 6G 34°S 141°E
Darlington 4 2E 54°N 1°W
Dart → 5 6C 50°N 3°W
Dartmoor 5 6C 50°N 4°W
Dartmouth 5 6C 50°N 3°W
Darwin 48 2E 12°S 130°E
Davao 45 6L 7°N 125°E
Davis Strait 50 3P 65°N 58°W
Dawa → 26 2C 4°N 42°E
Dawson 50 3F 64°N 139°W
De Aar 28 3C 30°S 24°E
Deal 5 5H 51°N 1°E
Death Valley 52 3C 36°N 116°W
Debrecen 39 2H 47°N 21°E
Debundscha 47 11M 4°N 8°E
Deccan 44 5F 18°N 79°E
Dee → 4 3D 53°N 3°W
Delaware 53 3L 39°N 75°W
Delhi 44 4F 28°N 77°E
Denizli 39 4J 37°N 29°E
Denmark 36 5N 55°N 9°E
Denmark Strait 50 3S 66°N 30°W
Denver 52 3F 39°N 105°W
Derby 4 4E 52°N 1°W
Derbyshire 9 5F 52°N 1°W
Derg, Lough 7 4C 53°N 8°W
Derwent →, Cumberland 4 2C 54°N 3°W
Derwent →, Derbyshire 4 3E 52°N 1°W
Derwent →, Yorkshire 4 3F 53°N 0°W
Detroit 53 2K 42°N 83°W
Devon 9 6E 50°N 3°W
Dieppe 37 8J 49°N 1°E
Dijon 37 9L 47°N 5°E
Dinaric Alps 39 3G 44°N 16°E
Dingle 7 4A 52°N 10°W
Dingwall 6 2D 57°N 4°W
Djerba 38 5F 33°N 10°E
Djerid, Chott 38 5E 33°N 8°E
Djibouti 46 3H 12°N 43°E
Dnepr → 39 1K 46°N 32°E
Dnepropetrovsk 39 2K 48°N 35°E
Dnestr → 39 2J 46°N 30°E
Dodecanese 39 4J 36°N 27°E
Dodoma 46 5G 6°S 35°E
Doha 44 4D 25°N 51°E
Dolgellau 4 4C 52°N 3°W
Dominica 55 4M 15°N 61°W
Dominican Republic 55 4K 19°N 70°W
Don → 40 5E 47°N 39°E
Don →, Aberdeen 6 2F 57°N 2°W
Don →, Yorkshire 4 3E 53°N 0°W
Doncaster 4 3E 53°N 1°W
Donegal 7 2C 54°N 8°W
Donegal Bay 7 2C 54°N 8°W
Donetsk 39 2L 48°N 37°E
Doon → 6 4D 55°N 4°W
Dorchester 5 6D 50°N 2°W
Dordogne → 37 10J 45°N 0°W
Dornoch Firth 6 2E 57°N 4°W
Dorset 9 6E 50°N 2°W
Dortmund 36 7M 51°N 7°E
Douala 47 11M 4°N 9°E
Douglas 4 2B 54°N 4°W
Dourados 30 7E 22°S 54°W
Douro → 37 12D 41°N 8°W
Dove → 4 4E 52°N 1°W
Dover, U.K. 5 5H 51°N 1°E
Dover, U.S.A. 53 3L 39°N 75°W
Dover, Strait of 5 6H 51°N 1°E
Dovey → 5 4C 52°N 4°W
Down (county) 9 4D 54°N 5°W
Downpatrick 7 2F 54°N 5°W
Drakensberg 29 3D 31°S 28°E
Drammen 35 4C 59°N 10°E
Drava → 39 2G 45°N 18°E
Dresden 36 7Q 51°N 13°E
Driffield 4 2F 54°N 0°W
Drogheda 7 3E 53°N 6°W
Dublin 7 3E 53°N 6°W
Dubrovnik 39 3G 42°N 18°E
Dudley 5 4D 52°N 2°W
Duero → 37 12F 41°N 8°W
Dumbarton 6 4D 55°N 4°W
Dumfries 6 4E 55°N 3°W
Dumfries and Galloway 9 4E 55°N 4°W
Dunbar 6 3F 56°N 2°W
Duncansby Head 14 2E 58°N 3°W
Dundalk 7 2E 54°N 6°W
Dundee 6 3E 56°N 3°W
Dunedin 48 12M 45°S 170°E
Dunfermline 6 3E 56°N 3°W
Dungannon 7 2E 54°N 6°W
Dungarvan 7 4D 52°N 7°W
Dunkery Beacon 5 5C 51°N 3°W
Dunmore Hd. 7 4A 52°N 10°W
Dunnet Head 6 1E 58°N 3°W
Dunoon 6 4D 55°N 4°W
Durango 54 3D 24°N 104°W
Durban 29 2E 29°S 31°E
Durham 4 2E 54°N 1°W
Durham (county) 9 4F 54°N 1°W
Dushanbe 40 7F 38°N 68°E
Düsseldorf 37 7M 51°N 6°E
Dvina, North → 40 5C 64°N 40°E
Dvina, West → 35 4F 56°N 24°E
Dzhezkazgan 40 7E 47°N 67°E
Dzungaria 44 2G 44°N 88°E

East China Sea 45 4L 30°N 126°E
East Indies 45 7K 0° 120°E
East Kilbride 6 4D 55°N 4°W
East London 29 3D 33°S 27°E
East Lothian 9 4E 55°N 3°W
East Riding 9 5F 53°N 0°W
East Siberian Sea 41 16B 73°N 160°E
East Sussex 9 6G 51°N 0°E
East Timor 45 7L 9°S 125°E
Eastbourne 5 6G 50°N 0°E
Easter Island 49 10T 27°S 109°W
Eastern Ghats 44 5F 14°N 78°E
Eastern Province 26 2B 0° 38°E
Eastleigh 5 6E 50°N 1°W
Ebbw Vale 5 5C 51°N 3°W
Ebro → 37 12J 40°N 0°E
Ecuador 51 4D 2°S 78°W
Eday 6 7F 59°N 2°W
Eddystone 5 6B 50°N 4°W
Eden → 4 2D 54°N 3°W
Edinburgh 6 4E 55°N 3°W
Edmonton 50 4H 53°N 113°W
Egadi Islands 22 6C 37°N 12°E
Egypt 46 2G 28°N 31°E
Eigg 6 3B 56°N 6°W
El Aaiun 46 2B 27°N 13°W
El Fâsher 46 3F 13°N 25°E
El Obeid 46 3G 13°N 30°E
El Paso 54 1C 31°N 106°W
El Salvador 54 5G 13°N 89°W
Elba 22 3C 42°N 10°E
Elbe → 36 6P 53°N 9°E
Elbert, Mount 52 3E 39°N 106°W
Elbrus, Mount 34 7Q 43°N 42°E
Elche 37 13H 38°N 0°W
Eldoret 26 2B 0°N 35°E
Elefantes → 29 1E 24°S 32°E
Elgin 6 2E 57°N 3°W
Elgon, Mount 26 2A 1°N 34°E
Ellesmere Island 50 2M 79°N 80°W
Ellesmere Port 4 3D 53°N 2°W
Ellon 6 2F 57°N 2°W
Ely 5 4G 52°N 0°E
Embu 26 3B 0°S 37°E
England 36 6G 53°N 2°W
English Channel 5 6D 50°N 2°W
Ennis 7 4C 52°N 8°W
Enniscorthy 7 4E 52°N 6°W
Enniskillen 7 2D 54°N 7°W
Entebbe 26 2A 0°N 32°E
Enugu 47 10M 6°N 7°E
Equatorial Guinea 46 4D 2°N 8°E
Erfurt 36 7P 50°N 11°E
Eriboll, Loch 6 1D 58°N 4°W
Erie, Lake 53 2K 42°N 81°W
Eritrea 46 3G 14°N 38°E
Errigal 7 1C 55°N 8°W
Esbjerg 36 5N 55°N 8°E
Esfahan 44 3D 33°N 51°E
Esk →, Scotland 6 4E 54°N 3°W
Esk →, Yorkshire 4 2F 54°N 0°W
Esk, North → 6 3F 56°N 2°W
Esk, South → 6 3F 56°N 3°W
Eskişehir 39 4K 39°N 30°E
Espírito Santo 30 7G 20°S 40°W
Essen 36 7M 51°N 6°E
Essequibo → 55 6N 6°N 58°W
Essex 9 6G 51°N 0°E
Estonia 35 4F 58°N 25°E
Ethiopia 46 4H 8°N 40°E
Ethiopian Highlands 46 4G 10°N 37°E
Etna, Mount 38 4F 37°N 15°E
Etosha Pan 47 8E 18°S 16°E
Ettrick Water → 6 4F 55°N 2°W
Euphrates → 44 3C 31°N 47°E
Everest, Mount 44 4G 28°N 86°E
Everglades, The 53 5K 25°N 81°W
Evesham 5 4E 52°N 1°W
Ewaso → 26 2B 0°N 39°E
Exe → 5 6C 50°N 3°W
Exeter 5 6C 50°N 3°W
Exmoor 5 5C 51°N 3°W
Exmouth 5 6C 50°N 3°W
Eyemouth 6 4F 55°N 2°W
Eyre, Lake 48 5F 29°S 137°E

Fair Isle 14 2F 59°N 1°W
Fairbanks 50 3E 64°N 147°W
Faisalabad 44 3F 31°N 73°E
Falkirk 6 4E 56°N 3°W
Falkland Islands 51 9F 51°S 59°W
Falmouth 5 6A 50°N 5°W
Fareham 5 6E 50°N 1°W
Farewell, Cape 50 4Q 59°N 43°W
Farne Islands 4 1E 55°N 1°W
Faroe Islands 36 2E 62°N 7°W
Fastnet Rock 7 5B 51°N 9°W
Faya-Largeau 46 3E 17°N 19°E
Fdérik 46 2B 22°N 12°W
Fear, Cape 53 4L 33°N 77°W
Feira de Santana 30 5H 12°S 38°W
Felixstowe 5 5H 51°N 1°E
Fens, The 4 4F 52°N 0°E
Fermanagh 9 4C 54°N 7°W
Fermoy 7 4C 52°N 8°W
Ferrara 22 2C 44°N 11°E
Fès 46 1C 34°N 5°W
Fetlar 6 8K 60°N 0°W
Fife 9 3E 56°N 3°W
Fiji 49 9K 17°S 179°E
Findhorn → 6 2E 57°N 3°W
Finland 35 3F 63°N 27°E
Finland, Gulf of 35 4F 60°N 26°E
Fish → 28 2B 28°S 17°E
Fishguard 5 5B 51°N 4°W
Flamborough Head 4 2F 54°N 0°W
Flannan Islands 6 1A 58°N 7°W
Flattery, Cape 52 1B 48°N 124°W
Fleetwood 4 3C 53°N 3°W
Flensburg 36 5N 54°N 9°E
Flinders Island 48 7H 40°S 148°E
Flinders Ranges 48 6F 31°S 138°E
Florence 22 3C 43°N 11°E
Flores Sea 45 7K 6°S 120°E
Florianópolis 30 8F 27°S 48°W
Florida 53 5K 28°N 82°W
Florida Keys 53 6K 24°N 81°W
Florida Strait 53 5L 25°N 80°W
Foggia 22 4E 41°N 15°E
Folkestone 5 5H 51°N 1°E
Forfar 6 3F 56°N 2°W
Formosa Bay 26 3C 2°S 40°E
Fort Augustus 6 2D 57°N 4°W
Fort-de-France 55 5M 14°N 61°W
Fort Lauderdale 55 2H 26°N 80°W
Fort William 6 3C 56°N 5°W
Fort Worth 53 4G 32°N 97°W
Fortaleza 30 3H 3°S 38°W
Forth → 6 3D 56°N 3°W
Forth, Firth of 6 3F 56°N 2°W
Foula 6 8J 60°N 2°W
Fouta Djalon 46 3B 11°N 12°W
Foyle, Lough 7 1D 55°N 7°W
Foz do Iguaça 30 8E 25°S 54°W
France 37 9J 47°N 3°E
Frankfort 53 3K 38°N 84°W
Frankfurt 36 7N 50°N 8°E
Franz Josef Land 56 1F 81°N 60°E
Fraserburg 28 3C 31°S 21°E
Fraserburgh 6 2F 57°N 2°W
Fredrikstad 35 4C 59°N 10°E
Freeport 55 2J 26°N 78°W
Freetown 46 4B 8°N 13°W
Freiburg 37 8M 48°N 7°E
Fremantle 48 6B 32°S 115°E
French Guiana 51 3F 4°N 53°W
Frisian Islands 36 6L 53°N 6°E
Fuji, Mount 24 2F 35°N 138°E
Fukui 24 2E 36°N 136°E
Fukuoka 24 3B 33°N 130°E
Fukushima 43 3D 37°N 140°E
Fukuyama 24 2C 34°N 133°E
Funabashi 24 2G 35°N 140°E
Fushun 45 2L 41°N 123°E
Fuzhou 45 4K 26°N 119°E
Fyne, Loch 6 4C 56°N 5°W

Gabon 46 5E 0°S 10°E
Gaborone 28 1D 24°S 25°E
Gainsborough 4 3F 53°N 0°W
Gairdner, Lake 48 6F 31°S 136°E
Galana → 26 3C 3°S 40°E
Galapagos Islands 51 4B 0°N 89°W
Galashiels 6 4F 55°N 2°W
Galati 39 2J 45°N 28°E
Galdhøpiggen 35 3B 61°N 8°E
Gällivare 35 2E 67°N 20°E
Galloway, Mull of 6 5D 54°N 4°W
Galtymore 7 4C 52°N 8°W
Galway 7 3B 53°N 9°W
Galway Bay 7 3B 53°N 9°W
Gambia 46 3B 13°N 16°W
Ganges → 44 4H 23°N 90°E
Garanhuns 30 4H 8°S 36°W
Garda, Lake 22 2C 45°N 10°E
Garissa 26 3B 0°S 39°E
Garonne → 37 10H 45°N 0°W
Garoua 47 10N 9°N 13°E
Gateshead 4 2E 54°N 1°W
Gävle 35 3D 60°N 17°E
Gaza Strip 39 5K 31°N 34°E
Gaziantep 39 4L 37°N 37°E
Gdańsk 35 5D 54°N 18°E
Geelong 48 7G 38°S 144°E
Gemsbok National Park 28 2C 25°S 21°E
Geneva 37 9M 46°N 6°E
Geneva, Lake 37 9M 46°N 6°E
Genoa 22 2B 44°N 8°E
Genoa, Gulf of 22 2B 44°N 9°E
George 28 3C 33°S 22°E
George Town 45 6J 5°N 100°E
Georgetown 55 6N 6°N 58°W
Georgia, Asia 40 5E 42°N 43°E
Georgia, U.S.A. 53 4K 32°N 83°W
Geraldton 48 5A 28°S 114°E
Germany 36 7N 52°N 10°E
Germiston 29 2D 26°S 28°E
Ghana 47 10K 8°N 1°W
Ghats, Eastern 44 5F 14°N 78°W
Ghent 36 7K 51°N 3°E
Ghudāmis 46 1D 30°N 9°E
Giants Causeway 7 1E 55°N 6°W
Gibraltar 37 14F 36°N 5°W
Gibraltar, Strait of 37 14E 35°N 5°W
Gibson Desert 48 4C 24°S 126°E
Gifu 24 2E 35°N 136°E
Gijon 37 11F 43°N 5°W
Gillingham 5 5G 51°N 0°E
Gironde → 37 10H 45°N 1°W
Girvan 6 4D 55°N 4°W
Gladstone 48 4J 23°S 151°E
Glåma 35 2P 59°N 10°E
Glasgow 6 4D 55°N 4°W
Glen Mor 6 2D 57°N 4°W
Glenrothes 6 3E 56°N 3°W
Gloucester 5 5D 51°N 2°W
Gloucestershire 9 6E 51°N 2°W
Gobi 41 11E 44°N 111°E
Godavari → 44 5F 16°N 82°E
Godthab = Nuuk 50 3P 64°N 51°W
Goiânia 30 6F 16°S 49°W
Goiás 30 5F 12°S 48°W
Gold Coast 48 5J 28°S 153°E

Golspie 6 2 E 57°N 3°W
Gomel 35 5 G 52°N 31° E
Good Hope, Cape of 28 3 B 34°S 18° E
Goole 4 3 F 53°N 0°W
Gorey 7 4 E 52°N 6°W
Gosport 5 6 E 50°N 1°W
Götaland 35 4 C 58°N 14° E
Gothenburg 35 4 C 40°N 100°W
Gotland 35 4 D 57°N 18° E
Gotsu 24 2 C 35°N 132° E
Göttingen 36 7 N 51°N 9° E
Governador Valadares 30 6 G 18°S 41°W
Graaff-Reinet 28 3 C 32°S 24° E
Grahamstown 28 3 D 33°S 26° E
Grampian Mountains 6 3 D 56°N 4°W
Gran Chaco 51 6 E 25°S 61°W
Granada 37 14 G 37°N 3°W
Grand Bahama Island 55 2 J 26°N 78°W
Grand Canyon 52 3 D 36°N 112°W
Grand Cayman 55 4 H 19°N 81°W
Grand Teton 52 2 D 43°N 111°W
Grantham 4 4 F 52°N 0°W
Grantown-on-Spey 6 2 E 57°N 3°W
Gravesend 5 5 G 51°N 0° E
Graz 39 2 G 47°N 15° E
Great Australian Bight 48 6 D 33°S 130° E
Great Barrier Reef 48 3 H 18°S 146° E
Great Basin 52 2 C 39°N 116°W
Great Bear Lake 50 3 G 65°N 120°W
Great Divide 48 6 J 23°S 146° E
Great Fish → 28 3 D 33°S 27° E
Great Karoo 28 3 C 31°S 21° E
Great Kei → 29 3 D 32°S 27° E
Great Khingan Mountains 45 2 L 47°N 121° E
Great Lakes 50 5 L 46°N 85°W
Great Malvern 5 4 D 52°N 2°W
Great Ouse → 4 4 G 52°N 0° E
Great Plains 52 1 E 47°N 105°W
Great Salt Lake 52 2 D 41°N 112°W
Great Salt Lake Desert 52 3 D 40°N 113°W
Great Sandy Desert 48 4 C 21°S 124° E
Great Slave Lake 50 3 H 61°N 115°W
Great Victoria Desert 48 5 D 29°S 126° E
Great Wall 45 3 J 38°N 109° E
Great Yarmouth 4 4 H 52°N 1° E
Greater Antilles 51 2 D 17°N 74°W
Greater London 9 6 F 51°N 0°W
Greater Manchester 9 5 E 53°N 2°W
Greece 39 4 H 40°N 23° E
Greenland 50 2 Q 66°N 45°W
Greenland Sea 56 H 73°N 10°W
Greenock 6 4 D 55°N 4°W
Greenwich 5 5 G 51°N 0°W
Grenada 55 5 M 12°N 61°W
Grenoble 37 10 L 45°N 5° E
Gretna Green 6 4 E 55°N 3°W
Grimsby 4 3 F 53°N 0°W
Groningen 36 6 M 53°N 6° E
Groot Karasberge 28 2 B 27°S 18° E
Grootvloer 28 3 C 30°S 20° E
Guadalajara 54 3 D 20°N 103°W
Guadalquivir → 38 4 C 36°N 6°W
Guadeloupe 55 4 M 16°N 61°W
Guadiana → 38 4 B 37°N 7°W
Guam 49 6 G 13°N 144° E
Guangzhou 45 4 K 23°N 113° E
Guaporé → 30 5 B 11°S 65°W
Guatemala 54 4 F 15°N 90°W
Guaviare → 55 7 K 4°N 67°W
Guayaquil 51 4 D 2°S 79°W
Guernsey 5 7 D 49°N 2°W
Guiana Highlands 51 3 E 5°N 60°W
Guildford 5 5 F 51°N 0°W
Guinea 46 3 B 10°N 11°W
Guinea Bissau 46 3 B 12°N 15°W
Guinea, Gulf of 46 4 C 3°N 2° E
Guiyang 45 4 J 26°N 106° E
Gulf, The 44 4 D 27°N 50° E
Gulu 26 2 A 2°N 32° E
Gusau 47 9 M 12°N 6° E
Guyana 55 6 N 5°N 59°W
Gwynedd 9 5 D 53°N 4°W
Gyandzha 40 5 E 40°N 46° E

Hachioji 24 2 F 35°N 139° E
Hadrian's Wall 4 1 D 55°N 2°W
Hague, Cap de la 37 8 G 49°N 1°W
Hague, The 36 6 L 52°N 4° E
Hainan 45 5 J 19°N 110° E
Haiphong 45 4 J 20°N 106° E
Haiti 55 4 K 19°N 72°W
Hakodate 43 2 D 41°N 140° E
Halifax, Canada 50 5 N 44°N 63°W
Halifax, U.K. 4 3 E 53°N 1°W
Halle 36 7 Q 51°N 12° E
Halmahera 45 6 L 0°N 128° E
Halton 9 5 E 53°N 2°W
Hamada 24 2 C 34°N 132° E
Hamamatsu 24 2 E 34°N 137° E
Hamburg 36 6 P 53°N 9° E
Hamersley Range 48 4 B 22°S 117° E
Hamilton, Bermuda 55 1 M 32°N 64°W
Hamilton, Canada 53 2 L 43°N 79°W
Hamilton, New Zealand 48 10 N 37°S 175° E
Hamilton, U.K. 6 4 D 55°N 4°W
Hammerfest 35 1 E 70°N 23° E
Hampshire 9 6 F 51°N 1°W
Hangzhou 45 3 L 30°N 120° E
Hanoi 45 4 J 21°N 105° E
Hanover 36 6 N 52°N 9° E
Harare 47 6 G 17°S 31° E
Harbin 45 2 L 45°N 126° E
Hardanger Fjord 35 3 B 60°N 6° E
Harlow 5 5 G 51°N 0° E
Harris 6 2 B 57°N 6°W
Harrogate 4 3 E 53°N 1°W
Hartford 53 2 M 41°N 72°W
Hartland Point 5 5 B 51°N 4°W
Hartlepool 4 2 E 54°N 1°W
Harts → 28 2 C 28°S 24° E
Harwich 5 5 H 51°N 1° E
Hastings 5 6 G 50°N 0° E
Hatteras, Cape 50 6 M 35°N 75°W
Havana 55 3 H 23°N 82°W
Havant 5 6 F 50°N 0°W
Haverfordwest 5 5 B 51°N 4°W
Hawaii 52 8 Q 19°N 156°W
Hawick 6 4 F 55°N 2°W
Hay-on-Wye 5 4 C 52°N 3°W
Hebrides 36 4 E 57°N 7°W
Hebrides, Inner 6 2 B 57°N 6°W
Hebrides, Outer 6 2 A 57°N 7°W
Hegang 41 13 E 47°N 130° E
Helena 52 1 D 46°N 112°W
Helensburgh 6 3 D 56°N 4°W
Helmsdale 6 1 E 58°N 3°W
Helsingborg 35 4 C 56°N 12° E
Helsinki 35 3 E 60°N 25° E
Hemel Hempstead 5 5 F 51°N 0°W
Henderson Lake 52 1 A 49°N 125°W
Herat 44 3 E 34°N 62° E
Hereford 5 4 D 52°N 2°W
Hermosillo 54 2 B 32°N 114°W
Herne Bay 5 5 H 51°N 1° E
Hertford 5 5 F 51°N 0°W
Hertfordshire 9 6 F 51°N 0°W
Hexham 6 5 F 54°N 2°W
Heysham 4 2 D 54°N 2°W
Higashiosaka 24 2 D 34°N 135° E
High Willhays 5 6 B 50°N 3°W
High Wycombe 5 5 F 51°N 0°W
Highland (region) 9 3 D 57°N 5°W
Hiiumaa 35 4 E 58°N 22° E
Himalaya 44 4 G 29°N 84° E
Himeji 24 2 D 34°N 134° E
Homs 39 5 L 34°N 36° E
Hinckley 5 4 E 52°N 1°W
Hindu Kush 44 3 F 36°N 71° E
Hiroshima 24 2 C 34°N 133° E
Hitachi 24 1 G 36°N 140° E
Ho Chi Minh City 45 5 J 10°N 106° E
Hobart 48 8 H 42°S 147° E
Hofu 24 2 B 34°N 131° E
Hoggar 46 2 D 23°N 6° E
Hokkaido 43 2 D 43°N 143° E
Holderness 4 3 F 53°N 0°W
Holguín 55 3 J 20°N 76°W
Holy Island, Anglesey 4 3 B 53°N 4°W
Holy Island, Northumb'land 4 1 E 55°N 1°W
Holyhead 4 3 B 53°N 4°W
Honduras 54 5 G 14°N 86°W
Honduras, Gulf of 54 4 G 16°N 87°W
Hong Kong 45 4 K 22°N 114° E
Honiara 48 1 K 9°S 159° E
Honolulu 52 8 R 21°N 157°W
Honshu 43 3 C 36°N 138° E
Hormuz, Strait of 44 4 D 26°N 56° E
Horn, Cape 51 9 E 55°S 67°W
Horsham 5 5 F 51°N 0°W
Houghton-le-Spring 4 2 E 54°N 1°W
Houston 53 5 G 29°N 95°W
Hove 5 6 F 50°N 0°W
Howth Head 7 3 E 53°N 6°W
Hoy 6 6 E 58°N 3°W
Huambo 46 6 E 12°S 15° E
Huddersfield 4 3 E 53°N 1°W
Hudson Bay 50 4 L 60°N 86°W
Hudson Strait 50 3 M 62°N 70°W
Hudson → 53 2 M 40°N 74°W
Huelva 37 14 E 37°N 6°W
Hull → 4 3 F 53°N 0°W
Humber → 4 3 F 53°N 0°W
Hungary 39 2 G 47°N 19° E
Hunsberge 28 2 B 27°S 17° E
Huntingdon 5 7 E 52°N 0°W
Huntly 6 2 F 57°N 2°W
Huron, Lake 53 2 K 45°N 83°W
Hwang-Ho → 45 3 K 37°N 118° E
Hyderabad, India 44 5 F 17°N 78° E
Hyderabad, Pakistan 44 4 E 25°N 68° E

Iasi 39 2 J 47°N 27° E
Ibadan 47 10 L 7°N 3° E
Ibagué 55 7 J 4°N 75°W
Ibiza 37 13 J 38°N 1° E
Içá → 30 3 B 2°S 67°W
Iceland 56 1 H 64°N 19°W
Ichinomiya 24 2 E 35°N 136° E
Idaho 52 2 C 45°N 115°W
Ifrane 38 5 B 33°N 5°W
Iguaçu Falls 51 6 F 25°S 54°W
Ilfracombe 5 5 B 51°N 4°W
Ilhéus 30 5 H 14°S 39°W
Ilkeston 4 4 E 52°N 1°W
Illinois 53 3 J 40°N 89°W
Ilorin 47 10 L 8°N 4° E
Imabari 24 2 C 34°N 133° E
Imandra, Lake 35 2 G 67°N 33° E
Imperatriz 30 4 F 5°S 47°W
In Salah 46 2 D 27°N 2° E
Ina 24 2 E 35°N 137° E
India 44 4 F 20°N 78° E
Indian Ocean 61 4 N 5°S 75° E
Indian → 53 5 K 27°N 80°W
Indiana 53 2 J 40°N 86°W
Indianapolis 53 3 J 39°N 86°W
Indonesia 45 7 K 5°S 115° E
Indore 44 4 F 22°N 75° E
Indus → 44 4 E 24°N 67° E
Inishbofin 7 3 A 53°N 10°W
Inishmore 7 3 B 53°N 9°W
Inishowen Peninsula 7 1 D 55°N 7°W
Inishturk 7 3 A 53°N 10°W
Inland Sea 24 2 C 34°N 133° E
Inner Hebrides 6 2 B 57°N 6°W
Inner Mongolia 41 12 E 42°N 112° E
Innsbruck 37 9 P 47°N 11° E
International Date Line 49 5 L 15°N 180° E
Inveraray 6 3 C 56°N 5°W
Invercargill 48 12 L 46°S 168° E
Invergordon 6 2 D 57°N 4°W
Inverness 6 2 D 57°N 4°W
Inverurie 6 2 F 57°N 2°W
Ionian Islands 39 4 H 38°N 20° E
Ionian Sea 39 4 G 37°N 17° E
Iowa 53 2 H 42°N 93°W
Ipswich 5 4 H 52°N 1° E
Iqaluit 50 3 N 63°N 68°W
Iquitos 51 4 D 3°S 73°W
Iráklion 39 4 J 35°N 25° E
Iran 44 3 D 33°N 53° E
Iraq 44 3 C 33°N 44° E
Ireland 7 3 D 53°N 8°W
Ireland's Eye 7 3 E 53°N 6°W
Irian Jaya 49 8 F 4°S 137° E
Irish Sea 36 6 F 54°N 5°W
Irkutsk 41 11 D 52°N 104° E
Irrawaddy → 45 4 H 15°N 95° E
Irtysh → 40 7 C 61°N 68° E
Irvine 6 4 D 55°N 4°W
Ischia 22 4 D 40°N 13° E
Ise Bay 24 2 E 34°N 136° E
Islamabad 44 3 F 33°N 73° E
Islay 6 4 B 55°N 6°W
Ismâ'ilîya 39 5 K 30°N 32° E
Isparta 39 4 K 37°N 30° E
Israel 44 3 B 32°N 34° E
Istanbul 39 3 J 41°N 29° E
Itabuna 30 5 H 14°S 39°W
Itaituba 30 3 D 4°S 55°W
Italy 22 3 D 42°N 13° E
Itchen → 5 5 E 50°N 1°W
Ivory Coast 46 4 C 7°N 5°W
Iwaki 43 3 D 37°N 140° E
Izmir 39 4 J 38°N 27° E
Izmit 39 3 J 40°N 29° E

Jabalpur 44 4 F 23°N 79° E
Jackson 53 4 H 32°N 90°W
Jacksonville 53 4 K 30°N 81°W
Jaffna 44 6 G 9°N 80° E
Jaipur 44 4 F 27°N 75° E
Jakarta 45 7 J 6°S 106° E
Jamaica 55 4 J 18°N 77°W
Jamshedpur 44 4 G 22°N 86° E
Jan Mayen Island 56 H 71°N 9°W
Japan 45 3 M 36°N 136° E
Japan Trench 49 4 G 32°N 142° E
Japan, Sea of 43 3 B 40°N 135° E
Japurá → 30 3 B 3°S 65°W
Java 45 7 K 7°S 110° E
Jedburgh 6 4 F 55°N 2°W
Jedda 44 4 B 21°N 39° E
Jerez de la Frontera 37 14 E 36°N 6°W
Jersey 5 7 D 49°N 2°W
Jinan 45 3 K 36°N 117° E
Jinja 26 2 A 0°N 33° E
Jixi 43 1 B 45°N 130° E
João Pessoa 30 4 J 7°S 34°W
Joensuu 35 3 F 62°N 29° E
Johannesburg 29 2 D 26°S 28° E
John o'Groats 6 1 E 58°N 3°W
Johnstone 6 4 D 55°N 4°W
Joinville 30 8 F 26°S 48°W
Jönköping 35 4 C 57°N 14° E
Jordan 44 3 B 31°N 36° E
Jotunheimen 36 2 M 61°N 8° E
Juan Fernández Archipelago 49 10 V 33°S 80°W
Juàzeiro 30 4 G 9°S 40°W
Juàzeiro do Norte 30 4 H 7°S 39°W
Juba 46 4 G 4°N 31° E
Juiz de Fora 30 7 G 21°S 43°W
Juneau 50 4 F 58°N 134°W
Jura 6 4 C 56°N 5°W
Jura, Sound of 6 4 C 55°N 5°W
Juruá → 30 3 B 2°S 65°W
Juruena → 30 4 D 7°S 58°W
Jutland 36 4 N 56°N 9° E
Jyväskylä 35 3 F 62°N 25° E

K2 44 3 F 35°N 76° E
Kabul 44 3 E 34°N 69° E
Kaduna 47 9 M 10°N 7° E
Kagoshima 24 4 B 31°N 130° E
Kainji Reservoir 47 9 L 10°N 4° E
Kakamega 26 2 A 0°N 34° E
Kalahari Desert 28 1 C 24°S 21° E
Kalahari-Gemsbok National Park 28 2 C 25°S 20° E
Kalemie 46 5 F 5°S 29° E
Kalgoorlie-Boulder 48 6 C 30°S 121° E
Kaliningrad 35 5 E 54°N 20° E
Kam → 28 1 B 24°S 17° E
Kamchatka Peninsula 41 16 D 57°N 160° E
Kampala 46 4 G 0°N 32° E
Kampuchea = Cambodia 45 5 J 12°N 105° E
Kananga 46 5 F 5°S 22° E
Kanazawa 24 1 E 36°N 136° E
Kangaroo Island 48 7 F 35°S 137° E
Kano 47 9 M 12°N 8° E
Kanpur 44 4 G 26°N 80° E
Kansas 52 3 G 38°N 99°W
Kansas City 53 3 H 39°N 94°W
Kansk 41 10 D 56°N 95° E
Kanye 28 1 D 24°S 25° E
Kaohsiung 45 4 L 22°N 120° E
Kara Kum 40 6 E 39°N 60° E
Kara Sea 40 7 B 75°N 70° E
Karachi 44 4 E 24°N 67° E
Karaganda 40 8 E 49°N 73° E
Karakoram Range 44 3 F 47°N 102° E
Karatsu 24 3 A 33°N 129° E
Kareeberge 28 3 C 30°S 21° E
Karelia 35 3 G 62°N 33° E
Kariba, Lake 46 6 F 16°S 28° E
Karlsruhe 37 8 N 49°N 8° E
Karoo 47 8 F 31°S 21° E
Kasai → 46 5 F 3°S 16° E
Kassel 36 7 N 51°N 9° E
Katmandu 44 4 G 27°N 85° E
Katowice 39 2 G 50°N 19° E
Katrine, Loch 6 3 D 56°N 4°W
Katsina 47 9 M 13°N 7° E
Kattegat 35 4 C 57°N 11° E
Kaunas 35 5 E 54°N 23° E
Kawagoe 24 2 F 35°N 139° E
Kawaguchi 24 2 F 35°N 139° E
Kawasaki 24 2 F 35°N 139° E
Kayseri 39 4 L 38°N 35° E
Kazakstan 40 6 E 50°N 70° E
Kazan 40 5 D 55°N 49° E
Keetmanshoop 28 2 B 26°S 18° E
Keighley 4 3 E 53°N 1°W
Keith 6 2 F 57°N 2°W
Kelso 6 4 F 55°N 2°W
Kemi 35 2 E 65°N 24° E
Kendal 4 2 D 54°N 2°W
Kenmare 7 5 B 51°N 9°W
Kennet → 5 5 E 51°N 0°W
Kent 9 6 G 51°N 0° E
Kentucky 53 3 J 37°N 84°W
Kenya 26 2 B 1°N 38° E
Kenya, Mount 26 3 B 0°S 37° E
Kerguelen Islands 61 5 N 49°S 69° E
Kericho 26 3 B 0°S 35° E
Kermadec Islands 49 11 K 30°S 178°W
Kermadec Trench 49 11 L 30°S 176°W
Kerman 44 3 D 30°N 57° E
Kerry 9 5 B 52°N 9°W
Keswick 4 2 C 54°N 3°W
Kettering 5 4 F 52°N 0°W
Khabarovsk 41 14 E 48°N 135° E
Khanka, Lake 43 2 B 45°N 132° E
Kharkov 39 2 L 49°N 36° E
Khartoum 46 3 G 15°N 32° E
Khios 39 4 J 38°N 26° E
Khutse Game Reserve 28 1 C 23°S 24° E
Kidderminster 5 4 D 52°N 2°W
Kiel 36 5 P 54°N 10° E
Kiel Canal 36 5 N 54°N 9° E
Kielder Water 4 1 D 55°N 2°W
Kiev 35 5 G 50°N 30° E
Kigali 46 5 G 1°S 30° E
Kii Channel 24 3 D 33°N 135° E
Kildare 7 3 E 53°N 6°W
Kilimanjaro 46 5 G 3°S 37° E
Kilkee 7 4 B 52°N 9°W
Kilkenny 7 4 D 52°N 7°W
Killarney 7 4 B 52°N 9°W
Killiecrankie, Pass of 6 3 E 56°N 3°W
Killybegs 7 2 C 54°N 8°W
Kilmarnock 6 4 D 55°N 4°W
Kilrush 7 4 B 52°N 9°W
Kimberley, Australia 48 3 D 32°S 141° E
Kimberley, South Africa 28 2 C 28°S 24° E
Kimchaek 43 2 A 40°N 129° E
King Island 48 7 G 39°S 144° E
King's Lynn 4 4 G 52°N 0° E
Kingston 55 4 J 18°N 76°W
Kingston upon Hull 4 3 F 53°N 0°W
Kingston-upon-Thames 5 5 F 51°N 0°W
Kingstown 55 5 M 13°N 61°W
Kingussie 6 2 D 57°N 4°W
Kinross 6 3 E 56°N 3°W
Kinshasa 46 5 E 4°S 15° E
Kintyre 6 4 C 55°N 5°W
Kintyre, Mull of 6 4 C 55°N 5°W
Kinyeti 26 2 A 4°N 33° E
Kiribati 49 7 K 5°S 176° E
Kiritimati 49 7 N 1°N 157°W
Kirkcaldy 6 3 E 56°N 3°W
Kirkcudbright 6 5 D 54°N 4°W
Kirkenes 35 2 F 69°N 30° E
Kirkwall 6 6 E 58°N 2°W
Kirov 40 5 D 54°N 34° E
Kiruna 35 2 E 67°N 20° E
Kisangani 46 4 F 0°N 25° E
Kisii 26 3 A 0°S 34° E
Kismayu 46 5 H 0°S 42° E
Kisumu 26 3 A 0°S 34° E
Kitakyushu 24 3 B 33°N 130° E
Kitale 26 2 B 1°N 35° E
Kitwe 46 6 F 12°S 28° E
Klaipėda 35 4 E 55°N 21° E
Knock 7 3 C 53°N 8°W
Knockmealdown Mountains 7 4 C 52°N 8°W
Kobe 24 2 D 34°N 135° E
Koblenz 36 7 M 50°N 7° E

Kochi	24	3 C	33°N	133° E
Kofu	24	2 F	35°N	138° E
Kola Peninsula	35	2 H	67°N	38° E
Kolkata	44	4 G	22°N	88° E
Kolyma Range	41	16 C	63°N	157° E
Kompasberg	28	3 C	31°S	24° E
Konya	39	4 K	37°N	32° E
Korea Strait	43	4 A	34°N	129° E
Korea, North	45	2 L	40°N	127° E
Korea, South	45	3 L	36°N	128° E
Kos	39	4 J	36°N	27° E
Kosciuszko, Mount	48	7 H	36°S	148° E
Košice	39	2 H	48°N	21° E
Kosovo	39	3 H	42°N	21° E
Kota Kinabalu	45	6 K	6°N	116° E
Kotlas	40	5 C	61°N	46° E
Kraai →	28	3 D	30°S	26° E
Kraków	35	5 D	50°N	19° E
Krasnodar	39	2 L	45°N	39° E
Krasnovodsk	40	6 E	40°N	52° E
Krasnoyarsk	41	10 D	56°N	93° E
Kristiansand	35	4 B	58°N	8° E
Kristiansund	35	3 B	63°N	7° E
Krivoy Rog	39	2 K	47°N	33° E
Kroonstad	28	2 D	27°S	27° E
Kruger National Park	29	1 E	23°S	31° E
Krugersdorp	28	2 D	26°S	27° E
Kuala Lumpur	45	6 J	3°N	101° E
Kucing	45	6 K	1°N	110° E
Kumamoto	24	3 B	32°N	130° E
Kumasi	47	10 K	6°N	1°W
Kunlun Shan	44	3 G	36°N	86° E
Kunming	45	4 J	25°N	102° E
Kuopio	35	3 F	62°N	27° E
Kurashiki	24	2 C	34°N	133° E
Kurayoshi	24	2 C	35°N	133° E
Kure	24	2 C	34°N	132° E
Kuril Islands	49	3 H	45°N	150° E
Kuril Trench	49	3 H	44°N	153° E
Kursk	39	1 L	51°N	36° E
Kuruman	28	2 C	26°S	20° E
Kuruman →	28	2 C	26°S	20° E
Kurume	24	3 B	33°N	130° E
Kuwait	44	4 C	29°N	47° E
KwaMashu	29	2 E	29°S	30° E
Kyle of Lochalsh	6	2 C	57°N	5°W
Kyoga, Lake	26	2 A	1°N	33° E
Kyoto	24	2 D	35°N	135° E
Kyrgyzstan	40	8 E	42°N	75° E
Kyushu	24	3 B	33°N	131° E

La Coruña	37	11 D	43°N	8°W
La Paz, Bolivia	51	5 E	16°S	68°W
La Paz, Mexico	54	3 B	24°N	110°W
La Perouse Strait	43	1 D	45°N	142° E
La Plata	51	7 F	35°S	57°W
La Rochelle	37	9 H	46°N	1°W
La Spezia	22	2 C	44°N	9° E
Labrador	50	4 N	53°N	61°W
Laccadive Islands	44	5 F	10°N	72° E
Ladoga, Lake	35	3 G	61°N	30° E
Lagan →	7	2 F	54°N	5°W
Lagos	47	10 L	6°N	3° E
Lahore	44	3 F	31°N	74° E
Lahti	35	3 F	60°N	25° E
Lairg	6	1 D	58°N	4°W
Lak Dera →	26	2 C	0°N	42° E
Lake District	4	2 C	54°N	3°W
Lakshadweep Islands	44	5 F	10°N	72° E
Lanark	6	4 E	55°N	3°W
Lancashire	9	5 E	53°N	2°W
Lancaster	4	2 D	54°N	2°W
Land's End	5	6 A	50°N	5°W
Lansing	53	2 K	42°N	84°W
Lanzhou	45	3 J	36°N	103° E
Laois	9	5 C	53°N	7°W
Laos	45	5 J	17°N	105° E
Lapland	35	2 F	68°N	24° E
Laptev Sea	41	13 B	76°N	125° E
Largs	6	4 D	55°N	4°W
Larne	7	2 F	54°N	5°W
Las Palmas	46	1 B	28°N	15°W
Las Vegas	52	3 C	36°N	115°W
Latakia	39	4 L	35°N	35° E
Latvia	35	4 E	56°N	24° E
Launceston	48	8 H	41°S	147° E
Lausanne	37	9 M	46°N	6° E
Le Havre	37	8 J	49°N	0° E
Le Mans	37	8 J	48°N	0° E
Lebanon	44	3 B	34°N	36° E
Lee →	7	5 C	51°N	8°W
Leeds	4	3 E	53°N	1°W
Leeward Islands	55	4 M	16°N	63°W
Leicester	5	4 E	52°N	1°W
Leicestershire	9	5 F	52°N	1°W
Leinster	7	3 D	53°N	7°W
Leipzig	36	7 Q	51°N	12° E
Leith Hill	5	5 F	51°N	0°W
Leitrim	9	4 B	54°N	8°W
Lembomboberge	29	1 E	24°S	31° E
Lena →	41	13 B	72°N	126° E
León, Mexico	54	3 D	21°N	101°W
León, Spain	37	11 F	42°N	5°W
Lérida	37	12 J	41°N	0° E
Lerwick	6	8 J	60°N	1°W
Lesbos	39	4 J	39°N	26° E
Lesotho	29	2 D	29°S	28° E
Lesser Antilles	51	2 E	15°N	61°W
Letchworth	5	5 F	51°N	0°W
Lethbridge	52	1 D	49°N	112°W
Letterkenny	7	2 D	54°N	7°W
Lewes	5	6 G	50°N	0° E
Lewis	6	1 B	58°N	6°W
Lhasa	44	4 H	29°N	91° E
Liberia	46	4 C	6°N	9°W
Libreville	46	4 D	0°N	9° E
Libya	46	2 E	27°N	17° E
Libyan Desert	46	2 F	25°N	25° E
Liechtenstein	37	9 N	47°N	9° E
Liepaja	35	4 E	56°N	21° E
Liffey →	7	3 E	53°N	6°W
Ligurian Sea	22	3 B	43°N	9° E
Likasi	46	6 F	10°S	26° E
Lille	37	7 K	50°N	3° E
Lillehammer	35	3 C	61°N	10° E
Lilongwe	46	6 G	14°S	33° E
Lima	51	5 D	12°S	77°W
Limassol	39	5 K	34°N	33° E
Limerick	7	4 C	52°N	8°W
Limoges	37	10 J	45°N	1° E
Limpopo →	47	7 F	25°S	33° E
Linares	37	13 G	38°N	3°W
Lincoln, U.K.	4	3 F	53°N	0°W
Lincoln, U.S.A.	53	2 G	40°N	96°W
Lincolnshire	9	5 F	53°N	0°W
Line Islands	49	8 N	7°N	160°W
Linköping	35	4 D	58°N	15° E
Linz	37	8 Q	48°N	14° E
Lipari Islands	22	5 E	38°N	14° E
Lisbon	37	13 D	38°N	9°W
Lisburn	7	2 E	54°N	6°W
Listowel	7	4 B	52°N	9°W
Lithuania	35	4 E	55°N	24° E
Little Karoo	28	3 C	33°S	21° E
Little Minch	6	2 B	57°N	6°W
Little Ouse →	5	4 G	52°N	0° E
Little Rock	53	4 H	34°N	92°W
Littlehampton	5	6 F	50°N	0°W
Liverpool	4	3 D	53°N	3°W
Liverpool Bay	14	5 E	53°N	3°W
Livingston	6	4 E	55°N	3°W
Livingstone	47	6 F	17°S	25° E
Livorno	22	3 C	43°N	10° E
Lizard	5	7 A	49°N	5°W
Ljubljana	38	2 F	46°N	14° E
Llandovery	5	4 C	51°N	3°W
Llandrindod Wells	5	4 C	52°N	3°W
Llandudno	4	3 C	53°N	3°W
Llanelli	5	5 B	51°N	4°W
Llangollen	4	4 C	52°N	3°W
Lochgilphead	6	3 C	56°N	5°W
Lochy, Loch	6	2 D	57°N	4°W
Lockerbie	6	4 E	55°N	3°W
Lodwar	26	2 B	3°N	35° E
Łódź	35	5 D	51°N	19° E
Lofoten Islands	35	2 C	68°N	15° E
Loire →	37	9 G	47°N	2°W
Lomé	47	10 L	6°N	1° E
Lomond, Loch	6	3 D	56°N	4°W
London	5	5 F	51°N	0°W
Londonderry	7	2 D	55°N	7°W
Londrina	30	7 E	23°S	51°W
Long Eaton	4	4 E	52°N	1°W
Longford	7	3 D	53°N	7°W
Loop Head	7	4 B	52°N	9°W
Lorient	37	9 G	47°N	3°W
Lorn, Firth of	6	3 C	56°N	5°W
Los Angeles	52	4 C	34°N	118°W
Los Mochis	54	2 C	25°N	108°W
Loughborough	4	4 E	52°N	1°W
Loughrea	7	3 C	53°N	8°W
Louisiana	53	4 H	30°N	92°W
Louisville	53	3 J	38°N	85°W
Louth (county)	9	5 C	53°N	6°W
Louth, Ireland	7	3 E	53°N	6°W
Louth, U.K.	4	3 F	53°N	0°W
Lower California	54	2 B	28°N	115°W
Lower Lough Erne	7	2 D	54°N	7°W
Lowestoft	5	4 H	52°N	1° E
Luanda	46	5 E	8°S	13° E
Lubango	46	6 E	14°S	13° E
Lübeck	36	6 P	53°N	10° E
Lublin	35	5 E	51°N	22° E
Lubumbashi	46	6 F	11°S	27° E
Luce Bay	6	5 D	54°N	4°W
Lucknow	44	4 G	26°N	81° E
Lüderitz	28	2 L	26°S	15° E
Lugansk	39	2 B	48°N	39° E
Lugnaquilla	7	4 E	52°N	6°W
Lule →	35	2 E	65°N	22° E
Luleå	35	2 E	65°N	22° E
Lundy	5	5 B	51°N	4°W
Lune →	4	2 D	54°N	2°W
Lurgan	7	2 E	54°N	6°W
Lusaka	46	6 F	15°S	28° E
Luton	5	5 F	51°N	0°W
Luxembourg	37	8 M	49°N	6° E
Luzon	45	5 L	16°N	121° E
Lvov	39	2 H	49°N	24° E
Lyme Bay	14	6 E	50°N	2°W
Lyme Regis	5	6 D	50°N	2°W
Lyons	37	10 L	45°N	4° E

Macapá	30	2 E	0°N	51°W
Macau	45	4 K	22°N	113° E
Macclesfield	4	3 D	53°N	2°W
MacDonnell Ranges	48	4 E	23°S	133° E
Macduff	6	2 F	57°N	2°W
Macedonia	39	3 H	41°N	21° E
Maceió	30	4 H	9°S	35°W
Macgillycuddy's Reeks	7	4 B	52°N	9°W
Machakos	26	3 B	1°S	37° E
Machu Picchu	51	5 D	13°S	72°W
Mackay	48	4 H	21°S	149° E
Mackenzie →	50	3 G	69°N	134°W
Madadeni	29	2 E	27°S	30° E
Madagascar	47	6 H	20°S	47° E
Madeira	46	1 B	32°N	17°W
Madeira →	30	3 C	3°S	58°W
Madison	53	2 J	43°N	89°W
Madras = Chennai	44	5 G	13°N	80° E
Madre, Laguna	53	5 G	27°N	97°W
Madrid	37	12 G	40°N	3°W
Madurai	44	6 F	9°N	78° E
Maebashi	24	1 F	36°N	139° E
Mafikeng	28	2 D	25°S	25° E
Magadan	41	16 D	59°N	150° E
Magdalena →	51	3 D	11°N	74°W
Magdeburg	36	6 P	52°N	11° E
Magellan, Strait of	51	9 E	52°S	75°W
Maggiore, Lake	22	2 B	45°N	8° E
Mahajanga	46	6 H	15°S	46° E
Maidenhead	5	5 F	51°N	0°W
Maidstone	5	5 G	51°N	0° E
Maiduguri	47	9 N	12°N	13° E
Maine	53	1 N	45°N	69°W
Mainland, Orkney	6	7 E	59°N	3°W
Mainland, Shetland	6	8 J	60°N	1°W
Maizuru	24	2 D	35°N	135° E
Majorca	37	13 K	39°N	3° E
Makgadikgadi Salt Pans	47	7 F	20°S	25° E
Malacca, Strait of	45	6 H	3°N	101° E
Málaga	37	14 F	36°N	4°W
Malawi	46	6 G	11°S	34° E
Malawi, Lake	46	6 G	12°S	34° E
Malay Peninsula	45	6 J	7°N	100° E
Malaysia	45	6 J	5°N	110° E
Maldives	44	6 F	5°N	73° E
Malé	44	6 F	4°N	73° E
Mali	46	3 C	17°N	3°W
Malin Head	7	1 D	55°N	7°W
Malindi	26	3 C	3°S	40° E
Mallaig	6	2 C	57°N	5°W
Mallow	7	4 C	52°N	8°W
Malmö	36	5 Q	55°N	12° E
Malta	38	4 F	35°N	14° E
Malton	4	2 F	54°N	0°W
Mamoré →	30	5 B	10°S	65°W
Man, Isle of	4	2 B	54°N	4°W
Managua	54	5 G	12°N	86°W
Manama	44	4 D	26°N	50° E
Manaus	30	3 B	3°S	60°W
Manchester	4	3 D	53°N	2°W
Manchuria	45	2 L	44°N	126° E
Mandalay	45	4 H	22°N	96° E
Manila	45	5 L	14°N	121° E
Manisa	39	4 J	38°N	27° E
Manizales	55	6 J	5°N	75°W
Mannheim	37	8 N	49°N	8° E
Mansfield	4	3 E	53°N	1°W
Manyara, Lake	26	3 B	3°S	35° E
Manzhouli	41	12 E	49°N	117° E
Manzini	29	2 E	26°S	31° E
Maputo	47	7 G	25°S	32° E
Maputo, Bahia de	29	1 E	25°S	32° E
Mar del Plata	51	7 F	38°S	57°W
Marabá	30	4 F	5°S	49°W
Maracaibo	55	5 K	10°N	71°W
Maracaibo, Lake	55	6 K	9°N	71°W
Maracay	55	5 L	10°N	67°W
Maranhão	30	4 F	5°S	46°W
Marathon	39	4 H	38°N	23° E
Marbella	37	14 F	36°N	4°W
Maree, Loch	6	2 C	57°N	5°W
Margate	5	5 H	51°N	1° E
Mariana Trench	49	6 G	13°N	145° E
Marico →	28	1 D	23°S	26° E
Mariental	28	1 B	24°S	18° E
Mariupol	39	2 L	47°N	37° E
Maroua	47	9 N	10°N	14° E
Marquesas Islands	49	8 Q	9°S	140°W
Marrakesh	46	1 C	31°N	8°W
Marsabit	26	2 B	2°N	38° E
Marseilles	37	11 L	43°N	5° E
Marshall Islands	49	6 K	9°N	171° E
Martinique	55	5 M	14°N	61°W
Maryland	53	3 L	39°N	76°W
Masaka	26	3 A	0°S	31° E
Maseru	28	2 D	29°S	27° E
Mashhad	40	6 F	36°N	59° E
Mask, Lough	7	3 B	53°N	9°W
Massachusetts	53	2 M	42°N	72°W
Massif Central	37	10 K	44°N	3° E
Masuda	24	2 B	34°N	131° E
Matamoros	54	2 E	25°N	97°W
Matanzas	55	3 H	23°N	81°W
Matlock	4	3 E	53°N	1°W
Mato Grosso	30	5 D	14°S	55°W
Mato Grosso do Sul	30	6 D	18°S	55°W
Mato Grosso, Plateau of	51	5 F	15°S	54°W
Matroosberg	28	3 B	33°S	19° E
Matsue	24	2 C	35°N	133° E
Matsumoto	24	1 F	36°N	138° E
Matsuto	24	1 E	36°N	136° E
Matsuyama	24	3 C	33°N	132° E
Maturín	55	6 M	9°N	63°W
Mauna Kea	52	9 S	19°N	155°W
Mauna Loa	52	9 S	19°N	155°W
Mauritania	46	3 B	20°N	10°W
Mauritius	61	4 M	20°S	57° E
Mayo	9	5 B	53°N	9°W
Mayotte	46	6 H	12°S	45° E
Mazatlán	54	3 C	23°N	106°W
Mbabane	29	2 E	26°S	31° E
Mbale	26	2 A	1°N	34° E
Mbandaka	46	5 E	0°N	18° E
Mbeya	46	5 G	8°S	33° E
Mbini	46	4 E	1°N	10° E
Mbuji-Mayi	46	5 F	6°S	23° E
McKinley, Mount	50	3 D	63°N	151°W
Mead, Lake	52	3 D	36°N	114°W
Meath	9	5 C	53°N	6°W
Mecca	44	4 B	21°N	39° E
Medan	45	6 H	3°N	98° E
Medellín	55	6 J	6°N	75°W
Medina	44	4 B	24°N	39° E
Mediterranean Sea	38	4 F	35°N	15° E
Medway Towns	9	6 G	51°N	0° E
Medway →	5	5 G	51°N	0° E
Meekatharra	48	5 B	26°S	118° E
Mekong →	45	5 J	9°N	106° E
Melanesia	49	8 H	4°S	155° E
Melbourne	48	7 H	37°S	145° E
Melilla	38	4 C	35°N	2°W
Melrhir, Chott	38	5 E	34°N	6° E
Melton Mowbray	4	4 F	52°N	0°W
Melville Island	48	2 E	11°S	131° E
Memphis	53	3 J	35°N	90°W
Mendip Hills	5	5 D	51°N	2°W
Mendocino, Cape	52	2 B	40°N	124°W
Mendoza	51	7 E	32°S	68°W
Mérida	54	3 G	20°N	89°W
Mérida, Cordillera de	55	6 K	9°N	71°W
Merrick	6	4 D	55°N	4°W
Mersey →	14	5 E	53°N	2°W
Merseyside	9	5 E	53°N	2°W
Mersin	39	4 K	36°N	34° E
Merthyr Tydfil	5	5 C	51°N	3°W
Meru, Kenya	26	2 B	0°N	37° E
Meru, Tanzania	26	2 B	3°S	36° E
Mesopotamia	44	3 C	33°N	44° E
Messina, Italy	22	5 E	38°N	15° E
Messina, South Africa	29	1 E	22°S	30° E
Messina, Strait of	39	4 G	38°N	15° E
Metz	37	8 M	49°N	6° E
Meuse →	37	8 L	50°N	5° E
Mexicali	54	1 B	32°N	115°W
Mexico	54	3 D	25°N	105°W
Mexico, Gulf of	54	2 E	25°N	90°W
Miami	53	5 K	25°N	80°W
Michigan	53	2 J	44°N	85°W
Michigan, Lake	53	2 J	44°N	87°W
Micronesia	49	7 J	0°N	163° E
Micronesia, Federated States of	49	7 G	9°N	150° E
Middelburg	28	3 D	31°S	25° E
Middlesbrough	4	2 E	54°N	1°W
Midlothian	9	4 E	55°N	3°W
Midway Islands	49	5 K	28°N	177°W
Midwest	53	2 J	42°N	90°W
Milan	22	2 B	45°N	9° E
Milford Haven	5	5 A	51°N	5°W
Milltown Malbay	7	4 B	52°N	9°W
Milton Keynes	5	4 F	52°N	0°W
Milwaukee	53	2 J	43°N	87°W
Milwaukee Deep	51	2 E	19°N	68°W
Minas Gerais	30	6 F	18°S	46°W
Mindanao	45	6 L	8°N	125° E
Mindanao Trench	49	6 E	12°N	126° E
Minehead	5	5 C	51°N	3°W
Minna	47	10 M	9°N	6° E
Minneapolis	53	2 H	44°N	93°W
Minnesota	53	1 H	46°N	94°W
Minorca	37	12 L	40°N	4° E
Minsk	35	5 F	53°N	27° E
Mississippi	53	4 J	33°N	90°W
Mississippi River Delta	53	5 J	29°N	89°W
Mississippi →	53	5 J	29°N	89°W
Missouri	53	3 H	38°N	92°W
Missouri →	53	3 H	38°N	90°W
Mitchell →	48	3 G	15°S	141° E
Mito	24	1 G	36°N	140° E
Miyake Islands	24	2 F	34°N	139° E
Miyakonojo	24	4 B	31°N	131° E
Miyazaki	24	3 B	32°N	131° E
Mjøsa	36	2 N	60°N	11° E
Mmabatho	28	2 D	25°S	25° E
Modena	22	2 C	44°N	10° E
Mogadishu	46	4 H	2°N	45° E
Mogalakwena →	29	1 D	22°S	28° E
Mogilev	35	5 G	53°N	30° E
Mojave Desert	52	3 C	35°N	116°W
Mold	4	3 C	53°N	3°W
Moldova	39	2 J	47°N	28° E
Moloko →	29	1 D	23°S	27° E
Molopo →	28	2 C	27°S	20° E
Moluccas	45	7 L	1°S	127° E
Mombasa	26	3 B	4°S	39° E
Monaco	37	11 M	43°N	7° E
Monaghan	7	2 E	54°N	6°W
Mongolia	41	10 E	47°N	103° E
Mongolia, Plateau of	45	2 J	44°N	100° E
Monmouth	5	5 D	51°N	2°W
Monrovia	46	4 B	6°N	10°W
Montana	52	1 D	47°N	110°W
Montenegro	39	3 G	42°N	19° E
Montería	55	6 J	8°N	75°W
Monterrey	54	2 D	25°N	100°W
Montes Claros	30	6 G	16°S	43°W
Montevideo	51	7 F	34°S	56°W
Montgomery	53	4 J	32°N	86°W
Montpelier	53	2 M	44°N	72°W
Montpellier	37	11 K	43°N	3° E
Montreal	53	1 M	45°N	73°W
Montrose	6	3 F	56°N	2°W
Morar, Loch	6	3 C	56°N	5°W
Morava →	39	3 H	44°N	20° E
Moray Firth	6	2 E	57°N	3°W
Morecambe	4	2 D	54°N	2°W
Morecambe Bay	4	2 C	54°N	3°W
Morocco	46	1 C	32°N	5°W
Moroto	26	2 A	2°N	34° E
Morpeth	4	1 E	55°N	1°W
Moscow	35	4 H	55°N	37° E
Moselle →	37	8 M	50°N	7° E
Moshi	26	3 B	3°S	37° E

Mosselbaai 28 3 C 34°S 22° E
Mossoró 30 4 H 5°S 37°W
Mostaganem 38 4 D 35°N 0° E
Mosul 44 3 C 36°N 43° E
Motherwell 6 4 E 55°N 4°W
Moulmein 45 5 H 16°N 97° E
Mount Gambier 48 7 G 37°S 140° E
Mount Isa 48 4 F 20°S 139° E
Mourne Mountains 7 2 E 54°N 6°W
Mourne → 7 2 D 54°N 7°W
Moville 7 1 D 55°N 7°W
Mozambique 47 6 G 19°S 35° E
Mozambique Channel 47 7 H 17°S 42° E
Mpumalanga 29 2 E 29°S 30° E
Mudanjiang 43 2 A 44°N 129° E
Mulhacén 38 4 C 37°N 3°W
Mulka 48 5 F 28°S 138° E
Mull 6 3 C 56°N 6°W
Mullet Peninsula 7 2 A 54°N 10°W
Mullingar 7 3 D 53°N 7°W
Multan 44 3 F 30°N 71° E
Mumbai = Bombay 44 5 F 18°N 72° E
Munich 37 8 P 48°N 11° E
Münster, Germany 36 7M 51°N 7° E
Munster, Ireland 7 4 B 52°N 9°W
Murchison Falls 26 2 A 2°N 31° E
Murcia 37 13 H 38°N 1°W
Murmansk 35 2 G 68°N 33° E
Murray → 48 6 G 35°S 139° E
Murrumbidgee → 48 6 H 34°S 143° E
Muscat 44 4 D 23°N 58° E
Musgrave Ranges 48 5 E 26°S 132° E
Musoma 26 3 A 1°S 33° E
Musselburgh 6 4 E 55°N 3°W
Mwanza 26 3 A 2°S 32° E
Mweru, Lake 46 5 G 9°S 28° E

Naas 7 3 E 53°N 6°W
Nafud Desert 44 4 C 29°N 40° E
Nagano 24 1 F 36°N 138° E
Nagasaki 24 3 A 32°N 129° E
Nagoya 24 2 E 35°N 136° E
Nagpur 44 4 F 21°N 79° E
Nairn 6 2 E 57°N 3°W
Nairobi 26 3 B 1°S 36° E
Nakuru 26 3 B 0°S 36° E
Namaland 28 2 B 26°S 17° E
Namib Desert 47 7 E 22°S 15° E
Namib-Naukluft Park 28 1 B 24°S 15° E
Namibia 47 7 E 22°S 18° E
Nan Shan 45 3 H 38°N 99° E
Nanao 24 1 E 37°N 137° E
Nanchang 45 4 K 28°N 115° E
Nancy 37 8M 48°N 6° E
Nanjing 45 3 K 32°N 118° E
Nanking = Nanjing 45 3 K 32°N 118° E
Nanning 45 4 J 22°N 108° E
Nantes 37 9 H 47°N 1°W
Naples 22 4 D 40°N 14° E
Narvik 35 2 D 68°N 17° E
Nashville 53 3 J 36°N 86°W
Nassau 55 2 J 25°N 77°W
Nasser, Lake 46 2 G 23°N 32° E
Natal 30 4 H 5°S 35°W
Natron, Lake 26 3 B 2°S 36° E
Nauru 49 8 K 1°S 166° E
Ndjamena 46 3 E 12°N 14° E
Ndola 46 6 F 13°S 28° E
Ndoto Mountains 26 2 B 2°N 37° E
Neagh, Lough 7 2 E 54°N 6°W
Neath 5 5 C 51°N 3°W
Nebraska 52 2 F 41°N 99°W
Negro → 30 3 C 3°S 60°W
Neisse → 36 7 R 52°N 14° E
Nelson, New Zealand 48 11M 41°S 173° E
Nelson, U.K. 4 3 D 53°N 2°W
Nelspruit 29 2 E 25°S 30° E
Neman → 35 5 E 55°N 21° E
Nene → 4 4 G 52°N 0° E
Nepal 44 4 G 28°N 84° E
Ness, Loch 6 2 D 57°N 4°W
Netherlands 36 6 L 52°N 5° E
Netherlands Antilles 55 5 L 12°N 69°W
Nevada 52 3 C 39°N 117°W
New Caledonia 49 10 J 21°S 165° E
New Delhi 44 4 F 28°N 77° E
New England 53 2M 43°N 73°W
New Forest 5 6 E 50°N 1°W
New Guinea 49 8 F 4°S 136° E
New Hampshire 53 2M 44°N 71°W
New Jersey 53 2M 40°N 74°W
New Mexico 52 4 E 34°N 106°W
New Orleans 53 5 J 30°N 90°W
New Siberian Islands 41 14 B 75°N 140° E
New South Wales 48 6 H 33°S 146° E
New York 53 2M 42°N 76°W
New Zealand 48 11M 40°S 176° E
Newark 4 3 F 53°N 0°W
Newbury 5 5 E 51°N 1°W
Newcastle-under-Lyme 4 3 D 53°N 2°W
Newcastle-upon-Tyne 4 2 E 54°N 1°W
Newcastle West 7 4 B 52°N 9°W
Newcastle, Australia 48 6 J 33°S 151° E
Newcastle, U.K. 36 5 H 54°N 1°W
Newfoundland 50 5 P 53°N 58°W
Newhaven 5 6 G 50°N 0° E
Newman 48 4 B 23°S 119° E
Newport, Isle of Wight 5 6 E 50°N 1°W
Newport, Wales 5 5 D 51°N 3°W
Newquay 5 6 A 50°N 5°W
Newry 7 2 E 54°N 6°W
Newton Stewart 6 5 D 54°N 4°W
Newtown 5 4 C 52°N 3°W
Newtownards 7 2 F 54°N 5°W

Niagara Falls 50 5M 43°N 79°W
Niamey 47 9 L 13°N 2° E
Nicaragua 54 5 G 11°N 85°W
Nicaragua, Lake 54 5 G 12°N 85°W
Nice 37 11M 43°N 7° E
Nicobar Islands 44 6 H 9°N 93° E
Nicosia 39 4 K 35°N 33° E
Nidd → 4 2 E 54°N 1°W
Niger 46 3 D 17°N 10° E
Niger Delta 47 11M 4°N 5° E
Niger → 47 10M 5°N 6° E
Nigeria 47 10M 8°N 8° E
Nii Islands 24 2 F 34°N 139° E
Niihama 24 3 C 33°N 133° E
Nikolayev 39 2 K 46°N 32° E
Nile → 46 2 G 30°N 31° E
Nîmes 37 11 L 43°N 4° E
Nith → 6 4 E 55°N 3°W
Nizhniy Novgorod 40 5 D 56°N 44° E
Nobeoka 24 3 B 32°N 131° E
Nogata 24 3 B 33°N 130° E
Nore → 7 4 D 52°N 7°W
Norfolk, U.K. 9 5 G 52°N 1° E
Norfolk, U.S.A. 53 3 L 36°N 76°W
Norilsk 41 9 C 69°N 88° E
Norrköping 35 4 D 58°N 16° E
North America 50 5 K 40°N 100°W
North Berwick 6 3 F 56°N 2°W
North Cape, New Zealand 48 9M 34°S 173° E
North Cape, Norway 35 1 F 71°N 25° E
North Carolina 53 3 K 35°N 80°W
North Dakota 52 1 F 47°N 100°W
North Downs 5 5 G 51°N 0° E
North Dvina → 40 5 C 64°N 40° E
North Eastern Province 26 2 C 1°N 40° E
North Esk → 6 3 F 56°N 2°W
North Foreland 14 6 G 51°N 1° E
North Island 48 10M 38°S 175° E
North Korea 45 2 L 40°N 127° E
North Magnetic Pole 56 1 L 77°N 102°W
North Minch 6 1 C 58°N 5°W
North Pole 56 1 B 90°N 0°W
North Ronaldsay 6 7 F 59°N 2°W
North Sea 36 4 K 56°N 4° E
North Tyne → 4 1 D 54°N 2°W
North Uist 6 2 A 57°N 7°W
North West Cape 48 4 A 21°S 114° E
North West Highlands 6 2 C 57°N 5°W
North York Moors 4 2 F 54°N 0°W
North Yorkshire 9 4 F 54°N 1°W
Northallerton 4 2 E 54°N 1°W
Northampton 5 4 F 52°N 0°W
Northamptonshire 9 5 F 52°N 0°W
Northern Ireland 7 2 E 54°N 7°W
Northern Marianas 49 6 G 17°N 145° E
Northern Territory 48 4 E 20°S 133° E
Northumberland 9 4 E 55°N 2°W
Norway 35 3 C 63°N 11° E
Norwich 4 4 H 52°N 1° E
Noss Head 6 1 E 58°N 3°W
Nossob → 28 2 C 26°S 20° E
Nottingham 4 4 E 52°N 1°W
Nottinghamshire 9 5 F 53°N 1°W
Nouakchott 46 3 B 18°N 15°W
Nova Iguaçu 30 7 G 22°S 43°W
Nova Scotia 50 5 N 45°N 63°W
Novara 22 2 B 45°N 8° E
Novaya Zemlya 40 6 B 75°N 56° E
Novgorod 35 4 G 58°N 31° E
Novokuznetsk 40 9 D 53°N 87° E
Novosibirsk 40 9 D 55°N 83° E
Nuevo Laredo 54 2 E 27°N 99°W
Nullarbor Plain 48 6 D 31°S 129° E
Numazu 24 2 F 35°N 138° E
Nuneaton 5 4 E 52°N 1°W
Nuremburg 37 8 P 49°N 11° E
Nuuk 50 3 P 64°N 51°W
Nuweveldberge 28 3 C 32°S 21° E
Nyanza Province 26 2 A 0°S 34° E
Nyeri 26 3 B 0°S 36° E

Oaxaca 54 4 E 17°N 96°W
Ob → 40 7 C 66°N 69° E
Ob, Gulf of 40 8 C 69°N 73° E
Oban 6 3 C 56°N 5°W
Odawara 24 2 F 35°N 139° E
Odense 35 5 P 55°N 10° E
Oder → 36 6 R 53°N 14° E
Odessa 39 2 K 46°N 30° E
Offaly 9 5 C 53°N 7°W
Ogaki 24 2 E 35°N 136° E
Ogbomosho 47 10 L 8°N 4° E
Ogooué → 46 5 D 1°S 9° E
Ohio 53 2 K 40°N 82°W
Ohio → 53 3 J 36°N 89°W
Oita 24 3 B 33°N 131° E
Okavango Swamps 47 6 F 18°S 22° E
Okaya 24 1 F 36°N 138° E
Okayama 24 2 C 34°N 133° E
Okazaki 24 2 E 34°N 137° E
Okeechobee, Lake 63 5 K 27°N 80°W
Okhotsk 41 15 D 59°N 143° E
Okhotsk, Sea of 41 15 D 55°N 145° E
Oki Islands 24 1 C 36°N 133° E
Oklahoma 52 3 G 35°N 97°W
Oklahoma City 52 3 G 35°N 97°W
Olbia 22 4 B 40°N 9° E
Oldenburg 36 6 N 53°N 8° E
Oldham 4 3 D 53°N 2°W
Olifants → 28 2 B 25°S 19° E
Olympia 52 1 B 47°N 122°W
Olympus, Mount 39 3 H 40°N 22° E
Omagh 7 2 D 54°N 7°W
Oman 44 4 D 23°N 58° E
Oman, Gulf of 44 4 D 24°N 58° E
Omdurman 46 3 G 15°N 32° E
Omiya 24 2 F 35°N 139° E
Omsk 40 8 D 55°N 73° E
Omuta 24 3 B 33°N 130° E
Onega → 35 3 H 63°N 37° E
Onega, Lake 35 3 H 62°N 35° E
Onitsha 47 10M 6°N 6° E
Ontario, Lake 53 2 L 43°N 78°W
Oporto 37 12 D 41°N 8°W
Oran 46 1 C 35°N 0°W
Orange → 28 2 B 28°S 16° E
Ørebro 35 4 D 59°N 15° E
Oregon 52 2 B 44°N 121°W
Orense 37 11 E 42°N 7°W
Orinoco → 55 6M 9°N 61°W
Orkney Isles 6 7 E 59°N 3°W
Orlando 53 5 K 28°N 81°W
Orléans 37 9 J 47°N 1° E
Ormskirk 4 3 D 53°N 2°W
Osaka 24 2 D 34°N 135° E
Osizweni 29 2 E 27°S 30° E
Oslo 35 4 C 59°N 10° E
Osnabrück 36 6 N 52°N 8° E
Østersund 35 3 C 63°N 14° E
Osumi Channel 24 4 B 30°N 131° E
Oswestry 4 4 C 52°N 3°W
Otranto, Strait of 22 4 G 40°N 18° E
Otsu 24 2 D 35°N 135° E
Ottawa 53 1 L 45°N 75°W
Ouagadougou 47 9 K 12°N 1°W
Oujda 38 5 C 34°N 1°W
Oulu 35 3 F 65°N 25° E
Oulu, Lake 35 3 F 64°N 27° E
Ouse →, Cambridgeshire 5 4 F 52°N 0° E
Ouse →, Sussex 5 5 G 50°N 0° E
Ouse →, Yorkshire 4 3 E 53°N 0°W
Outer Hebrides 6 2 A 57°N 7°W
Oxford 5 5 E 51°N 1°W
Oxfordshire 9 6 F 51°N 1°W
Oyo 47 10 L 7°N 3° E
Ozark Plateau 53 3 H 37°N 93°W
Ozarks, Lake of the 53 3 H 38°N 92°W

Pacaraima, Sierra 55 7M 4°N 63°W
Pacific Ocean 49 7M 10°N 140°W
Padang 45 7 J 1°S 100° E
Padua 22 2 C 45°N 11° E
Paisley 6 4 D 55°N 4°W
Pakistan 44 4 E 30°N 70° E
Palau 49 7 F 7°N 134° E
Palawan 45 6 K 9°N 118° E
Palembang 45 7 J 3°S 104° E
Palermo 22 5 D 38°N 13° E
Palma 37 13 K 10°S 40° E
Palmerston North 48 11 N 40°S 175° E
Palmira 55 7 J 3°N 76°W
Pamir 44 3 F 37°N 73° E
Pampas 51 7 E 35°S 63°W
Panama 55 6 H 8°N 79°W
Panama Canal 51 3 C 9°N 79°W
Panama, Gulf of 55 6 J 8°N 79°W
Panama, Isthmus of 55 6 J 9°N 79°W
Pantelleria 22 6 D 36°N 11° E
Papua New Guinea 49 8 G 8°S 145° E
Pará 30 3 E 3°S 52°W
Paraguay 51 6 F 23°S 57°W
Paraguay → 51 6 F 27°S 58°W
Paraíba 30 4 H 7°S 36°W
Parakou 47 10 L 9°N 2° E
Paramaribo 51 3 F 5°N 55°W
Paraná 30 7 E 24°S 51°W
Paraná → 51 6 F 33°S 59°W
Pare Mountains 26 3 B 4°S 37° E
Paris 37 8 K 48°N 2° E
Parma 22 2 C 44°N 10° E
Parnaiba → 30 3 G 3°S 41°W
Parow 28 3 B 33°S 18° E
Passo Fundo 30 8 E 28°S 52°W
Patagonia 51 8 E 45°S 69°W
Pate Island 26 3 C 2°S 41° E
Patna 44 4 G 25°N 85° E
Patrai 39 4 H 38°N 21° E
Pau 37 11 H 43°N 0°W
Peak, The 14 5 F 53°N 1°W
Pecos → 54 2 D 29°N 101°W
Peebles 6 4 E 55°N 3°W
Peking = Beijing 45 3 K 39°N 116° E
Peloponnese 39 4 H 37°N 22° E
Pelotas 30 9 E 31°S 52°W
Pemba Island 46 5 G 5°S 39° E
Pembroke 5 5 B 51°N 4°W
Pennines 4 2 D 54°N 2°W
Pennsylvania 53 2 L 40°N 77°W
Penrith 4 2 D 54°N 2°W
Pentland Firth 6 1 E 58°N 3°W
Penza 40 5 D 53°N 45° E
Penzance 5 6 A 50°N 5°W
Pereira 55 7 J 4°N 75°W
Perm 40 6 D 58°N 56° E
Pernambuco 30 4 H 8°S 37°W
Perpignan 37 11 K 42°N 2° E
Persian Gulf = The Gulf 44 4 D 27°N 50° E
Perth, Australia 48 6 B 31°S 115° E
Perth, U.K. 6 3 E 56°N 3°W
Peru 51 4 D 4°S 75°W
Perugia 22 3 D 43°N 12° E
Pescara 22 3 D 42°N 14° E
Peterborough 5 4 F 52°N 0°W
Peterhead 6 2 G 57°N 1°W
Peterlee 4 2 E 54°N 1°W
Petrozavodsk 35 3 G 61°N 34° E
Philadelphia 53 2 L 40°N 75°W
Philippines 45 5 L 12°N 123° E
Phnom Penh 45 5 J 11°N 104° E
Phoenix 52 4 D 33°N 112°W
Phoenix Islands 49 8 L 3°S 172°W
Piacenza 22 2 B 45°N 9° E
Piauí 30 4 G 7°S 43°W
Pierre 52 2 F 44°N 100°W
Pietermaritzburg 29 2 E 29°S 30° E
Pietersburg 29 1 D 23°S 29° E
Pindus Mountains 39 4 H 40°N 21° E
Piracicaba 30 7 F 22°S 47°W
Pisa 22 3 C 43°N 10° E
Pitcairn Island 49 10 Q 25°S 130°W
Pitlochry 6 3 E 56°N 3°W
Pittsburgh 53 2 K 40°N 79°W
Ploesti 39 3 J 44°N 26° E
Plovdiv 39 3 H 42°N 24° E
Plymouth 5 6 B 50°N 4°W
Plynlimon 5 4 C 52°N 3°W
Plzen 36 8 Q 49°N 13° E
Po → 22 2 C 44°N 12° E
Pobedy, Peak 40 8 E 42°N 79° E
Pointe-à-Pitre 55 4M 16°N 61°W
Pointe Noire 46 5 E 4°S 11° E
Poitiers 37 9 J 46°N 0° E
Poland 35 5 D 52°N 20° E
Polynesia 49 8M 10°S 162°W
Pompei 38 3 F 40°N 14° E
Ponta Grossa 30 8 E 25°S 50°W
Pontchartrain Lake 53 4 J 30°N 90°W
Pontianak 45 7 J 0°S 109° E
Pontine Mountains 39 3 L 41°N 35° E
Pontypool 5 5 C 51°N 3°W
Pontypridd 5 5 C 51°N 3°W
Poole 5 6 D 50°N 1°W
Poopo, Lake 51 5 E 18°S 67°W
Popocatepetl 54 4 E 19°N 98°W
Pori 35 3 E 61°N 21° E
Port-au-Prince 55 4 K 18°N 72°W
Port Augusta 48 6 F 32°S 137° E
Port Elizabeth 28 3 D 33°S 25° E
Port Harcourt 47 11M 4°N 7° E
Port Hedland 48 4 B 20°S 118° E
Port Laoise 7 3 D 53°N 7°W
Port Lincoln 48 6 F 34°S 135° E
Port Moresby 49 8 G 9°S 147° E
Port Nolloth 28 2 B 29°S 16° E
Port of Spain 55 5M 10°N 61°W
Port Pirie 48 6 F 33°S 138° E
Port Said 39 5 K 31°N 32° E
Port Sudan 46 3 G 19°N 37° E
Port Talbot 5 5 C 51°N 3°W
Port Vila 49 9 J 17°S 168° E
Portadown 7 2 E 54°N 6°W
Porthmadog 4 4 B 52°N 4°W
Portland Bill 5 6 D 50°N 2°W
Portland, Maine 53 2M 43°N 70°W
Portland, Oregon 52 1 B 45°N 122°W
Pôrto Alegre 30 9 E 30°S 51°W
Porto Novo 47 10 L 6°N 2° E
Pôrto Velho 30 4 C 8°S 63°W
Portree 6 2 B 57°N 6°W
Portsmouth 5 6 E 50°N 1°W
Portugal 37 13 E 40°N 8°W
Potomac → 53 3 L 38°N 76°W
Potsdam 36 6 Q 52°N 13° E
Poulaphouca Reservoir 7 3 E 53°N 6°W
Powys 9 5 E 52°N 3°W
Poznań 35 5 D 52°N 16° E
Prague 36 7 R 50°N 14° E
Preston 4 3 D 53°N 2°W
Pretoria 29 2 D 25°S 28° E
Pripet → 39 1 J 51°N 30° E
Pskov 35 4 F 57°N 28° E
Puebla 54 4 E 19°N 98°W
Puerto Barrios 54 4 G 15°N 88°W
Puerto Rico 55 4 L 18°N 66°W
Pune 44 5 F 18°N 73° E
Punta Arenas 56 L 53°S 71°W
Purus → 30 3 C 3°S 61°W
Pusan 45 3 L 35°N 129° E
Putumayo → 30 3 B 3°S 67°W
Pwllheli 4 4 B 52°N 4°W
Pyongyang 45 3 L 39°N 125° E
Pyrenees 37 11 J 42°N 0° E

Qandahar 44 3 E 31°N 65° E
Qatar 44 4 D 25°N 51° E
Qingdao 45 3 L 36°N 120° E
Qiqihar 45 2 L 47°N 124° E
Quebec 53 1M 46°N 71°W
Queen Charlotte Islands 50 4 F 53°N 132°W
Queen Elizabeth Islands 50 1 H 76°N 95°W
Queen Maud Land 56 B 72°S 12° E
Queensland 48 4 G 22°S 142° E
Queenstown 28 3 D 31°S 26° E
Querétaro 54 3 D 20°N 100°W
Quetta 44 3 E 30°N 66° E
Quezon City 45 5 L 14°N 121° E
Quibdo 55 6 J 5°N 76°W
Quilpie 48 5 G 26°S 144° E
Quimper 37 9 F 48°N 4°W
Quito 51 4 D 0°S 78°W

Rabat 46 1 C 34°N 6°W
Race, Cape 50 5 P 46°N 53°W
Rainier, Mount 52 1 B 46°N 121°W
Rangoon 45 5 H 16°N 96° E
Rannoch, Loch 6 3 D 56°N 4°W
Rathlin Island 7 1 E 55°N 6°W

Ravenna 22 2D 44°N 12° E
Reading 5 5F 51°N 0°W
Recife 30 4H 8°S 35°W
Red Sea 46 2G 25°N 36° E
Red → 53 4H 31°N 91°W
Redcar 4 2E 54°N 1°W
Redditch 5 4E 52°N 1°W
Ree, Lough 7 3D 53°N 8°W
Regensburg 37 8Q 49°N 12° E
Reggio di Calabria 22 5E 38°N 15° E
Reggio nell' Emilia 22 2C 44°N 10° E
Rehoboth 28 1B 23°S 17° E
Reigate 5 5F 51°N 0°W
Reims 37 8L 49°N 4° E
Rennes 37 8H 48°N 1°W
Réunion 61 4M 21°S 56° E
Reykjavík 56 1H 64°N 21°W
Reynosa 54 2E 26°N 98°W
Rhine → 36 7M 51°N 6° E
Rhode Island 53 2M 41°N 71°W
Rhodes 39 4J 36°N 28° E
Rhodope Mountains 39 3H 41°N 24° E
Rhondda 5 5C 51°N 3°W
Rhône → 37 11L 43°N 4° E
Rhyl 4 3C 53°N 3°W
Ribble → 4 3D 54°N 2°W
Ribeirão Prêto 30 7F 21°S 47°W
Richards Bay 29 2E 28°S 32° E
Richmond, U.K. 4 2E 54°N 1°W
Richmond, U.S.A. 53 3L 37°N 77°W
Richtersveld National Park 28 2B 28°S 17° E
Rift Valley Province 26 2B 0°N 36° E
Riga 35 4E 56°N 24° E
Riga, Gulf of 35 4E 57°N 23° E
Rimini 22 2D 44°N 12° E
Rio Branco 30 4B 9°S 67°W
Rio de Janeiro 30 7G 23°S 43°W
Rio de la Plata → 51 7F 34°S 57°W
Rio Grande, Brazil 30 9E 32°S 52°W
Rio Grande, Mexico 54 3C 23°N 103°W
Rio Grande do Norte 30 3E 3°S 53°W
Rio Grande do Sul 30 9E 30°S 53°W
Rio Grande → 54 2E 25°N 97°W
Ripon 4 2E 54°N 1°W
Rivadavia 51 7E 35°S 62°W
Riviera 22 2B 44°N 8° E
Riyadh 44 4C 24°N 46° E
Rochdale 4 3D 53°N 2°W
Rockhampton 48 4J 23°S 150° E
Rocky Mountains 52 2E 55°N 121°W
Roggeveldberge 28 3C 32°S 20° E
Romania 39 2H 46°N 25° E
Rome 22 4D 41°N 12° E
Romford 5 5G 51°N 0° E
Romney Marsh 5 5G 51°N 0° E
Rondônia 30 5C 11°S 63°W
Rondonópolis 30 6E 16°S 54°W
Roodepoort 28 2D 26°S 27° E
Roraima 30 2C 2°N 61°W
Roraima, Mount 55 6M 5°N 60°W
Rosario 51 7E 33°S 60°W
Roscommon 7 3C 53°N 8°W
Roscrea 7 4D 52°N 7°W
Roseau 55 4M 15°N 61°W
Ross Ice Shelf 56 H 80°S 180° E
Ross-on-Wye 5 5D 51°N 2°W
Ross Sea 56 H 74°S 178° E
Rosslare 7 4E 52°N 6°W
Rostock 36 5Q 54°N 12° E
Rostov 39 2L 47°N 39° E
Rother → 5 5G 50°N 0° E
Rotherham 4 3E 53°N 1°W
Rothesay 6 4C 55°N 5°W
Rotorua 48 10N 38°S 176° E
Rotterdam 36 7L 51°N 4° E
Rouen 37 8J 49°N 1° E
Rousay 6 7E 59°N 3°W
Rovaniemi 35 2F 66°N 25° E
Rugby 5 4E 52°N 1°W
Rum 6 3B 57°N 6°W
Runcorn 4 3D 53°N 2°W
Russia 40 6C 60°N 80° E
Rutland 9 5F 52°N 0°W
Rwanda 46 5G 2°S 30° E
Ryan, Loch 6 5C 55°N 5°W
Rybinsk Reservoir 35 4H 58°N 38° E
Rye → 4 2F 54°N 0°W
Ryukyu Islands 45 4L 26°N 126° E

Saarbrücken 37 8M 49°N 6° E
Saaremaa 35 4E 58°N 22° E
Sabah 45 6K 6°N 117° E
Sabine → 53 5H 29°N 93°W
Sacramento 52 3B 38°N 121°W
Sacramento Mountains 52 4E 32°N 105°W
Sacramento Valley 52 3B 39°N 122°W
Sado 43 3C 38°N 138° E
Sahara Desert 46 2D 25°N 9° E
Saiki 24 3B 32°N 131° E
Saimaa 39 4E 61°N 28° E
Saint Albans 5 5F 51°N 0°W
Saint Andrews 6 3F 56°N 2°W
Saint Austell 5 6B 50°N 4°W
Saint David's Head 5 5A 51°N 5°W
Saint-Étienne 37 10L 45°N 4° E
Saint George's 55 5M 12°N 61°W
Saint George's Channel 7 5E 52°N 6°W
Saint Helena 46 6C 15°S 5°W
Saint Helens 4 3D 53°N 2°W
Saint Helens, Mount 52 1B 46°N 122°W
Saint Helier 5 7D 49°N 2°W
Saint Ives 5 6A 50°N 5°W
Saint John's, Antigua 55 4M 17°N 61°W
Saint John's, Canada 50 5P 47°N 52°W
Saint Kilda 14 3B 57°N 8°W
Saint Kitts & Nevis 55 4M 17°N 62°W
Saint Lawrence → 53 1M 49°N 66°W
Saint Louis 53 3H 38°N 9°W
Saint Lucia 55 5M 14°N 60°W
Saint Lucia, Cape 29 2E 28°S 32° E
Saint Lucia, Lake 29 2E 28°S 32° E
Saint-Malo 37 8H 48°N 2°W
Saint Mary's 5 8J 49°N 6°W
Saint-Nazaire 37 9G 47°N 2°W
Saint Neots 5 7E 52°N 0°W
Saint Paul 53 2H 44°N 93°W
Saint Peter Port 5 7D 49°N 2°W
Saint Petersburg 35 4G 59°N 30° E
Saint Vincent 55 5M 13°N 61°W
Sakai 24 2D 34°N 135° E
Sakhalin 41 15D 51°N 143° E
Salamanca 39 12F 40°N 5°W
Saldanha 28 3B 33°S 17° E
Sale 4 3D 53°N 2°W
Salerno 22 4E 40°N 14° E
Salford 4 3D 53°N 2°W
Salisbury 5 5E 51°N 1°W
Salisbury Plain 5 5E 51°N 1°W
Salt Lake City 52 2D 40°N 111°W
Salto 51 7F 31°S 57°W
Salton Sea 52 4C 33°N 115°W
Salvador 30 5H 13°S 38°W
Salvador, El 54 5G 13°N 89°W
Salween → 45 5H 16°N 97° E
Salzburg 37 9Q 47°N 13° E
Samara 40 6D 53°N 50° E
Samarkand 40 7F 39°N 66° E
Samoa 49 9L 13°S 172°W
Samos 39 4J 37°N 26° E
Samsun 39 3L 41°N 36° E
San Andreas Fault 52 3B 38°N 120°W
San Antonio 52 5G 29°N 98°W
San Bernardino 52 4C 34°N 117°W
San Blas, Cape 53 5J 29°N 85°W
San Cristóbal 55 6K 7°N 72°W
San Diego 52 4C 32°N 117°W
San Francisco 52 3B 37°N 122°W
San Joaquin Valley 52 3B 37°N 121°W
San José 55 6H 9°N 84°W
San Juan, Argentina 51 7E 31°S 68°W
San Juan, Puerto Rico 55 4L 18°N 66°W
San Lucas, Cape 50 7H 22°N 110°W
San Luis Potosí 54 3D 22°N 100°W
San Marino 22 3C 43°N 12° E
San Pedro Sula 54 4G 15°N 88°W
San Salvador 54 5G 13°N 89°W
San Sebastian 37 11H 43°N 1°W
Sana 44 5C 6°S 79°W
Sanaga → 47 11N 3°N 9° E
Sanday 6 7F 59°N 2°W
Sanquhar 6 4E 55°N 3°W
Santa Catarina 30 8F 27°S 48°W
Santa Clara 55 3H 22°N 80°W
Santa Cruz 51 5E 17°S 63°W
Santa Fé, Argentina 51 7E 31°S 60°W
Santa Fe, U.S.A. 52 3E 35°N 105°W
Santander 37 11G 43°N 3°W
Santarém 30 3E 2°S 54°W
Santiago de Compostela 37 11D 42°N 8°W
Santiago de Cuba 55 3J 20°N 75°W
Santiago, Chile 51 7D 33°S 70°W
Santiago, Dominican Republic 55 4K 19°N 70°W
Santo Domingo 55 4L 18°N 69°W
Santos 30 7F 24°S 46°W
São Francisco do Sul 30 8F 26°S 48°W
São Francisco → 30 5H 10°S 36°W
São José do Rio Prêto 30 7F 20°S 49°W
São Luis 30 3G 2°S 44°W
São Paulo 30 7F 23°S 46°W
São Tomé and Principé 46 4D 0°N 6° E
Saône → 37 10L 45°N 4° E
Sapporo 43 2D 43°N 141° E
Sarajevo 39 3G 43°N 18° E
Saratov 40 5D 51°N 46° E
Sarawak 45 6K 2°N 113° E
Sardinia 22 4B 40°N 9° E
Sargasso Sea 55 2K 27°N 72°W
Sarh 46 4E 9°N 18° E
Sark 5 7D 49°N 2°W
Sarmiento 58 8E 45°S 69°W
Sasebo 24 3A 33°N 129° E
Sassari 22 4B 40°N 8° E
Saudi Arabia 44 4C 26°N 44° E
Savannah 53 4K 32°N 81°W
Savannah → 53 4K 32°N 80°W
Sayan Mountains 42 3M 52°N 94° E
Scafell Pike 4 2C 54°N 3°W
Scandinavia 42 4A 64°N 12° E
Scarborough 4 2F 54°N 0°W
Schwarzrand 28 2B 25°S 17° E
Scilly Isles 5 8J 49°N 6°W
Scotland 6 3D 57°N 4°W
Scottish Borders 9 4E 55°N 2°W
Scunthorpe 4 3F 53°N 0°W
Seattle 52 1B 47°N 122°W
Seeheim 28 2B 26°S 17° E
Seine → 37 8J 49°N 0° E
Sekondi-Takoradi 47 11K 4°N 1°W
Selvas 51 4E 6°S 67°W
Semarang 45 7K 7°S 110° E
Sendai 24 4B 31°N 130° E
Senegal 46 3B 14°N 14°W
Sénégal → 46 3B 15°N 16°W
Seoul 45 3L 37°N 126° E
Seram 45 7L 3°S 129° E
Serengeti Plain 26 3A 2°S 35° E
Sergipe 30 5H 10°S 37°W
Serov 40 7D 59°N 60° E
Sese Islands 26 3A 0°S 32° E
Sevastopol 39 3K 44°N 33° E
Severn → 5 5D 51°N 2°W
Severnaya Zemlya 41 10B 79°N 100° E
Seville 37 14F 37°N 6°W
Seychelles 61 4M 5°S 56° E
Sfax 46 1E 34°N 10° E
Shanghai 45 3L 31°N 121° E
Shannon → 7 3C 52°N 9°W
Shapinsay 6 7F 59°N 2°W
Shibele → 46 4H 2°N 44° E
Sheerness 5 5G 51°N 0° E
Sheffield 4 3E 53°N 1°W
Shenyang 45 2L 41°N 123° E
Shetland Isles 6 8J 60°N 1°W
Shikoku 24 3C 33°N 133° E
Shimonoseki 24 3B 33°N 130° E
Shingu 24 3D 33°N 135° E
Shiono, Cape 24 3D 33°N 135° E
Shiraz 44 4D 29°N 52° E
Shizuoka 24 2F 34°N 138° E
Shrewsbury 4 4D 52°N 2°W
Shropshire 9 5E 52°N 2°W
Sian = Xi'an 45 3J 34°N 109° E
Siberia 40 9D 60°N 100° E
Sicily 22 6D 37°N 14° E
Sidmouth 5 6C 50°N 3°W
Sidra, Gulf of 46 1E 31°N 18° E
Siena 22 3C 43°N 11° E
Sierra Blanca 52 4E 31°N 105°W
Sierra Leone 46 4B 9°N 12°W
Sierra Madre 54 2C 16°N 93°W
Sierra Morena 37 13F 38°N 4°W
Sierra Nevada, Spain 37 14F 37°N 3°W
Sierra Nevada, U.S.A. 52 3B 39°N 120°W
Sikhote Alin Range 43 2B 45°N 136° E
Simbirsk 40 4D 54°N 48° E
Simpson Desert 48 5F 25°S 137° E
Singapore 45 6J 1°N 103° E
Siracusa 22 6E 37°N 15° E
Sishen 28 2C 27°S 22° E
Sivas 39 4L 39°N 36° E
Sjælland 36 5P 55°N 11° E
Skagen 35 4C 57°N 10° E
Skagerrak 35 4B 57°N 9° E
Skegness 4 3G 53°N 0° E
Skellefteå 35 3E 64°N 20° E
Skipton 4 3D 53°N 2°W
Skopje 39 3H 42°N 21° E
Skye 6 2B 57°N 6°W
Slaney → 7 4E 52°N 6°W
Slieve Donard 7 2E 54°N 5°W
Sligo 7 2C 54°N 8°W
Sligo Bay 7 2C 54°N 8°W
Slough 5 5F 51°N 0°W
Slovenia 38 2F 46°N 15° E
Smolensk 35 5G 54°N 32° E
Snaefell 4 2B 54°N 4°W
Snag 50 3E 62°N 140°W
Snake → 52 2C 46°N 119°W
Snowdon 4 3B 53°N 4°W
Snowy Mountains 48 7H 36°S 148° E
Sobradinho Reservoir 30 4G 9°S 42°W
Sobral 30 3G 3°S 40°W
Sochi 39 3L 43°N 39° E
Society Islands 49 9N 17°S 151°W
Sofia 39 3H 42°N 23° E
Sogne Fjord 35 3B 61°N 5° E
Sokoto 47 9M 13°N 5° E
Solapur 44 5F 17°N 75° E
Solihull 5 4E 52°N 1°W
Solimões → 30 3E 0°S 50°W
Solomon Islands 49 8J 6°S 155° E
Solway Firth 4 2C 54°N 3°W
Somali Peninsula 46 4H 8°N 45° E
Somali Republic 46 4H 7°N 47° E
Somerset 9 6E 51°N 3°W
Songkhla 45 6J 7°N 100° E
Sonora 52 5D 29°N 111°W
Sorano 22 3C 42°N 11° E
Soroti 26 2A 1°N 33° E
Sousse 38 4F 35°N 10° E
South Africa 28 3C 32°S 23° E
South America 51 5F 10°S 60°W
South Australia 48 5E 32°S 139° E
South Carolina 53 4K 34°N 81°W
South China Sea 45 5K 10°N 113° E
South Dakota 52 2F 44°N 100°W
South Downs 5 6F 50°N 0°W
South Esk → 6 3F 56°N 3°W
South Georgia 51 9H 54°S 37°W
South Island 48 11M 44°S 170° E
South Korea 45 3L 36°N 128° E
South Magnetic Pole 56 2F 64°S 138° E
South Orkney Islands 56 2M 63°S 45°W
South Pole 56 2J 90°S 0°W
South Ronaldsay 6 6F 58°N 2°W
South Sandwich Islands 56 2A 57°S 27°W
South Sandwich Trench 56 2A 56°S 24°W
South Shetland Islands 56 2M 62°S 59°W
South Shields 4 2E 54°N 1°W
South Uist 6 2A 57°N 7°W
South Yorkshire 9 5F 53°N 1°W
Southampton 5 6E 50°N 1°W
Southend 5 5G 55°N 5°W
Southern Alps 48 11M 43°S 170° E
Southern Ocean 56 2H 62°S 60° E
Southern Uplands 6 4E 55°N 3°W
Southport 4 3D 53°N 3°W
Soweto 29 2D 26°S 27° E
Spain 37 12G 39°N 4°W
Spalding 4 4F 52°N 0°W
Sparta 39 4H 37°N 22° E
Spencer Bay 28 2A 25°S 14° E
Spencer Gulf 48 6F 34°S 137° E
Sperrin Mountains 7 2D 54°N 7°W
Spey → 6 2E 57°N 3°W
Spezia 37 10N 44°N 9° E
Springfield 53 3J 39°N 89°W
Spurn Head 4 3G 53°N 0° E
Sredinnyy Range 41 16D 57°N 160° E
Sri Lanka 44 6G 7°N 80° E
Srinagar 44 3F 34°N 74° E
Stafford 4 4D 52°N 2°W
Staffordshire 9 5E 52°N 2°W
Staines 5 5F 51°N 0°W
Stanley 51 9F 51°S 59°W
Stanovoy Range 41 13D 55°N 130° E
Start Point 5 6C 50°N 3°W
Stavanger 35 4B 58°N 5° E
Stavropol 39 2M 45°N 42° E
Stevenage 5 5F 51°N 0°W
Stewart Island 48 12L 46°S 167° E
Stirling 6 3E 56°N 3°W
Stockholm 35 4D 59°N 18° E
Stockport 4 3D 53°N 2°W
Stockton 4 2E 54°N 1°W
Stoke on Trent 4 3D 53°N 2°W
Stonehaven 6 3F 56°N 2°W
Stonehenge 5 5E 51°N 1°W
Stornoway 6 1B 58°N 6°W
Stour →, Dorset 5 6D 50°N 1°W
Stour →, Suffolk 5 5H 51°N 1° E
Stourbridge 5 4D 52°N 2°W
Strabane 7 2D 54°N 7°W
Stranraer 6 5C 54°N 5°W
Strasbourg 37 8M 51°N 104°W
Stratford-upon-Avon 5 4E 52°N 1°W
Strath Spey 6 2E 57°N 3°W
Strathmore 6 3E 56°N 3°W
Stromboli 38 4F 38°N 15° E
Stromeferry 6 2C 57°N 5°W
Stronsay 6 7F 59°N 2°W
Stroud 5 5D 51°N 2°W
Stuttgart 37 8N 48°N 9° E
Sucre 51 5E 19°S 65°W
Sudan 46 3G 15°N 30° E
Suez 46 2G 29°N 32° E
Suez Canal 46 1G 31°N 32° E
Suffolk 9 5G 52°N 1° E
Suir → 14 5C 52°N 7°W
Sukhumi 39 3M 41°N 41° E
Sulu Archipelago 45 6L 6°N 121° E
Sulu Sea 45 6K 8°N 120° E
Sumatra 45 6J 0°N 100° E
Sumba 45 7L 9°S 119° E
Sumbawa 45 7K 8°S 117° E
Sumburgh Head 6 7J 59°N 1°W
Sumy 39 1K 50°N 34° E
Sunda Islands 45 7K 5°S 105° E
Sundays → 28 3D 33°S 25° E
Sunderland 4 2E 54°N 1°W
Sundsvall 35 3D 62°N 17° E
Superior, Lake 53 1J 47°N 87°W
Surabaya 45 7K 7°S 112° E
Surat 44 4F 21°N 72° E
Surgut 40 8C 61°N 73° E
Surinam 51 3F 4°N 56°W
Surrey 9 6F 51°N 0°W
Sutton Coldfield 5 4E 52°N 1°W
Sutton in Ashfield 4 3E 53°N 1°W
Suva 49 9K 18°S 178° E
Svalbard 56 1G 78°N 17° E
Svealand 35 3C 59°N 15° E
Swakopmund 28 1A 22°S 14° E
Swale → 4 2E 54°N 1°W
Swanage 5 6D 50°N 1°W
Swansea 5 5C 51°N 3°W
Swaziland 29 2E 26°S 31° E
Sweden 35 3D 57°N 15° E
Swilly, Lough 7 1D 55°N 7°W
Swindon 5 5E 51°N 1°W
Switzerland 37 9M 46°N 8° E
Sydney 48 6J 33°S 151° E
Syr Darya → 40 7E 46°N 61° E
Syria 44 3B 35°N 38° E
Szczecin 35 5C 53°N 14° E

Tabora 46 5G 5°S 32° E
Tabriz 40 5F 38°N 46° E
Tagus → 48 4B 38°N 9°W
Tahiti 49 9P 17°S 149°W
Taimyr Peninsula 41 10B 75°N 100° E
Taipei 45 4L 25°N 121° E
Taiwan 45 4L 23°N 121° E
Taiyuan 45 3K 38°N 112° E
Tajikistan 40 7F 38°N 70° E
Tajo → 38 3C 38°N 9°W
Takamatsu 24 2D 34°N 134° E
Takaoka 24 1E 36°N 137° E
Takasaki 24 1F 36°N 139° E
Takayama 24 1E 36°N 137° E
Takefu 24 2E 35°N 136° E
Takla Makan 44 3G 38°N 83° E
Tallahassee 53 4K 30°N 84°W
Tallinn 35 4E 59°N 24° E
Tamale 47 10K 9°N 0°W
Tamar → 5 6B 50°N 4°W
Tampa 53 5K 27°N 82°W
Tampere 35 3E 61°N 23° E
Tampico 54 3E 22°N 97°W
Tamworth 48 6J 31°S 150° E
Tana →, Norway 35 2F 70°N 28° E

Tana →, Kenya	26	3C	2°S	40°E
Tana, Lake	46	3G	13°N	37°E
Tanabe	24	3D	33°N	135°E
Tanami Desert	48	3E	18°S	132°E
Tanega Island	24	4B	30°N	131°E
Tanga	46	5G	5°S	39°E
Tanganyika, Lake	46	5F	6°S	30°E
Tangier	46	1C	35°N	5°W
Tanimbar Islands	45	7M	7°S	131°E
Tanzania	46	5G	6°S	34°E
Tapajós →	30	3E	2°S	54°W
Taranto	22	4F	40°N	17°E
Taranto, Gulf of	22	4F	40°N	17°E
Tarragona	37	12J	41°N	1°E
Tashkent	40	7E	41°N	69°E
Tasman Sea	49	11J	36°S	160°E
Tasmania	48	8H	42°S	146°E
Taunton	5	5C	51°N	3°W
Taurus Mountains	39	4K	37°N	35°E
Taw →	5	6C	51°N	4°W
Tay →	6	3E	56°N	3°W
Tay, Firth of	6	3F	56°N	3°W
Tbilisi	40	5E	41°N	44°E
Tees →	4	2E	54°N	1°W
Tegucigalpa	54	5G	14°N	87°W
Tehran	40	6F	35°N	51°E
Tehuantepec, Gulf of	54	4F	15°N	95°W
Tehuantepec, Isthmus of	54	4F	17°N	94°W
Teifi →	5	4B	52°N	4°W
Teign →	5	6C	50°N	3°W
Teles Pires →	30	4D	7°S	58°W
Telford	4	4D	52°N	2°W
Tema	47	10L	5°N	0°W
Temuco	51	7D	38°S	72°W
Tennessee	53	3J	36°N	86°W
Tennessee →	53	3J	37°N	88°W
Teófilo Otoni	30	6G	17°S	41°W
Teresina	30	4G	5°S	42°W
Terni	22	3D	42°N	12°E
Test →	5	5E	51°N	1°W
Tétouan	38	4B	35°N	5°W
Teviot →	6	4F	55°N	2°W
Texas	52	4F	31°N	98°W
Thabana Ntlenyana	29	2D	29°S	29°E
Thailand	45	5J	16°N	102°E
Thailand, Gulf of	45	5J	11°N	101°E
Thame →	5	5E	51°N	1°W
Thames Estuary	5	5H	51°N	0°E
Thames →	5	5G	51°N	0°E
Thar Desert	44	4F	28°N	72°E
Thessaloniki	39	3H	40°N	22°E
Thetford	5	4G	52°N	0°E
Thika	26	3B	1°S	37°E
Thimphu	44	4G	27°N	89°E
Thurrock	9	6G	51°N	0°E
Thurso	6	1E	58°N	3°W
Tian Shan	44	2G	43°N	84°E
Tianjin	45	3K	39°N	117°E
Tiber →	22	3D	41°N	12°E
Tibesti	46	2E	21°N	17°E
Tibet, Plateau of	44	3G	31°N	86°E
Tientsin = Tianjin	45	3K	39°N	117°E
Tierra del Fuego	51	9E	54°S	67°W
Tigris →	44	3C	37°N	42°E
Tijuana	54	1A	32°N	117°W
Timbuktu	46	3C	16°N	3°W
Timişoara	39	2H	45°N	21°E
Timor Sea	48	2D	12°S	127°E
Tipperary	7	4C	52°N	8°W
Tirane	39	3G	41°N	19°E
Tirat Zevi	44	3B	32°N	35°E
Tiree	6	3B	56°N	6°W
Tiruchchirappalli	44	5F	10°N	78°E
Titicaca, Lake	51	5E	15°S	69°W
Tiverton	5	6C	50°N	3°W
Toamasina	47	6H	18°S	49°E
Tobermory	6	3B	56°N	6°W
Tocantins	30	5F	10°S	48°W
Tocantins →	30	3F	1°S	49°W
Togo	47	10L	8°N	1°E
Tokelau Islands	49	8L	9°S	171°W
Tokushima	24	2D	34°N	134°E
Tokuyama	24	3B	33°N	131°E
Tokyo	24	2F	35°N	139°E
Toledo, Spain	37	13G	39°N	4°W
Toledo, U.S.A.	53	2K	41°N	83°W
Toliara	47	7H	23°S	43°E
Tombigbee →	53	4J	31°N	87°W
Tomsk	40	8D	56°N	85°E
Tonga	49	10L	19°S	174°W
Tonga Trench	49	10L	18°S	175°W
Tonkin, Gulf of	45	5J	20°N	108°E
Toowoomba	48	5J	27°S	151°E
Topeka	53	3G	39°N	95°W
Torbay	5	6C	50°N	3°W
Torfaen	9	6E	51°N	3°W
Toronto	53	2L	43°N	79°W
Torquay	5	6C	50°N	3°W
Torrens, Lake	48	6F	31°S	137°E
Torreón	54	2D	25°N	103°W
Torres Strait	48	2G	9°S	142°E
Torridge →	5	6B	50°N	4°W
Torridon, Loch	6	2C	57°N	5°W
Tórshavn	36	1E	62°N	6°W
Tory Island	7	1C	55°N	8°W
Tosa Bay	24	3C	32°N	132°E
Tottori	24	2D	35°N	134°E
Toubkal	46	1C	31°N	8°W
Toulon	37	11L	43°N	5°E
Toulouse	37	11J	43°N	1°E
Tours	37	9J	47°N	0°E
Townsville	48	3H	19°S	146°E
Toyama	24	1E	36°N	137°E
Toyohashi	24	2E	34°N	137°E
Toyota	24	2E	35°N	137°E
Trabzon	39	3L	41°N	39°E
Tralee	7	4B	52°N	9°W
Tramore	7	4D	52°N	7°W
Transylvanian Alps	39	2H	45°N	25°E
Trawsfynydd, Lake	14	5D	52°N	3°W
Trent →	4	3F	53°N	0°W
Trento	22	1C	46°N	11°E
Trenton	53	2M	40°N	74°W
Trieste	22	2D	45°N	13°E
Trinidad and Tobago	55	5M	10°N	61°W
Trinity →	53	5H	29°N	94°W
Tripoli	46	1E	32°N	13°E
Tristan da Cunha	60	4J	37°S	12°W
Tromsø	35	2D	69°N	18°E
Trondheim	35	3C	63°N	10°E
Troon	6	4D	55°N	4°W
Trowbridge	5	5D	51°N	2°W
Troyes	37	8L	48°N	4°E
Trudeau, Mount Pierre Elliot	50	3E	60°N	140°W
Trujillo	51	4D	8°S	79°W
Truro	5	6A	50°N	5°W
Tshabong	28	2C	26°S	22°E
Tshane	28	1C	24°S	21°E
Tsu	24	2E	34°N	136°E
Tsuruga	24	2E	35°N	136°E
Tsuyama	24	2D	35°N	134°E
Tuamotu Archipelago	49	9P	17°S	144°W
Tubuai Islands	49	10N	25°S	150°W
Tucson	52	4D	32°N	110°W
Tucumán	51	6E	26°S	66°W
Tugela →	29	2E	29°S	31°E
Tula	40	4D	54°N	37°E
Tullamore	7	3D	53°N	7°W
Tully	48	3H	17°S	145°E
Tunbridge Wells	5	5G	51°N	0°E
Tunis	46	1E	36°N	10°E
Tunisia	46	1D	33°N	9°E
Turin	22	2A	45°N	7°E
Turkana, Lake	26	2B	3°N	36°E
Turkey	39	4K	39°N	36°E
Turkmenistan	40	6F	39°N	59°E
Turks & Caicos Islands	55	3K	21°N	71°W
Turku	35	3E	60°N	22°E
Turriff	6	2F	57°N	2°W
Tuvalu	49	8K	8°S	178°E
Tuxtla Gutiérrez	54	4F	16°N	93°W
Tuz Gölü	39	4K	38°N	33°E
Tver	35	4H	56°N	35°E
Tweed →	6	4F	55°N	1°W
Tyne and Wear	9	4F	54°N	1°W
Tyne →	4	2E	54°N	1°W
Tynemouth	4	1E	55°N	1°W
Tyrone	9	4C	54°N	7°W
Tyrrhenian Sea	22	4D	40°N	12°E
Tyumen	40	7D	57°N	65°E
Tywi →	5	5B	51°N	4°W
Uaupes →	30	3B	0°S	67°W
Ubangi →	46	4E	0°S	17°E
Ube	24	3B	33°N	131°E
Uberlândia	30	6F	19°S	48°W
Ucayali →	51	4D	4°S	73°W
Udine	22	1D	46°N	13°E
Uganda	46	4G	2°N	32°E
Uitenhage	28	3D	33°S	25°E
Ujung Pandang	45	7K	5°S	119°E
Ukerewe Island	26	3A	1°S	33°E
Ukhta	40	6C	63°N	53°E
Ukraine	39	2K	49°N	32°E
Ulan Bator	41	11E	47°N	106°E
Ulan Ude	41	11D	51°N	107°E
Ullapool	6	2C	57°N	5°W
Ullswater	4	2D	54°N	2°W
Ulm	37	8N	48°N	9°E
Ulster	7	2E	54°N	6°W
Ulundi	29	2E	28°S	31°E
Umeå	35	3E	63°N	20°E
Umlazi	29	2E	29°S	30°E
Umtata	29	3D	31°S	28°E
Umuarama	30	7E	23°S	53°W
United Arab Emirates	44	4D	23°N	54°E
United Kingdom	36	5H	55°N	3°W
United States of America	50	6K	37°N	96°W
Unst	6	8K	60°N	0°W
Upington	28	2C	28°S	21°E
Upper Lough Erne	7	2D	54°N	7°W
Uppsala	35	4D	59°N	17°E
Ural Mountains	40	6D	60°N	59°E
Ural →	40	6E	47°N	51°E
Ure →	4	2E	54°N	1°W
Uruguaiana	30	8D	29°S	57°W
Uruguay	51	7F	32°S	56°W
Ürümqi	44	2G	43°N	87°E
Usambara Mountains	26	3B	4°S	38°E
Usk →	5	5C	51°N	2°W
Ust Ilimsk	41	11D	58°N	102°E
Ust Shchugor	40	6C	64°N	57°E
Utah	52	3D	39°N	111°W
Utrecht	36	6L	52°N	5°E
Utsunomiya	24	1F	36°N	139°E
Uwajima	24	3C	33°N	132°E
Uzbekistan	40	7E	41°N	65°E
Vaal-Dam	29	2D	27°S	28°E
Vaal →	28	2C	29°S	23°E
Vaasa	35	3E	63°N	21°E
Vadodara	44	4F	22°N	73°E
Vadsø	35	1F	70°N	29°E
Vaduz	37	9N	47°N	9°E
Valence	37	10L	44°N	4°E
Valencia, Spain	37	13H	39°N	0°W
Valencia, Venezuela	55	5L	10°N	68°W
Valencia Island	7	5A	51°N	10°W
Valladolid	37	12F	41°N	4°W
Valledupar	55	5K	10°N	73°W
Valletta	38	4F	35°N	14°E
Valparaiso	51	7D	33°S	71°W
Vancouver	52	1B	49°N	123°W
Vanda	56	2G	77°N	162°E
Vanderbiljpark	28	2D	26°S	27°E
Vänern, Lake	35	4C	58°N	13°E
Vanuatu	49	9J	15°S	168°E
Varanasi	44	4G	25°N	83°E
Vardø	35	1G	70°N	31°E
Varna	39	3J	43°N	27°E
Västerås	35	4D	59°N	16°E
Vatican City	22	4C	41°N	12°E
Vättern, Lake	35	4C	58°N	14°E
Venezuela	55	6L	8°N	66°W
Venice	22	2D	45°N	12°E
Vereeniging	29	2D	26°S	27°E
Verkhoyansk	41	14C	67°N	133°E
Verkhoyansk Range	41	13C	66°N	129°E
Vermont	53	2M	44°N	73°W
Verona	22	2C	45°N	10°E
Vesterålen	35	2C	68°N	15°E
Vesuvius	38	3F	40°N	14°E
Vicenza	22	2C	45°N	11°E
Victoria, Australia	48	7G	37°S	144°E
Victoria, Canada	52	1B	48°N	123°W
Victoria, Seychelles	44	7D	5°S	55°E
Victoria Falls	47	6F	17°S	25°E
Victoria Island	50	2H	71°N	111°W
Victoria Nile →	26	2A	2°N	31°E
Victoria West	28	3C	31°S	23°E
Victoria, Lake	26	3A	1°S	33°E
Vienna	39	2G	48°N	16°E
Vientiane	45	5J	17°N	102°E
Vietnam	45	5J	19°N	106°E
Vigo	37	11D	42°N	8°W
Villahermosa	54	4F	17°N	92°W
Vilnius	35	5F	54°N	25°E
Vinnitsa	39	2J	49°N	28°E
Vinson Massif	56	2L	78°S	85°W
Virgin Islands	55	4M	18°N	64°W
Virginia, South Africa	28	2D	28°S	26°E
Virginia, U.S.A.	53	3L	37°N	78°W
Vistula →	35	5D	54°N	18°E
Vitebsk	35	4G	55°N	30°E
Vitória	30	7G	20°S	40°W
Vitória da Conquista	30	5G	14°S	40°W
Vladivostok	41	14E	43°N	131°E
Volga →	40	5E	46°N	48°E
Volgograd	40	5E	48°N	44°E
Volta →	47	10L	5°N	0°E
Volta, Lake	47	10L	7°N	0°E
Vorkuta	41	18B	67°N	64°E
Voronezh	40	4D	51°N	33°E
Vostok Island	49	9N	10°S	152°W
Vryburg	28	2C	26°S	24°E
Vyborg	35	3F	60°N	28°E
Vyrnwy, Lake	4	4C	52°N	3°W
Wadi Halfa	46	2G	21°N	31°E
Wagga Wagga	48	7H	35°S	147°E
Wakayama	24	2D	34°N	135°E
Wake Island	49	6J	19°N	166°E
Wakefield	4	3E	53°N	1°W
Wales	5	4C	52°N	3°W
Wallasey	4	3C	53°N	3°W
Walney, Isle of	4	2C	54°N	3°W
Walsall	5	4E	52°N	1°W
Walvis Bay	28	1A	23°S	14°E
Walvisbaai	28	1A	23°S	14°E
Warrenpoint	7	2E	54°N	6°W
Warrington	4	3D	53°N	2°W
Warsaw	35	5E	52°N	21°E
Warwick	5	4E	52°N	1°W
Warwickshire	9	5F	52°N	1°W
Wash, The	4	3G	52°N	0°E
Washington, U.K.	4	2E	54°N	1°W
Washington, U.S.A.	52	1B	47°N	120°W
Washington D.C.	53	3L	38°N	77°W
Washington, Mount	53	2M	44°N	71°W
Waterford	7	4D	52°N	7°W
Watford	5	5F	51°N	0°W
Waveney →	5	4H	52°N	1°E
Wear →	4	2D	54°N	1°W
Weddell Sea	56	2M	72°S	40°W
Weipa	48	2G	12°S	141°E
Welkom	28	2D	28°S	26°E
Welland →	5	4F	52°N	0°W
Wellingborough	5	4F	52°N	0°W
Wellington	48	11M	41°S	174°E
Wells	4	4G	52°N	0°E
Welshpool	5	4C	52°N	3°W
Welwyn Garden City	5	5F	51°N	0°W
Wensleydale	4	2E	54°N	2°W
Weser →	36	6N	53°N	8°E
West Bank	39	5L	32°N	35°E
West Bromwich	5	4D	52°N	2°W
West Indies	51	1E	15°N	65°W
West Lothian	9	4E	55°N	3°W
West Midlands	9	5E	52°N	1°W
West Siberian Plain	40	8C	62°N	75°E
West Sussex	9	6F	50°N	0°W
West Virginia	53	3K	38°N	80°W
West Yorkshire	9	5F	53°N	1°W
Western Australia	48	4C	25°S	118°E
Western Ghats	44	5F	14°N	75°E
Western Isles	9	3C	57°N	7°W
Western Province	26	2A	0°N	34°E
Western Sahara	46	2B	25°N	13°W
Westmeath	9	5C	53°N	7°W
Weston-super-Mare	5	5D	51°N	2°W
Westport	7	3B	53°N	9°W
Westray	6	7F	59°N	3°W
Wexford	7	4E	52°N	6°W
Weymouth	5	6D	50°N	2°W
Whalsay	6	8K	60°N	1°W
Wharfe →	4	3E	53°N	1°W
Wharfedale	4	2D	54°N	2°W
Whernside	4	2D	54°N	2°W
Whitby	4	2F	54°N	0°W
White Nile →	46	3G	15°N	32°E
White Sea	35	2H	66°N	38°E
Whitehaven	4	2C	54°N	3°W
Whitney, Mount	50	6H	36°N	118°W
Whyalla	48	6F	33°S	137°
Wick	6	1E	58°N	3°W
Wicklow	7	4E	53°N	6°W
Wicklow Mountains	7	4E	53°N	6°W
Widnes	4	3D	53°N	2°W
Wiesbaden	36	7N	50°N	8°E
Wigan	4	3D	53°N	2°W
Wight, Isle of	5	6E	50°N	1°W
Wigtown	6	5D	54°N	4°W
Wilge →	29	2D	27°S	28°E
Willemstad	55	5L	12°N	69°W
Wiltshire	9	6F	51°N	2°W
Winchester	5	5E	51°N	1°W
Windermere	4	2D	54°N	2°W
Windhoek	28	1B	22°S	17°E
Windrush →	5	5E	51°N	1°W
Windsor	5	5F	51°N	0°W
Windward Islands	55	5M	13°N	61°W
Winnipeg	50	5K	49°N	97°W
Winnipeg, Lake	50	4K	52°N	97°W
Winterberge	28	3D	32°S	26°E
Wisconsin	53	2J	44°N	89°W
Witham →	4	3F	53°N	0°W
Withernsea	4	3G	53°N	0°E
Woking	5	5F	51°N	0°W
Wokingham	9	6F	51°N	0°W
Wollongong	48	6J	34°S	150°E
Wolverhampton	5	4D	52°N	2°W
Worcester, South Africa	28	3B	33°S	19°E
Worcester, U.K.	5	4D	52°N	2°W
Workington	4	2C	54°N	3°W
Worksop	4	3E	53°N	1°W
Worthing	5	6F	50°N	0°W
Wrangel Island	56	B	71°N	180°E
Wrath, Cape	6	1C	58°N	5°W
Wrexham	4	3C	53°N	3°W
Wrocław	35	5D	51°N	17°E
Wuhan	45	3K	30°N	114°E
Würzburg	36	8P	49°N	9°E
Wye →	5	5D	51°N	2°W
Wyndham	48	3D	15°S	128°E
Wyoming	52	2E	43°N	107°W
Xi'an	45	3J	34°N	109°E
Xingu →	30	3E	1°S	51°W
Yablonovyy Range	41	12D	53°N	114°E
Yakutsk	41	13C	62°N	129°E
Yalta	39	3K	44°N	34°E
Yangtse-Kiang →	45	3K	31°N	121°E
Yanji	43	2A	42°N	129°E
Yaoundé	47	11N	3°N	11°E
Yaqui →	54	2B	27°N	110°W
Yare →	5	4H	52°N	1°E
Yaroslavl	40	4D	57°N	39°E
Yatsushiro	24	3B	32°N	130°E
Yawatahama	24	3C	33°N	132°E
Yekaterinburg	40	7D	56°N	60°E
Yell	6	8J	60°N	1°W
Yellow Sea	45	3L	35°N	123°E
Yellowknife	50	3H	62°N	114°W
Yellowstone National Park	52	2D	44°N	110°W
Yemen	44	5C	15°N	44°E
Yenisei →	40	8C	71°N	82°E
Yeo →	5	5D	51°N	3°W
Yeovil	5	6D	50°N	2°W
Yerevan	40	5E	40°N	44°E
Yokkaichi	24	2E	34°N	136°E
Yokohama	24	2F	35°N	139°E
Yokosuka	24	2F	35°N	139°E
Yonago	24	2C	35°N	133°E
York	4	3E	53°N	1°W
York, Cape	48	2G	10°S	142°E
Yorkshire Wolds	4	2F	54°N	0°W
Youghal	7	5D	51°N	7°W
Yucatan	54	4G	20°N	89°W
Yucatan Strait	54	3G	22°N	86°W
Yugoslavia	39	3H	44°N	20°E
Yukon →	50	3D	62°N	165°W
Yuzhno-Sakhalinsk	41	15E	46°N	142°E
Zagreb	39	2G	45°N	16°E
Zagros Mountains	44	3D	33°N	48°E
Zambezi →	47	6G	18°S	36°E
Zambia	46	6F	15°S	28°E
Zamboanga	45	6L	6°N	122°E
Zanzibar	46	5G	6°S	39°E
Zaporozhye	39	2L	47°N	35°E
Zaragoza	37	12H	41°N	0°W
Zhitomir	35	5F	50°N	28°E
Zimbabwe	47	6F	19°S	30°E
Zonguldak	39	3K	41°N	31°E
Zürich	37	9N	47°N	8°E